Pillars of Government

Pillars of Government
and Other Essays on State and Society
c.1770–c.1880

Norman Gash
Emeritus Professor of History, University of St. Andrews

Edward Arnold

© Norman Gash 1986

First published in Great Britain 1986 by
Edward Arnold (Publishers) Ltd, 41 Bedford Square, London WC1B 3DQ

Edward Arnold (Australia) Pty Ltd, 80 Waverley Road, Caulfield East,
  Victoria 3145, Australia

Edward Arnold, 3 East Read Street, Baltimore, Maryland 21202,
  USA

British Library Cataloguing in Publication Data
Gash, Norman
  Pillars of government and other essays
  on state and society c. 1770–c. 1880.
  1. Great Britain—History—18th century
  2. Great Britain—History—19th century
  I. Title
  941   DA480

  ISBN 0 7131 6463 8

DA
530
628
.1986

Photoset in Linotron Plantin
by Northern Phototypesetting Co, Bolton
Printed and bound by
Billings & Sons Limited, Worcester

To Arnold Joseph Taylor
from whose friendship and erudition I have so often benefited

'The four pillars of government . . . (which are religion, justice, counsel, and treasure).'

Francis Bacon, 1561–1626
'Of Seditions and Troubles'

Contents

Preface

These fifteen essays were written at different times for different purposes. Less than half have previously been printed. Of these, two which seemed worth rescuing from oblivion date back more than forty years. Of the remainder, published and unpublished, ten have only been written in their present form within the last four years. In selecting articles for reprinting I refrained from including any from such well-known periodicals as *The English Historical Review*, *Transactions of the Royal Historical Society*, *Parliamentary History*, and *History Today*. I have confined myself to a few which appeared in less accessible publications. The one partial exception is the essay on 'Bonham and the Conservative Party' which incorporates most of the article on him in the *English Historical Review* of 1948. Since that date I had accumulated further information which seemed worth putting on record, though it was not of a kind that would form the basis of a separate, self-contained essay. The only course was to rewrite the original article in an extended form.

The other published articles are given here as first printed – with two minor infractions of that rule. In the article on 'Oxford Politics in the Chancellor's Election of 1834', Mary Dawson's letter was wrongly ascribed to her husband; this has now been put right. In the article on 'Peel and the Oxford University Election of 1829', written in 1938–9, I made some casual allusions to the 'Tory party' in the 1820s. Keith Feiling's attractive book *The Second Tory Party, 1714–1832* had just been published and the use of the phrase seemed at that time unexceptionable. I would be reluctant, however, to appear today to be endorsing the assumptions implicit in Feiling's title and I have therefore reworded a couple of sentences in the first two paragraphs.

Of the unpublished papers, that on 'The English Constitution in the Age of the American Revolution' is the text of the Hinkley inaugural lecture which I had the honour of giving in Baltimore in 1962. The first part of the essay entitled 'Some Reflections on History' contains a substantial part of my inaugural lecture at St Andrews in 1956. The essay on the 'State of the Nation, 1822' was written specifically for inclusion here. The subject had not, to my knowledge, been noticed by any other historian and it seemed to me to merit more attention than I was able to give it in my recent life of Lord Liverpool. The others, though only now cast into essay form, are on topics which I had been using for a number of years in talks to various historical audiences.

Because of their diverse origins these essays are designed to be read separately and not as a continuous whole. Though the chronological range is from the reign of George II to the closing decades of Queen Victoria, the largest concentration of material is in the period from 1815 to 1850. There was inevitably an occasional overlapping and repetition which could not be excised now without damage to the thread of the argument. I hope that readers observant enough to notice will be charitable enough to show a decent indulgence. The essays which conclude the volume stand apart from the others; though, like the epilogues which once customarily brought up the rear of a stage-play, they may perhaps be seen to have some relevance to what has gone before.

The origin of each essay is indicated in a footnote on its first page. I would like to thank the following who kindly allowed me to reprint articles from the periodicals which they represent: the editors of *The English Historical Review* (for no. 10); The Leeds Philosophical and Literary Society (for no. 7); Sir Anthony Meyer, MP (for no. 12); the editor of *Oxoniensia* (for no. 6); the Oxonian-Rewley Press Ltd. (for no. 8); the Peel Society of Tamworth (for no. 9); and the Prince Albert Society of Coburg (for nos. 2 and 5).

Norman Gash
November, 1985.

Langport, Somerset

Part I

Pillars of Government

1

The English Constitution in the Age of the American Revolution[1]

At the start of the eighteenth-century dispute between Britain and her American colonies, one of the chief arguments of the colonists was the appeal to fundamental English rights. These rights – or so ran the argument – were guaranteed to all British subjects by their constitution, could not be altered by either the supreme legislature or the supreme executive, and could not be forfeited merely by migration across the Atlantic. When it became regrettably clear that the English constitution was devoid of fundamental rules and recognized no rights outside the context of common and statute law, the disappointment was considerable; and few branches of the constitution escaped hostile comment on this [i.e. the American] side of the water. Every student of the crisis is familiar with the transition from criticism of parliamentary authority to an attack on ministerial policy and thence to a final onslaught on the executive action of the Crown. The First Continental Congress denounced the 'arbitrary proceedings of [the British] parliament'; the Second spoke of 'the designs of an arbitrary Ministry'; and for George III himself was reserved the solemn rhetoric of the Declaration of Independence – 'the history of the present King of Great Britain is a history of repeated injuries and usurpations . . . a Prince, whose character is thus marked by every act which may define a Tyrant, is unfit to be the ruler of a free People'.

This colonial attitude, which represented after all the final and far from transient impression of the English monarchy left on the emerging American states, was the more striking because of its contrast to the conventional contemporary view of the constitution. Englishmen (though not perhaps Irishmen) were under the impression that they enjoyed civil and religious liberty under the freest constitution on earth. Secure in that belief they looked with insular superiority on those unfortunate continental states whose inhabitants languished in the triple thraldom picturesquely symbolized to them by 'Popery, despotism and wooden shoes'. If they needed encouragement in this posture of satisfaction, they found it in the unsolicited testimony of European intellectuals. Voltaire during his exile in England in 1726–8, wrote approvingly that 'the English are the only people upon earth who have been able to prescribe limits to the power of Kings'.[2] Montesquieu in his classic work on the *Spirit of Laws*, first published in 1748, observed of Britain that this was the 'one nation in the world which has as the direct object of its constitution political liberty'.[3] Over twenty years later, in the middle of the

[1] Inaugural lecture as Hinkley Professor of English History at Johns Hopkins University, 1962. Not previously published.
[2] *Lettres sur les Anglais* (Eng. edn of 1741), Letter VIII.
[3] *De L'Esprit des Lois*, Book XI, ch. v.

contest with the American colonies, the Swiss jurist de Lolme in his book on the English Constitution[1] spoke of it as 'a constitution which at the same time as it carries liberty to its height, guards against what seem inevitable inconveniences'. To the Europe of the Enlightenment England presented a spectacle of intellectual and personal liberty all the more enviable because it was combined with economic wealth and naval strength. It was natural that more than one speculative continental mind sought to discover the secret of this free and powerful community.

There is therefore some irony in the fact that when analysing the English constitution the European philosophers of the eighteenth century defined the prescription for its boasted liberty in exactly the same formula as that employed by the fathers of the American Constitution when they came to draw up a legal framework for their own new and independent community: the formula, that is to say, of the separation of powers and of a system of checks and balances. So far from being a novel solution, the American Constitution derived from a European doctrine which saw in England its living exemplar. Even the humanist Voltaire noted in passing 'that mixture in the English government, that harmony between King, Lords and Commons'.[2] Montesquieu more systematically located the genius of the English constitution in the independence of the judiciary, the separation of the executive power, the division of the legislature into two branches, their mutual check on each other, and their joint relationship with the executive which both restrained and was restrained by them. The pedantic de Lolme expanded the craggy aphorisms of Montesquieu's monolithic chapter into a whole volume on 'the resources allotted to the different parts of the English government for balancing each other, and how their reciprocal actions and reactions produce the freedom of the Constitution, which is no more than an equilibrium between the ruling powers of the State'.[3] Nor was this the uncritical enthusiasm of the European intelligentsia alone. Blackstone, the great English constitutional writer who became Vinerian professor of law at Oxford, in the lectures he delivered there from 1753 onwards,[4] gave lapidary (and for most of his countrymen conclusive) expression to an identical doctrine. 'Herein indeed consists the true excellence of the English government, that all parts of it form a mutual check upon each other.' Analysing, in the characteristically rational and scientific language of the post-Newtonian age, the rival forces of Crown, Lords and Commons, he concluded that 'like three distinct powers in mechanics, they jointly impel the machine of government in a direction different from what either, acting by itself, would have done; but at the same time in a direction partaking of each, and formed out of all; a direction which constitutes the true line of the liberty and happiness of the community'.[5]

This notable disparity between the American and European attitudes towards the eighteenth-century English constitution can hardly fail to provoke two questions. Were the European philosophers right in discerning a system of separated powers, of checks and balances, leading to the almost automatic production of maximum civil and political liberty? And if so, how is this to be

[1] *Constitution de l'Angleterre* (Amsterdam 1771), Preface.
[2] *Lettres sur les Anglais*, Letter IX.
[3] Eng. edn (1784) p. 195.
[4] First published 1765–9.
[5] *Commentaries on the Laws of England*, Book I, ch. ii.

reconciled with the language and experience of the angry American colonists?

II

Less than fifty years ago the first question might have seemed ingenuous, the second irrelevant; the answer to both self-evident. Tory historians had painted a picture of the Whig ascendancy in the first fifty years of the Hanoverian dynasty – the 'Venetian oligarchy' of Disraeli's literary imagination – who dominated their captive and inarticulate German kings, corrupted parliament, and took the fleshpots of political power into their capacious and practised hands. Their Whiggish, and academically more reputable, colleagues countered with a portrait of a stupid and obstinate George III who under maternal tutorship tried to reverse the majestic evolution of the British Constitution by an assumption of obsolete monarchical power, and sacrificed an Empire on the altar of a 'Patriot King'. Both sides at least seemed to be in agreement on this: that the executive government was strong, that power was centralized, and that liberty was in danger. No reputable historian today is likely to advance such views. With greater knowledge of eighteenth-century politics has come greater perceptivity and in the process the scene has become more complex, more realistic and more balanced. Greater emphasis is laid on the real power exercised by the first two Hanoverian kings; on the general support enjoyed by George III in his limited and conscientious attempts not to subvert but to uphold the constitution as he and most of his contemporaries saw it; above all, on the indispensable function of the monarchy in an age when the absence of an organized party system made it impossible that there could be any permanent and satisfactory method of selecting executive ministers except by the Crown. Conversely there is more understanding of the practical limitations on even the most successful of the parliamentary politicians – men like Walpole, Henry Pelham, Lord North, and the younger Pitt; of the strong monarchical concept of government that coloured their vocabulary and behaviour; on their double and not easily reconcilable rôles as spokesmen of the Commons to the King and of the King to the Commons. Sir Robert Walpole, one of the last of a line of great royal ministers who go back through Godolphin and Clarendon to Elizabeth's Burleigh, and one of the first of the modern line of parliamentary statesmen continued in Pitt and Liverpool, personified the mixed and balanced nature of the limited monarchy he served. To eighteenth-century ministers royal and parliamentary confidence were equally necessary. Without parliamentary support royal favour alone could not maintain in supreme power unpopular or isolated individuals like Carteret, Bute and Shelburne; but equally so, parliament could not often impose and never long sustain a minister obnoxious to the king. Eighteenth-century politics were a dialogue between crown and legislature and only those who could interpret both languages could succeed.

The same limitations are apparent in the legislature. Secure in the massive gains made at the end of the seventeenth century, parliament had settled down under the steadying effect of the Septennial Act to the practice rather than the exploitation of the permanent place it had obtained in the working of the constitution. The House of Lords, though already perhaps the lesser chamber in point of power if not prestige, gave permanent seats to noble ministers of the Crown, acted as executioner for legislation which it was impolitic to block elsewhere, and through relatives, friends and clients in the Commons exerted an inconspicuous but important influence on the lower house. The House of Commons debated, criticized, required explanations, ventilated grievances, and examined requests for money with the jealousy to be expected of an assembly of tax-payers. Yet it conceived its prime duty was to support the Crown and the ministers of the Crown within the limits of its wider duty to the nation at large – that is to say, as long as those ministers were not peculiarly unpopular, inefficient or unfortunate. This restraint was not solely or even chiefly the product of bribery and other forms of undue and illicit influence. Much of the 'corruption' of the eighteenth-century was simply the by-product of an aristocratic society in which the monarch was the fountain of honours and rewards: a 'spoils-system' that was as much social as political, that concerned status as much as service. Where patronage was applied to sweeten political arrangements, reward a faithful hack, or convert a waverer, or where Treasury money and influence were used to bring a useful official into parliament or deny a seat to an opponent – the result was only to stiffen the ministerial majority in the legislature, not to manufacture it. In the House of Lords, with its restricted membership and absence of constituents, the ministers and court officials, reinforced by a phalanx of some two dozen bishops, formed the core of a government party in a peerage which habitually looked to the Court for guidance. In the House of Commons the most important single body of men were not the place-holders but the independent country gentlemen who scorned bribes, who shunned office, and were essentially 'amateurs in politics', enjoying their status for its social prestige rather than its material perquisities. It was these men who traditionally gave the king's government a support which was all the more effective because voluntary and unpaid. No ministry could long survive without their loyalty; and when they turned, however unwillingly and belatedly, against the government, it was a danger-signal that could not be ignored.

It was a mark of the moderation of the legislature that throughout the century a flavour of immorality clung to the notion of a 'formed opposition'. To oppose on a specific issue was legitimate; to oppose on system was factious. There were always ambitious politicians out of office who made it their business to produce as much inconvenience as possible until they got in. But even they had to pay lip-service to the conventions by claiming to be champions of the king against tyrannical and selfish ministers or expounders of the true interests of the empire against a misguided executive. 'Patriotism' was not so much the last refuge of a scoundrel as the uniform of an office-seeker. Only the presence from time to time of a politically active heir to the throne, providing the opportunity to support the future rather than the present wearer of the crown, to back the long-term prospects of the 'reversionary' against the present interest, gave a species of occasional legitimacy to an organized opposition-party. Only in the closing decades of the century could Burke, not without ulterior motives, suggest that the notion of party in politics might not be without constitutional value, or Fox endeavour unsuccessfully to anticipate parliamentary theories of the nineteenth century. But George III was in his grave before the phrase 'His Majesty's Opposition', thrown out jocularly in debate, passed into political vocabulary. Till then the legislature held that it had no business to tell the king what ministers he should employ. 'The House of Commons has a right,' observed the elder Fox in 1762, 'and has sometimes exerted it, to accuse a Minister and make it very inadvisable for a Prince to retain him in his favour. But I do not remember they ever undertook to say who should succeed him.'[1]

The more the eighteenth century is studied, in fact, the more apparent do certain features become: the absence of any overwhelming authority in any of its branches; the practical recognition of limitations; the readiness to work together. Not for nothing was this the Age of Reason; and the political realism that marked the maturity of the English aristocracy was equally present – though perhaps less often recognized – in the new dynasty of monarchs who had left their native Hanover to preside over the fortunes of an unfamiliar, unpredictable and notoriously turbulent nation. When Lord Hardwicke in his famous conversation with George II in January 1745 affirmed that 'your ministers, sir, are only your instruments of government', the king retorted 'ministers are kings in this country'. But he said it smilingly and could no more have believed in the literal accuracy of his remark than Hardwicke in his own diplomatic understatement. The truth lay somewhere between the two extremes, and monarchs and statesmen alike were content to leave it there without trying to determine too nicely its exact location. The king had to be something of a politician; while the politicians in their dealings with the king had to be diplomats. The crises which punctuate the narrative of eighteenth-century politics – the successful attack on Walpole in 1742, the mass resignation of the Pelham ministry in 1746, the assumption of office on their own terms by the Rockingham Whigs in 1782, the dismissal of the Fox – North coalition in 1783, the royal opposition to Catholic Emancipation and Pitt's resignation in 1801 – are merely boundary posts marking the limits of mutual tolerance. They delimit the working of the constitution; they do not describe it. What was more significant, though less spectacular, was the harmony that generally characterized eighteenth-century constitutional practice. The royal veto on legislation was never employed after Anne's reign; impeachment as a method of enforcing political responsibility was moribund; there were no major disputes between the two Houses of Parliament; nearly every parliament lasted out its full legal term; and the government never lost a general election.

All this is sufficiently established. What is less often noticed is that this is precisely the separation of powers, the checks and balances, the practical harmony described by the philosophic theorists of the constitution translated into the untidiness of events and personalities. The separation was not of course complete; the checks and balances were irregular in their operation. But all such obvious qualifications spring primarily from the fact that this was a living and working constitution as distinct from a paper scheme. The significant aspect is that contemporaries accepted these broad characteristics as essentials of their government and became practised in their manipulation without much speculation on whether some other system were either preferable or practical. Indeed, whenever historians of the eighteenth century turn to reasonably objective contemporaries for clues to what is happening, they find the answers staring them in the face. Horace Walpole's remark on the 1744 crisis: 'It is not easy to say where power resides at present; it is plain that it resides not in the King; and yet he has enough to hinder anyone else from having it', is one that might well be applied to

---

[1] *Life and Letters of Lady Sarah Lennox*, ed. Countess of Ilchester (1902), I, 76.

the whole period. And David Hume's description in 1741 of the House of Commons:

> The Crown has so many offices at its disposal that when assisted by the honest disinterested part of the House, it will always command the resolutions of the whole, so far, at least, as to preserve the ancient constitution from danger,[1]

is a singular anticipation of Sir Lewis Namier. Indeed, we seem almost driven to the conclusion that eighteenth-century Englishmen understood, a great deal better than their immediate posterity, the system on which they managed their affairs; to which may be added the rider that their system was in many respects nearer to the subsequent American Constitution than to the English constitution a century later.

III

The analogy may be extended to the third branch of the constitution – the judiciary. The judges, if no longer the seventeenth-century 'lions under the throne', were in no sense the tribunes of the people. Yet Englishmen, more apt to worship their constitution in this than perhaps in any other period in their history, saw in the equity of their laws and the impartiality of their judges virtues which ranked with the mildness of their religion and the freedom of their political system in making them the envy and admiration of the world. The eighteenth century had seen the emergence of the judiciary as an independent, powerful and venerated element in the constitution. Though appointed by the Crown the judges held office for life. Their status had been specifically safeguarded by the Act of Settlement in 1701 which prepared the way for the Hanoverian succession; and a further statute in 1760 provided for the permanence of their commissions even on the death of the sovereign. Since there was no formal written constitution, it was no part of their function to decide on the limits and locations of authority in the other branches of the constitution.[2] Yet by their application, interpretation and declaration of the law they came at certain points very close to this position. If they did not hold, at least they tried according to their lights to enforce, a balance between subject and sovereign; and some of the more important contributions of the eighteenth century to English constititional development came in the shape of judge-made law. It was one of the greatest judges of the period, Lord Mansfield, who in 1772 in the case of the negro Somerset gave the classic judicial ruling that in the absence of positive law to the contrary, no man could be held in a state of slavery on English soil. In the matter of general warrants[3] raised by Wilkes and No. 45 *North Briton* in the famous series of cases between 1763 and 1766, it was the judges again who condemned a well-established prerogative usage of arrest and interrogation employed by secretaries of

---

[1] Walpole, *Letters*, II, 66; Hume, *Essays Moral, Political and Literary*, Essay VI, 'Of the Independence of Parliament'.

[2] The *obiter dicta* of judges, such as Lord Camden's denunciation of the Declaratory Act of 1766 in the House of Lords as 'contrary to the fundamental laws of this constitution' had of course no legal or judicial validity.

[3] Orders issued by secretaries of state to arrest persons and impound papers. The main object was to obtain evidence that would justify a charge. They were not again employed after 1763.

state ever since the close of the seventeenth century and brought the practice to an abrupt end. They did so, moreover, in language that would not have seemed incongruous in the mouth of Jefferson or Sam Adams. 'Such a power . . . invested in a Secretary of State . . . may affect the person and property of every man in this kingdom, and is totally subversive of the liberty of the subject,' observed Chief Justice Pratt.[1] And when an application was made for a re-trial on grounds of excessive damages awarded to the plaintiffs (Wilkes and the printers) he upheld the severity of the jury on the grounds that they had been moved by 'a righteous indignation at the conduct of those who sought to exercise arbitrary power over all the King's subjects, to violate Magna Carta, and to destroy the liberty of the kingdom'.[2]

On the other hand, it was also the business of the judges to protect and strengthen legal authority, whether of the executive or the legislature, and in certain matters essential to any liberal concept of political freedom, such as the right of public discussion and criticism, they held a professionally narrow view of what was legally permissible. Schooled by the tradition of more anarchic centuries to believe that the habits of civil obedience were too fragile to endure deliberate tampering, they looked to the security of the state rather than to the satisfaction of the public.[3] On the central issue of criminal libel,[4] for example, the doctrine of the liberty of the press as defined by one judge – 'that every man may fearlessly advocate any new doctrine, provided he does so with proper respect to the religion and government of the country'[5] was one that was hardly calculated to encourage the exuberance of public debate. Franklin, the editor of the *Craftsman*, found himself in the dock on a charge of seditious libel for printing in January 1731 a news-letter which suggested (with complete accuracy as it turned out) that the government was about to throw over its ally France and make peace with the Emperor. Similarly, at the trial of the Gordon rioters in 1781, Lord Mansfield upheld from the bench the traditional but highly artificial doctrine of constructive treason. By this somewhat strained legal theory forcible action by numbers of persons for general or public objects[6] were held to be the technical equivalent of levying war against the king, and so treason and punishable by death – an antiquated and ferocious doctrine dating back to the period before the Riot Act of 1715 when the problem of controlling riotous crowds was one of great legal and administrative difficulty.

Yet even the professionalism of the judges and the rigour of the law had a

---

[1] In *Wilkes v. Wood* (1763).

[2] Quoted by C. D. Yonge, *Constitutional History of England 1760–1860* (2nd edn 1883) p. 18.

[3] LCJ Pratt (later Lord Camden) in 1763, for example, took a a higher view of parliamentary privilege in releasing Wilkes than the House of Commons was prepared to do and higher than Chief Justice Denman in 1839 in the case of *Stockdale v. Hansard*.

[4] Writings calculated to bring the government into hatred or contempt or to subvert the loyalty of the subject.

[5] Mr Justice Best in the case of *Sir Francis Burdett* in 1820. Fox's Libel Act did not of course alter the legal definition of seditious libel nor did it take away the judge's right to express his opinion in court on the character of the alleged libel.

[6] Such as for raising wages, opening prisons, destroying certain classes of buildings (chapels or brothels), resisting militia laws, throwing down enclosures, redressing real or imaginary grievances. It is significant, however, that the jury acquitted Lord George Gordon from the charge of high treason on which he was arranged.

compensating element in the jury system. Judges might direct on law but juries had to find on fact, and they frequently modified the effect of the judicial machinery by their own notions of what the law ought to be even if it were not. In law, until the passing of Fox's libel act in 1792, it was for the judges to decide whether a publication was seditious, the jury being merely required to find on the fact of publication and the meaning of the words and expressions used. But juries showed considerable tenacity and ingenuity (not without encouragement from defending counsel) in encroaching on the judicial function. Consider, for example, the case of William Owen, the bookseller, tried in 1752 on a charge of printing and publishing a seditious libel entitled 'The Case of Alexander Murray, esquire'. The pamphlet dealt with a recent disputed and riotous election at Westminster[1] and since it charged the House of Commons with being a partial, corrupt and unjust assembly, and the Court of the King's Bench with overturning *Habeas Corpus*, it was clearly libellous by contemporary judicial criteria. The fact of publication was admitted by the defence and Lord Chief Justice Lee accordingly directed the jury to deliver a verdict of guilty. But the jurymen brought in a verdict of not guilty on the case as a whole – fact, law, and justice – even though at the request of the Attorney-General they were recalled to court afterwards to be cross-examined on the sense of their verdict. In the better known case of the Dean of St Asaph (1783–4) where the Dean, Dr Shipley, was prosecuted for publishing a pamphlet on parliamentary reform, the jury gave a verdict of guilty of publishing only and so precipitated a series of re-trials and motions in arrest of judgement which finally ended in a technical acquittal. Shipley's case, conducted by the great advocate Erskine, roused a national controversy which led to the act of 1792, enabling the jury in cases of seditious libel to pass a verdict on the whole of the matter brought before them. But it is clear that even before the law was changed, the popular element of the jury, through sentiment, prejudice and plain partisanship, could materially modify the power of the judges and the enforcement of received doctrine in this sensitive area between politics and law. Even in the judicial system the balance-wheel could be seen in operation.

In the wider reaches of political conduct to which the judiciary could not extend its authority, there were in the last resort the forces of public opinion and popular agitation – never more significantly employed than when attempting to challenge the legislature. In a real sense there is a case for arguing that if constitutional liberties were in danger in the eighteenth century, the danger came not from the power of the limited monarchy but from the excesses of a privileged legislature. The haphazard and antiquated structure of representation, never completely logical even in its origins and made less so by the passage of time, gave a peculiarly insulated character to the House of Commons. Even the traditionally-minded Blackstone admitted that if the structure of parliament needed amendment, it was in the direction of a more complete representation of the people; and the theory of 'indirect representation', though popular with the politicians, increasingly failed to convince the public as the century wore on. Much friction and several constitutional crises occurred primarily because the House of Commons seemed more bent on demonstrating its power against the public than against the Crown.

---

[1] Murray had been called to account by the House of Commons but had refused to apologize and was committed to Newgate. See *State Trials*, ed. T. B. Howell (1813), XVIII, pp. 1203 ff.

Defences elaborated in the sixteenth and seventeenth centuries to protect the legislature against royal intimidation, were turned in the eighteenth century against the very electorate which the House of Commons claimed to represent. The powerful and quasi-judicial 'privileges' of parliament were used to protect secrecy of debate and decisions on disputed elections in a manner that was increasingly irritating to influential public opinion. In the early part of the century a typical case was that of Cave, the proprietor of the *Gentleman's Magazine*, who was brought to the bar of the House in 1747 for publishing an account of a recent debate and only obtained his liberty by humble submission and payment of heavy fees. But when the radically-minded City of London, the City magistracy, and the Middlesex mob were joined in 1763 by that astute and unscrupulous demagogue John Wilkes, a battle was opened which, though it lasted for nearly a decade, ended in the practical defeat of the House of Commons. If Wilkes remained excluded from parliament until 1774 and Crosby, the Lord Mayor of London, in 1771 enjoyed a popular and comfortable martyrdom at the hands of the Commons as prisoner in the Tower of London, the moral victory lay with the public. From then on reports of parliamentary debates were published with impunity; and after the belated admission in 1782 of the illegality of the Middlesex election decisions, it was tacitly taken for granted that the House of Commons could not by its mere declaration render any parliamentary candidate ineligible for election. Without any remedy at law being open to it, public opinion in the country had nevertheless inflicted a permanent defeat on a legislature which had overstepped the politically acceptable limits of its power; and in the constitutional conflicts of the Wilkes era are the first discernible roots of the movement for parliamentary reform. If the eighteenth-century constitution had its abuses, it could also furnish its own correctives.

IV

There were of course other aspects. The vaunted English liberty must have seemed somewhat tarnished to the Protestant Dissenter barred from public and municipal office by the Test and Corporation Acts; to the Roman Catholic leading his enclosed and alien life within the Protestant social community; to the men of the sea-ports and fishing-villages pressganged for the navy. Yet the Indemnity Acts, in a triumph of expediency over logic, annually protected Dissenters from the penalties of the law should they have chosen to break it; the savage penal legislation against Papists was rarely enforced;[1] and naval security at least exempted the mass of the male population from forcible conscription for service overseas. Hessian mercenaries abroad were a symbol of English freedom at home. It was true also that the liberty of the subject in the English eighteenth-century context had a legal rather than a social connotation. As defined by Blackstone it consisted in the free enjoyment of personal security, personal freedom, and private property, and in vindication of these the further right to regular and free administration of justice, the right of petitioning Crown and Parliament for the redress of grievances, and the right of bearing arms in self-defence. But by contemporary standards this was enough, for it provided the necessary frame-

---

[1] And by two statutes of 1778 and 1791 largely removed on condition of taking oaths of loyalty.

work for an even simpler concept of liberty – the right of men to live their lives as they wished, free from restraint, surveillance and control, subject only to the penalties of the law after they had infringed it. The eighteenth century in England was a profoundly individualistic and libertarian age. It is significant that not until the second quarter of the nineteenth century did Englishmen reluctantly accept the principle of a preventive police force; and not until the third quarter did they universally enforce it. Far more than the nineteenth, the eighteenth century was the age of economic liberalism, of *laisser-faire*, of self-help and free enterprise. It saw not only the writings of Adam Smith, Dean Tucker and Jeremy Bentham, but the practical disuse or repeal of a mass of Elizabethan and Stuart paternal legislation designed to regulate the lives of the poor and industrious; and the acceptance by parliament of the general thesis that industry flourished most where the state interfered least.

It was this which provided the wider setting for the constitution. If Englishmen regarded themselves as free, it was because they had reduced to a minimum the apparatus of the central executive. The task of government was to carry on those basic functions without which government can hardly be said to exist at all: the conduct of foreign policy, the defence of the realm, the enforcement of the law, the collection of taxes. But beyond this the eighteenth-century public and parliament showed a marked disinclination to extend the area of central executive activity. If this was fundamentally a distrust of power, it was also assisted by a justifiable prejudice. Governmental authority to them meant political influence; political influence meant jobbery and corruption; corruption meant extravagance and inefficiency. Moreover Hanoverian England was not a centralized society and did not wish to become one. For the great mass of the people who lived outside the few moderately sized towns, the historic units of county and shire, hundred and parish, under the ancient hierarchies of Lord Lieutenant, High Sheriff, Coroner, Custos Rotulorum, High Bailiff, High Constable, overseers of the poor, and parochial churchwardens, provided not only the juridical but also the social and administrative framework of their lives. If not quite a 'confederation of counties', England was at least deeply provincial; and slowness of communications in an age of dirt-roads and horse-transport gave the effect of great distance. Eighteenth-century administration reflected this quasi-federalistic structure. 'If we were asked,' wrote the greatest historians of English local government, 'to name a period in English history during which the country possessed the largest measure of self-government, when its local administrators were most effectively free from superior control, either by the National Executive, Parliament, or the Law Courts, we should suggest the years between 1689 and 1835, or, more precisely, the century that elapsed between the accession of the House of Hanover and the close of the Napoleonic Wars'.[1]

It was self-government in the sense at least of localized aristocratic government. The bulk of the work in this decentralized system had long been in the hands of the unpaid country gentry, acting singly as magistrates or collectively at Quarter Sessions. When it was necessary to create new powers for new tasks the legislature preferred to entrust them in regulated quantities to existing or specially created local authorities, self-financing or reimbursed from the county rate, rather than to

---

[1]   S. and B. Webb, *English Local Government, Parish and County* (1906), pp. 309–10.

a centrally controlled and nationally paid corps of officials. The residuary legatee of this devolution of administrative duty was the Justice of the Peace. He more than any other class in society was living proof of 'the inclination of the British monarchy', as one legal writer piously put it, 'to dispense the blessings of law and government, as well as to maintain the national defence, by the gratuitous instrumentality of the nobles and gentry'.[1] The JP was the maid of all work in the eighteenth as in the sixteenth century; but the factotum of the Tudors had become the domestic tyrant of the Hanoverians – and there was no Star Chamber, no Burleigh or Strafford to keep him in proper deference to the central power. Freed from the need to submit their actions to the scrutiny of either parliament or department of state, the eighteenth-century magistrates were even developing what the Webbs called 'inchoate provincial legislation' in the form of orders in Quarter Session which derived what strictly legal force they possessed from old statutes, common law, or the mere habit of unchallenged authority. Indeed the decay of central regulative statutes was to some extent offset by the justices' intervention, often carried to a remarkable extent, into the social life of their own neighbourhoods; so that, for example, the question whether a man's wages were subject to quasi-judicial regulation might depend entirely on the locality in which he lived. But even apart from the organic, sub-parliamentary growth of local administration, the statutory duties and jurisdiction of the JPs annually increased. The standard handbook on his office (Dr Richard Burn's *Justice of the Peace*) first published in 1754 had by 1793 reached its seventeenth edition in four fat volumes; and as the author himself complained shortly before his death[2] 'so many new matters are in every session of parliament brought under the jurisdiction of these justices, and so many alterations are made in the subjects of which before they had cognizance, that every new edition, in order to keep pace with the law, is in effect a new book.' The reason, however, is clear. Much was being done to meet the needs of the community – perhaps it would be better to say, of the different communities – but it was not being done by the government. Parliament, as a sovereign legislative power, might supply the authority; but as an assembly of provincial landowners it was putting that authority in the hands of its own class in their own neighbourhoods. It was not an efficient mode of administration. Indeed, as the century wore on, there accumulated that impenetrable thicket of competing and overlapping powers and jurisdictions which horrified reformers after Waterloo. But it worked; whatever was urgently wanted was accomplished: after a fashion, locally, and at surprisingly little cost to the public at large.

From this distrustful and parsimonious approach came the great paradox of the eighteenth century: a centralized legislature and a decentralized administration, a parliament legislating for the whole country but not always or often for the country as a whole. As Maitland long ago pointed out, the greater part of the legislation of this period was not law but regulation, involving not legal principles but administrative details. Private acts formed a substantial proportion of the annual crop of statutes; and even of the public acts, the majority perhaps were essentially concerned with private and local affairs. Take at random the volume of

---

[1] Gilbert Hutcheson, *A Treatise on the Office of Justice of the Peace* (Edinburgh, 1806), I, Preface, vii.
[2] In the 15th edn (1785).

parliamentary statutes for one of the mid-century years – 1763–4 (IV Geo. III). The public acts include the recurrent and familiar items of supplies, customs and excise, indemnity and mutiny acts, together with one to regulate whale fishing and another 'for granting certain duties in the British Colonies and plantations in America'. They also included acts relating to hackney coaches in Kent and Essex, the manufacture of cambric in Sussex, and small debts in Doncaster; one for repairing and widening the road from Shillingford in Oxfordshire to Reading in Berkshire and building a bridge over the Thames; one to levy a rate of 2*d*. Scots or $\frac{1}{6}d$. sterling, on every pint of ale sold at Dunbar, for improving the harbour and repairing the town-hall; another to enable the Bank of England to purchase lands and houses at Cornhill; others still for the relief of the poor and the establishment of a night-watch in specific towns and villages. The private acts, so officially classified, cover an even more variegated miscellany: to naturalize Govert Cassau; to enclose common lands at Heckington in Lincolnshire; to drain fen-lands at Helgay, co. Norfolk; to permit the executors of John Newport to lease his estate during his lunacy; to annex the rectory of East Lockinge in Berkshire to All Souls College; to enable an infant, lately called Richard Peers, to take the surname Symons; to dissolve the marriage of John Weller with Charlotte Wilson and to enable him to marry again. The sheer quantity as well as the content of this legislation is impressive. There were eighty-three of these private acts in this year and ninety-three public acts. But of the latter, only about thirty were genuinely public acts. In other words, about 145 of a total of 176 statutes passed in that session were primarily concerned with local and personal administrative matters. Parliament provided the necessary enabling power; the money came from the county rate or private purse; the work fell on local or statutory authorities in the shape of unpaid magistrates, private individuals, or *ad hoc* bodies of one kind or another. But the most significant aspect of all from a constitutional point of view was that this mass of detailed, cheap, amateurish administration was only made possible by the growing omnicompetence of parliamentary activities.

V

Here perhaps is the clue to the ultimate paradox of the constitution: the antithesis which justifies both Montesquieu and Jefferson. In this annual flow of administrative regulation was steady and commonplace proof that the separation of powers in the constitution did not imply separation of authority. The tripartite division of the legislature into King, Lords, and Commons, led for domestic purposes at least to a political limitation of powers; but their conjunction in the act of legislation produced that formidable sovereign authority of the constitution, the Crown in Parliament. Hidden in the constitutional machine, for all its careful assemblage of checks, balances, and counterweights, lay a force which was essentially that of Hobbes's *Leviathan*, the modern omnicompetent state. Indeed, it is exactly at this point that the orthodox Blackstone becomes momentarily indistinguishable from the heretical Hobbes. Few passages in Blackstone's *Commentaries* are more revealing than the lyrical phrases that sober lawyer employed when lost in contemplation of what he called this 'sovereign and uncontrollable authority', this 'absolute despotic power which must in all governments reside somewhere', which could do 'everything that is not naturally impossible'. But he was not exaggerating. This was a power which had set aside James II and put William and Mary on the throne; a power that with growing confidence had declared in 1719 that it had full authority to make laws to bind the kingdom and people of Ireland; and in 1766 to 'bind the colonies and people of America, subjects of the crown of Great Britain, in all cases whatsoever'.[1] But these were rare and exceptional declarations of imperial supremacy. What nourished the roots of parliamentary authority was the quiet and unchallenged exercise throughout the century of this limitless legislation on the multifarious affairs of the English community. A power flexible enough to descend from high matters of state to regulate twenty miles of muddy road in the Thames Valley or the private affairs of a fatherless family, was a domesticated Leviathan, but a Leviathan all the same. It seemed harmless, because it was applied to small matters, often in minute and single applications, and by the request of the recipients; and above all because it was not reflected in a powerful executive. Here was sovereignty, the great prime mover that lay at the centre of the constitution: but sovereignty deprived of despotism – a sovereignty which (to adapt without irreverence a phrase from Surtees's Mr Jorrocks) was the image of despotism, but with none of its danger and only 25 per cent of its expense.[2]

The eighteenth-century constitution had in fact solved for immediate and domestic purposes the problem of asserting the legal omnicompetence of parliament without setting up an omnipotent executive. It was almost unavoidable therefore that when it stumbled on the crisis of the American colonies it made large claims without waiting to enquire whether it had equally large means. To admit the colonists' argument of natural rights or inherent liberties distinct from law ran counter to the whole massive if silent development of parliamentary jurisdiction; and Chatham's contention that it was illegal to tax colonies without representation was both antiquated and invalid. What parliament, the public and the Crown had to face was the infinitely more difficult political axiom propounded by Burke: that it is of small account to hold legal power unless that power can be enforced and unless there is a readiness to face the consequences of enforcement. Burke's attitude was more realistic, but to adopt it parliament had to distinguish between legal sovereignty which is infinite and political government which is limited. Since both existed harmoniously side by side in eighteenth-century England, it had been given little practice in this problem; and when recognition came, it was too late. George III had to fight the battle of a sovereign legislature with the resources of a limited monarchy. It was not surprising either that from the other side of the Atlantic the rebellious colonists could see in fact in the sovereignty of the British parliament only the image of despotism; that they feared its danger; and grudged even 10 per cent of its expense.

---

[1] Declatory Act.

[2] It will be remembered that Mr Jorrocks described hunting as 'the sport of Kings, the image of war without its guilt, and only five-and-twenty per cent of its danger'.

2

The Crisis of the Anglican Establishment in the Early Nineteenth Century[1]

Like most churches the Church of England has rarely been free from internal controversy. The difficulties of the period 1815–1850, however, were of a different order to all previous controversies since 1660. It was a crisis of the Establishment and not merely *in* the Establishment. For the first time since the reign of Anne a century earlier there was a conviction among many churchmen that the Church itself was in danger. This fear was not unreasonable. The nature of the attacks on the Church, in particular the demand for disestablishment, was something to find a parallel for which it was necessary to go back to the Puritan Revolution of the seventeenth century. The outward events of the crisis are well known. What is less often discussed is why the danger seemed so great, and why in the end it was overcome with such apparent ease.

It has been said that a church established is a church disarmed. Ever since the Henrician reformation of the sixteenth century there had been an undeniable truth in this maxim as far as the Church of England was concerned. The power of the Crown to appoint bishops and archbishops, and the authority of the Crown in parliament to legislate on the doctrine, discipline and liturgy of the church, placed the Establishment firmly under secular control. Between 1689 and 1714 there was another period of crisis when Church and State seemed to be pulling in opposite directions on the great issue of the time, namely the dynastic revolution of 1688 and the religious legislation which was part of the so-called Revolution Settlement. As a result the Hanoverian accession in 1714 was soon followed by the imposition of even tighter control by the politicians over the clerics of the Establishment. To get rid of a centre of possible political dissidence the regular meetings of Convocation (the representative assembly of the Church) were suspended in 1717 and were not resumed for another century and a half. The selection of bishops was increasingly subject to political and even party considerations. The two dozen bishops and two archbishops who sat in the House of Lords became an important element in the almost permanent government majority. Attendance during the now regular sessions of parliament, pamphleteering for the ready writers and debating for the ready speakers, became an expected part of a bishop's political duty; and since the inequality of episcopal stipends made translation from poorer to richer dioceses a natural object of episcopal ambition, government possessed a powerful source of influence over bishops even after appointment. For this there was a price to pay. Long and frequent absences from their dioceses, and the political flavour which surrounded their appointments and

[1] A paper read at the Coburg Seminar of the Prince Albert Society on 'Church, State and Society in the Nineteenth Century' in September 1983. Subsequently published in *Prince Albert Studies*, vol. II (Munich, 1984).

promotions, did much to separate the bishops, the ostensible leaders of the Church, from the lower clergy.

These were not the only points of weakness in the Establishment. The legislative supremacy of parliament meant that few changes in the constitution or organization of the Church could take place without parliamentary authority. The suspension of Convocation meant that the Church had no national forum of debate for its principles and policies. Effectively the Church of England was a church without government – certainly it was without government of a type that could initiate and direct change, exercise serious control over its clergy, or even provide for the proper training of its ordinands. Not surprisingly the Church fell victim to the abuses and obsolescence which affected most of the great institutions of the country during the prosperous and peaceful eighteenth century. The defects of the Church's organization at the start of the nineteenth century are notorious and need no more than a mention here – the maldistribution of its resources, the inequality of stipends, widespread pluralism and its inevitable concomitant absenteeism, and the decay of episcopal discipline. In 1800 the Irish Act of Union had provided for a union of the two established churches of England and Ireland. This union, though never more than nominal, was a source of further weakness since the Church of Ireland was even more defective as an organization, and even less defensible as an establishment, than its senior partner. At the start of the nineteenth century, therefore, the structure of the Church was weak and ungainly; certainly in no shape to meet the challenge of the age of criticism and protest which came with the return of peace in 1815.

By that date the Church of England had come to reflect to a large extent the characteristics of the secular state to which it was bound by so many legal and social ties. The Establishment was not an isolated institution; its strengths and weaknesses derived from its identification with the ruling classes. In the course of the eighteenth century the Church, which had been regarded as a potential danger to the governing system in the age of George I and Walpole, had become the steadfast ally of the governing system in the age of George III and the younger Pitt. This important transformation was a direct result of the assimilation of the clergy to the aristocracy and gentry who ruled the country after 1714. It was also one of the reasons why the Hanoverian period was one of domestic calm compared with the turbulent Stuart period. The Church, it could be said, had escaped from Stuart despotism only to fall into the hands of the Whig oligarchy. This in effect was the price of the Hanoverian succession; from a secular point of view it was a price well worth paying.

This assimilation was apparent at different levels. The episcopate had become not only a political ally of the government but to a considerable degree the preserve of the aristocracy. The peak of aristocratic influence on the composition of the bench of bishops in the House of Lords probably reached its height between 1783 and 1830. George III and George IV as monarchs, Pitt and Liverpool as prime ministers, all showed a decided preference in their appointments for men of aristocratic birth or connection. In an age of social unrest and equalitarian demands this became a deliberate act of policy. As George IV put it to Bishop Howley in 1827, it was 'very desirable to connect the Bench of bishops with the nobility of the country'. Of the hundred bishops in the period 1783–1852 whose social origins are ascertainable, nearly two-thirds were con-

nected by birth or marriage to the peerage or landed gentry. The social assimilation did not stop there. The laicization which was an inevitable part of the
process affected the parochial clergy as well. Though precise statistical analyses
are lacking, the general evidence suggests that the gentry and professional classes
provided the bulk of the incumbents in the more lucrative benefices; while the
curates, especially those unfortunates who languished for years in that ill-paid
capacity, were drawn from the humble classes with little wealth or family backing
to assist them.

This social stratification is not surprising when one reflects that the right of
presentation of about half of all benefices were held by lay patrons, and a further
tenth by town and other corporations and the Crown. Since the ecclesiastical
patrons who presented to the remaining two-fifths included the Oxford and
Cambridge colleges, who customarily sought to provide for members of the
college, it is clear that influence and connection counted for more than virtuous-
ness or scholarship in the distribution of the better livings within the Establishment.

There was in addition what could be called an administrative assimilation
which further linked the Church to the state. A body of men resident all over the
country, educated and presumed to be of good character, were too valuable to be
overlooked by a central government which lacked any large number of professional administrators and could not have afforded to pay them even if they had
existed. We find therefore that between 1815 and 1830 about a quarter of the
magistrates were supplied by the parochial clergy. In addition clergy played a part
not only in the administration of justice and repression of crime but in such local
government activities as poor law and highway management. Even when not
appointed magistrates, the parochial clergy found themselves part of the
machinery of the state. The parish was a unit not only of ecclesiastical but civil
government; the parish council (sometimes called the vestry from its traditional
meeting-place in the parish church) formed the lowest tier of provincial administration. Since it was a democratic body, usually elected by the body of rate-
payers, it frequently included dissenters and radicals over whom the parish
minister had to preside, often to his acute discomfort.

This identification of the Church with the governing system was in some
respects a source of strength even if it detracted from the spiritual authority of the
clergy; but only if the system was stable. It ceased to be so once the system itself
came under political attack. The misfortune of the Church after 1815 was that
historical factors over which it had little or no control were increasingly disturb-
ing the stability of the social and administrative structure in which the clergy
played so prominent a part. It was in fact a combination of its own internal
weaknesses and extrinsic national weaknesses which constituted the heart of the
problem for the Church of England at the start of the nineteenth century.

One difficulty was the distribution of its resources. The existing parochial
system was pre-industrial, virtually medieval, in its origins, that is to say, its
organization was based on a historic distribution of population that was densest in
the south and south-east, thinnest in the north and north-west. The startling
growth of population after 1770 had not only strained existing parish resources
but further compounded their inadequacies by a shift in distribution towards the
midlands and the north. The double problem created by the growth of new

industrial areas and the growth of towns could be dramatically seen, for example, in the town of Leeds in the west riding of Yorkshire which in 1831 had a population of 123,000 crammed within the boundaries of its one parish.

The second and entirely ifferent problem for the Establishment was the competition from other denominations. The Methodist movement of the eighteenth century had attracted adherents who by 1815 were probably as numerous as all the other non-Anglicans put together. Historic Protestant dissent, which had nearly disappeared in the reign of George I, had also revived under the stimulus of the Evangelical movement. Roman Catholicism, as a result of the re-emergence of the Irish problem in English politics after 1770 and the Union of the two countries in 1800, now presented a separate and formidable form of rivalry within the United Kingdom. Even without this new Irish dimension to the problem, it was clear by the first decade of the new century that the Church of England, for the first time in its history, was rapidly ceasing to be the church of the majority of English people.

Yet the law and the constitution still rested on the fiction that the Church of England represented the people of England in their religious aspect. This had never been true, even at the time of the Elizabethan settlement; but it was now more dangerously untrue than ever before. Nevertheless, the letter of the law and the practice of the constitution still upheld a principle which patently did not correspond to the facts and which was increasingly resented by the growing body of non-Anglicans. Legislation of the late seventeenth century, in particular the Test and Corporation Acts of Charles II's reign and the Oaths of Allegiance and Supremacy reframed at the Revolution of 1688, effectively excluded Roman Catholics from the legislature and in theory excluded Protestant dissenters, as well as Roman Catholics, from offices in local government and under the Crown. The Church of England in addition possessed a monopoly of officially recording births, deaths and marriages. Membership of the Church was a condition of obtaining degrees at Oxford and Cambridge, on which among other things entry into the professions of law and medicine depended. Though there were some excellent Dissenting Academies, secondary education was largely in the hands of public and grammar schools which were not only Anglican in spirit but normally staffed by Anglican clergy. In secular society at large householders, irrespective of their religion, were liable to pay church rates for the upkeep of the fabric of the parish church. Landowners and farmers were frequently subject to payment of tithe for the support of the Anglican parochial clergy.

At almost all levels of English society there were permanent points of friction arising from the privileged position of the Established Church and the inferior position accorded by state and society to other denominations. With more people than ever before outside the pale of the Establishment, the concept of a confessional state embodied in the constitution seemed more than ever an anachronism.

It was inevitable therefore that when all the great institutions of the state came under fire after 1815, the Church of England was not spared. The growth of radical political thought, under the stimulus of the American and French Revolutions, resulted in the formulation of demands for wide-ranging reforms; the economic and social difficulties of English society that came with the peace provided the stimulus for action. The Church was regarded by many reformers as part of a class-ridden, reactionary state and was attacked in the same way as the monarchy, the aristocracy, and the legislature. Indeed, the *Extraordinary Black Book*, the bible of radical reformers between 1828 and 1834, which styled itself 'An Exposition of Abuses in Church and State', devoted the first two chapters to the Church of England and its third to the Church of Ireland, before moving on to a consideration of the revenues of the Crown and other aspects of civil government.

The popular feeling against the Church reached its height, perhaps, in 1831 when by an unfortunate numerical coincidence twenty-one bishops in the House of Lords cast their votes against the parliamentary reform bill which, if they had been given in its favour, would have secured its passage. The government's Lord Chancellor, Henry Brougham, wrote privately that 'the bishops have done for themselves'; and in public *The Times* newspaper thundered against the 'mitred Iscariots' who had sold their country for a handful of silver. Bishops were burnt in effigy and in the reform riots at Bristol later that year the bishop's palace was burnt to the ground. When the reform bill finally passed in 1832 it was not so much hoped as confidently expected that it would be followed by immediate and fundamental changes in the structure and finance of the Established Church. It was in these years that the cry of 'Free Trade in Religion', echoing the dominant economic catchword of the day, was first heard; meaning by that a demand for equality of opportunity for all forms of Christianity without help or hindrance from the state.

For the Church of England the years between 1828 and 1841 represented one long crisis. In 1828 the Test and Corporation Acts were repealed, giving political equality to all Protestant dissenters. In 1829 came Catholic Emancipation, allowing entry to the legislature and most high offices of state for Roman Catholics. The Reform Act of 1832 strengthened the electoral influence of radicals and dissenters. In 1833 the Irish Church Act abolished ten Irish bishoprics of the Established Church. In 1837 the government introduced a bill to abolish church rates. Between 1833 and 1838 there was a prolonged battle in the House of Commons to pass a measure appropriating part of the revenues of the Church of Ireland for non-ecclesiastical purposes. In 1839 a Whig plan for national education was put forward involving a new principle of non-confessional education.

In the intense controversies surrounding these measures all the fundamental issues of church–state relationship came up for public and often passionate debate: the autonomy of the Church of England, its historical authority, the legitimacy of state support, the right of the Church to its property and revenues, the position of the bishops in the House of Lords, and above all, the question of disestablishment. For seven painful years from 1828 to 1835 the Church of England was thrown completely on the defensive and many of its leaders were pessimistic over the outcome of the struggle. 'The Church, as it now stands', wrote Arnold, the famous clerical headmaster of Rugby School in June 1832, 'no human power can save.' A month earlier Archbishop Whately of Dublin had written to the prime minister Lord Grey, more perhaps with hope than assurance, that it would be 'a difficult but great and glorious feat for your Lordship's ministry to preserve the Establishment from utter overthrow'.

Yet from about 1835 onward the tide slowly turned. The king's dismissal of the reforming Whig government in 1834, mainly on the grounds of his opposition to his ministers' Irish Church policy, allowed the Conservative opposition leader Sir

Robert Peel to form a brief ministry in the winter of 1834–5. Though weak politically he was able to make a significant contribution to the defence of the Church. During his few months of office he set up an Ecclesiastical Commission, a mixed body of churchmen and sympathetic laymen, charged with the task of reforming the Church from within. The church rates abolition bill was defeated in 1837; the government abandoned the appropriation principle in 1838; and withdrew their educational plan in 1839. The foundation of the Anti-State Church Society in 1844, which changed its name in 1853 to the less aggressive title of the 'Society for the Liberation of Religion from State Patronage and Control', attracted publicity and support but failed in its professed object. Though it provoked the counter-phenomenon of the 'Church Defence' movement in the years 1857–63, by that time there was little heat left in the old establishment controversy.

To what then did the Establishment owe its preservation? The answer is complex. In the first place the Church of England, because it was the church of the ruling classes, was entrenched in the seats of power: in the House of Lords, the House of Commons, the old universities, the learned professions; in the public schools, and in the two large political parties. It is true that among the grandees of the Whig Party at the beginning of Victoria's reign there was still an oligarchic tradition, republican, erastian, anti-ecclesiastical, stemming from its seventeenth-century origin. Men like Lord Holland, Lord Melbourne, were intellectual sceptics; Lord John Russell a utilitarian rationalist who believed neither in the dogmas nor in the authority of the Church of England. Nevertheless among the Whig gentry in the House of Commons were many who had the traditional loyalty of their class to the Anglican Church; and it was their reluctance which prevented their leaders from abolishing church rates in 1837. As for the Conservative party it was from the start a 'Church and State' party. Indeed it could fairly be argued that the Anglican reaction to the events of 1828–32 was one of the roots of the new party's strengths. Lord Stanley, who succeeded Peel as leader of the party, wrote later that 'in the main it is undoubted that . . . the Conservative Party was formed upon questions affecting the maintenance of the Established Church, and the integrity of the institutions of the country.'

This secular, political support was crucial. Indeed there is a strong case for saying that the Church of England was saved by its laity. Foremost among them would be two prime ministers. Lord Liverpool as early as 1818 extracted from parliament a grant of a million pounds for building new churches and followed that up with another half-million in 1824. Sir Robert Peel's creation of the Ecclesiastical Commission in 1835 proved a turning-point in the history of church reform in the nineteenth century. It has been said indeed that if any one man saved the Church of England it was Peel; and though such large claims ought not perhaps to be made for any individual, there can be little doubt that the Commission, along with his subsequent legislation like the Populous Parishes Act of 1843 enabling the Commission to form new parishes, was the largest single contribution to the church reform movement. For what it did was not only to create the machinery for a reform of the organization and finances of the Church but, equally important, to place the initiative and responsibility for reform legislation on the leaders of the Church themselves.

Behind the political leaders and the parties was the broad mass of the Anglican middle classes. The motives influencing them were no doubt very mixed. Genuine piety, historic loyalty, class habits, social snobbery, political partisanship, all these played their part. What is important is that then, and for many years to come, religious questions were taken seriously and greatly influenced political behaviour. England was still in that sense a religious society. Religion and church membership were essential elements in both public and private life. Indeed, without a knowledge of contemporary religious issues, the politics of the 1815–52 period are largely unintelligible.

There was another aspect. The Church of England was not so defective and corrupt as its enemies made out. Probably it never had been even in the worst days of the eighteenth century. But those days were far behind and certainly the work of regeneration had started long before 1830. It would be historically true to say that the reform of the Church in the early nineteenth century was part of, and not simply a result of, the political 'Age of Reform'. This is something not always comprehended even in England. In the recent celebrations of the 150th anniversary of the Oxford Movement some commentators, more fervent than scholarly, claimed for the Tractarians a pioneer role in the reform of the Church of England. Keble's sermon on National Apostasy in 1833, generally regarded as the start of the movement, was by some described as an appeal to the nation to return to the ways of Christianity. In fact, as any student of the Oxford Movement knows, it was a denunciation of the Whig government for imposing reform on the Church and of the public for demanding such reforms. It was the public acceptance of the need for reform which constituted in Keble's eyes 'apostasy'; not irreligion. In its origins therefore, the Oxford Movement was a reaction against reform. For the beginnings of the internal movement of reform one must go back to the eighteenth century, to the Evangelical Movement which not only sought higher moral standards for the laity but better pastoral care by the parochial clergy. A generation before the young Tractarian curates were coming down from Oxford to spread the gospel of the beauty of holiness in the parish churches of England, Simeon of Cambridge was sending out his ardent young evangelical clergy to rival the Methodists in missionary work in the industrial towns of northern England.

Evangelicalism was not the only inspiration for reform in the period before the Reform Act. There was also a powerful High Church movement which, however moved by dread of evangelical competition, had a profound influence on the pastoral activities of the Establishment. One could cite, for instance, that London group of laity and clergy known as the Clapton sect (an echo of the better-known Evangelical Clapham sect, both Clapham and Clapton being then residential suburbs of the capital). Also known as the Hackney Phalanx, it was this wealthy and influential pressure group under the leadership of the two Watsons and their church allies which was responsible for the foundation of the National Society in 1811 to start new Anglican schools, and for persuading the government to set up the Church Building Commission in 1818.

Paradoxically, therefore, the Church was beginning to reform and revitalize itself even before the worst of the attacks from without fell upon it. Already in the 1820s there was a perceptible spirit of change and renewal in the Church of England and many reforming bishops were already at work in their dioceses. Though the bishops as a body were never in the van of progress, several bishops, notably Archbishop Howley and Bishop Blomfield of London, were strong allies of the reforming laity. Had it not been so, Peel's Ecclesiastical Commission would never have succeeded since the essence of Peel's policy was to force the Church to put its house in order as the only alternative to having reform thrust upon it from outside. Indeed, within half a dozen years the Commission was largely in hands of bishops. They themselves as a class were changing their character. The prime ministers in power after 1830 – Grey, Melbourne, Peel and Russell – appointed far fewer men from the higher aristocracy than their immediate predecessors. None indeed of Peel's four bishops were of aristocratic origin. Though the clergy as a body continued to be drawn from the educated gentry and professional classes, the episcopate was becoming a socially more varied caste; and one much more aware of its social and pastoral responsibilities.

By the 1840s the Church was again active and confident. The pessimism of the reform era was giving way to optimism; in some cases (as in the young Gladstone's book on *The State in its relations with the Church* 1839) an exaggerated optimism. The home missionary work was extending from building new churches to the creation of new diocesan training colleges for teachers and a great wave of new Anglican schools. Between 1818 and 1856 in fact over three hundred new churches were built by the Church Building Commission alone and perhaps ten times that number by private initiative and subscriptions. In a variety of ways the Church had become more efficient and more professional. It is true that the fear of Popery, aroused by the Oxford Movement and a few well-publicized conversions of leading Tractarians to the church of Rome, temporarily damaged the reputation of the Church of England in the 1840s. The abandonment of the Conservative government's educational scheme in 1843, which would have favoured Anglicans, was largely due to the opposition of the Methodists who were alarmed by the apparent spread of Roman Catholic influence in the Establishment.

Despite this success, however, it is now clear that the enemies and critics of the Church of England were in reality never so powerful nor so united as they appeared to be in the years between 1828 and 1835. Their unity was more in their demands for redress of dissenting grievances than in their attack on the Establishment. The leadership of the large and well-organized Methodist movement was politically conservative under the dominating figure of Jabez Bunting (1779–1858) and the movement as a whole only slowly relinquished its original organic connection with the Church of England. The educational controversy of 1843 was in fact the first time that the Methodist leadership joined with historic Protestant Dissent to oppose Anglican interests. The dissenting churches themselves were divided internally on such central issues as state education and disestablishment. Not all dissenters wanted to see an end to the state church; not all objected to state assistance for their own ministers and schools. Some were ready to accept cooperation with Anglicans in such bodies as the Evangelical Alliance, founded in 1845 in the hope of evolving in the course of time a common policy on these difficult issues. The main body of dissenters were increasingly preoccupied by their own success and worldly prosperity. Their internal tasks of consolidation and organization, of chapel and school building, of training teachers and raising funds, absorbed much of their time and energy. They were in effect becoming more institutionalized and more conservative; more concerned to meet the needs of their own membership than to indulge in aggressive rivalry with other churches. Moreover, by the middle of the century few thoughtful clergy, whatever their denomination, could help being painfully aware of the great mass of irreligion – 'infidelity' in the contemporary phrase – presented by the urban poor on which, despite their collective efforts, the churches seemed to be making little impact. By the 1860s also there was growing recognition that, much as the churches had done collectively in founding schools and training teachers, the problem of national education was too great for their combined resources and that the state would have to take a more direct responsibility.

What had also contributed to the lessening of dissenting hostility was a sense that their main grievances had been recognized and remedies provided. The Whigs are rarely depicted – and would scarcely have regarded themselves – as friends of the Establishment. Yet in their reforms of the 1830s they made a significant contribution to the salvation of the Church from its enemies. The legislation of 1836, for example, provided practical solutions for many irritating problems which had vexed dissenters. Machinery was set up for the official state registration of births, deaths and marriages; an act was passed for the legalizing of dissenting marriages. The grant of a charter to London University the same year enabled non-Anglicans to obtain university degrees. Twenty years later first degrees at Oxford and Cambridge were thrown open to non-Anglicans. Other legislation of the 1850s dealt with such matters as burial grounds and chapel registrations; and though compulsory payment of church rates was not abolished until 1868, local agreements had by then left little intact of the old system.

By the middle of the century the crisis of the Establishment was virtually over. The Church had passed through a dangerous era with – to all appearances – its position intact. The Crown was still by law confined to Anglicans; the coronation service was still an Anglican ceremony; bishops still sat in the House of Lords; the property, buildings and revenues of the Church had not been confiscated. Admittedly the Church of Ireland was disestablished by Gladstone in 1869 but this was primarily a move to protect the Church of England by getting rid of its indefensible partner rather than a prelude to disestablishment of the Anglican counterpart. The close connection with Oxford and Cambridge, with the great public schools, with the aristocracy and gentry, still continued. Yet appearances were deceptive. Certainly the Church retained all the outward trappings of the Establishment; but it did so because – and perhaps only because – it had surrendered many of its historic rights and privileges. It could no longer claim a monopoly of sacramental ceremonies, of public offices for its communicants, of the superintendence of univeristy and secondary education. The internal reforms which had made the Church so efficient and confident had gone hand in hand with external concessions. The legal theory – or fiction – of the confessional state had been tacitly abandoned. The Church no longer possessed the historic position in the state it had enjoyed in 1815. It could, for instance, no longer call on the resources of the state to supply its wants. Few things are more significant in the history of the Church of England in the nineteenth century than the contrast between 1818 and 1842. In 1818, under Lord Liverpool, parliament had made a grant of one million pounds to build new churches. In 1842, after another conservative prime minister Sir Robert Peel had come to power, he was urged by many of his supporters to do something similar. He refused on the grounds that the time had passed when the body of taxpayers at large could be called upon to contribute to the national church and that the attempt would only damage the

Establishment. Equally significant in its way was the financial support made available by the state from 1833 onward for schools of all denominations, dissenting as well as anglican; and, as a special example, the greatly increased grant in 1845 to the Roman Catholic training college at Maynooth in Ireland. Unpopular as that was with many Conservatives, it demonstrated beyond doubt the principle of state impartiality towards all the major churches in the Un..ed Kingdom.

Behind the façade of the Anglican Establishment in fact there had been a perceptible distancing of Church and State. Two events in the 1850s could be taken as symbols of the altered relationship. The revival of Convocation in 1854–5 returned to the Church of England a measure of ecclesiastical autonomy; the admission of Jews to parliament in 1858 (to join Protestant dissenters and Roman Catholics and in another generation professed agnostics) illustrated how far parliament had ceased to be a professedly Christian, let alone an exclusively Anglican body.

It remained true, of course, that the Church of England still possessed an indelibly national character. It was still the residuary church of the English people: the church of all those English people who never went to church except to be christened, married and buried. It is interesting, for example, that in 1846 eight times as many marriages took place in Anglican churches as in those of other denominations; although the religious census of 1851 showed that the Established Church could only claim little more than half the regular church-going population. Social conventions apart, however, it was clear that the Church of England was becoming more like the independent churches – in its private initiative, self-help, reliance on its laity, and competitiveness – just as the dissenting churches were coming to resemble the Established Church in their organization, hierarchy, training and general institutionalism. Free Trade in religion, though no longer heard as a slogan, had to a large extent become a fact. The Established Church had shown adaptability, a responsiveness to changes in society and to altered opinions. In the process it had both gained and lost. It had gained as a church, lost as an establishment. For many Victorian churchmen this was clearly regarded not only as inevitable but as the proper choice.

3

'The State of the Nation' (1822)[1]

Between 1816 and 1827 Lord Liverpool's administration never enjoyed the degree of support from the newspaper press which it needed and modestly believed it deserved. The distress and discontents of the post-war years, and the growing political consciousness of the classes outside the aristocratic system, clearly made it difficult to bridge the gap between governors and governed. For ministers this lack of public support, of which the state of the press was the most obvious symptom, was always a source of regret and often of concern. Both the 'Peterloo' year of 1819 and the 'queen's trial' year of 1820 saw discussions within the administration on the need to secure better publicity. Practical efforts were in fact made through newspapers and pamphlets to present the ministerial case to the public. Important pro-government speeches were reprinted; sympathetic press articles were circulated among provincial editors; pamphlets were prepared under the supervision of the law officers. If Croker's remarks in old age are to be trusted, Peel and Palmerston about 1818–19 were actually writing articles for the *Courier* in an attempt to revive the languishing circulation of that government paper. How far all this had the desired effect is impossible to tell. The difficulty was, and had been for many years, that circulation counted for more in the eyes of newspaper proprietors than subsidies. The able, scurrilous and independent journal *John Bull*, started by Theodore Hook in December 1820, was generally thought to have done more to damage the queen's cause than anything emanating from government offices.

The ministry survived the protracted crisis of the queen's trial but their parliamentary position remained precarious in the succeeding session. The House of Commons still pressed hard and unreasonably for more economies, more tax-reductions; opposition Whigs and disgruntled agriculturalists combined to force the abolition of the tax on farm-horses; there were signs that the principle of transferring rotten-borough seats to new towns was gaining ground even among the country gentry; and a bill to enfranchise Roman Catholics actually got through the Commons. The king was still sulky after the collapse of his divorce project and there were personal difficulties over the internal reconstruction of the ministry. In the following winter there was a strong agitation among farmers and small landowners for the relief of the agricultural industry. Various instant remedies were pressed on ministers, none of them to their liking – the total prohibition of imports of foreign corn, more tax reductions, a reform of parliament, an arbitrary cut in the interest on government stock, and the abolition of tithes.

[1] Not previously published.

In retrospect the slack-water of the 1821 session can be seen as marking the turn of the tide for the hard-pressed ministry. Before the end of the year, with the king reconciled, a political alliance created with the Grenvillites, the entry of Peel into the cabinet, and an honourable exit arranged for Canning, ministers could feel with some justification that they had regained the initiative. Nevertheless, what the *Annual Register* called 'the clamorous outcries' of the landed interest at the start of 1822 gave little hope of a more peaceful session. It was at this point (and it was perhaps a sign of its new confidence) that the government took the unusual step of issuing a defence, not of its record in the previous session nor of its handling of the queen's affair, but of the whole of its policy since the end of the war. It appeared anonymously as a pamphlet, *The State of the Nation*, in January. The title seems curious to a modern eye since it dealt with the conduct of the ministry rather than the state of the country. The phrase, however, was a familiar one to contemporaries. Brougham had used it for a pamphlet he had published in 1806 attacking the whole record of Pitt's recent administration. Whitbread had moved for a committee on the 'state of the nation' in 1807. The precedent most likely to have been in the minds of the ministers, however, was Tierney's motion for a committee on the state of the nation in May 1819 when he called for a wide-ranging enquiry into relations with foreign powers, commercial policy, and finance. Two years later, in their own way and at a time of their own choosing, the government felt able to retort in kind.

The pamphlet was published by Hatchards of Piccadilly, a firm which printed two of Liverpool's major speeches in these years. Though it bore no official stamp of authority (which would in any case have been unprecedented for a work of this kind), no attempt was made to conceal its origin. The style, wavering uncertainly between pretended objectivity and unaffected partisanship, the quantity of statistical information, the assurance with which government policy was stated, the departmental layout of the material, and the sustained advocacy of the arguments, all proclaimed its provenance. The press and the public entertained no doubts about its authorship. Von Neumann, the Austrian minister in London, even thought he knew why the government had decided to resort to such an unusual step. In his diary for February 1822 he recorded that

> the country gentlemen, in spite of all the measures taken by the Government to reinforce Grenville's party, appear so little anxious to support the Ministers that the latter, three weeks before the opening of Parliament, foresaw their dismissal, and in order to prepare public opinion, issued a pamphlet entitled *The State of the Nation*, giving an exact account of their administration since they had assumed office. This did some good.[1]

Neumann exaggerated the cabinet's pessimism over their survival but the public shared his view that the pamphlet was the authentic voice of the government. A month later *The Times* deigned to take notice of it.

> Most of our readers must be aware, that immediately before the opening of the session, Ministers issued a sort of manifesto on the state of the nation. . . . This manifesto, though it had not an avowed official stamp upon it, but appeared in the

---

[1] *The Diary of Philipp von Neumann*, trans. and ed. by F. Beresford Chancellor (2 vols. 1928), I, 91.

guise of a bulky pamphlet, price 5s. 6d., yet was well understood to emanate from authority, and was of course in great demand.[1]

The Times, then in opposition, was free with its sarcasms on the ministerial effort, and there was at least one rejoinder to the pamphlet in the shape of Joshua Collier's *Reply to a Pamphlet on the State of the Nation*. Nevertheless, within twelve months of publication, it had gone through at least seven editions.[2] Given its price and the not inconsiderable demands it made on its readers (95 pages of close type, some 47,000 words in all) this was a notable success, due as much as anything perhaps to its semi-official character. From the style, content, and liberal use of classical quotations (the trademark of the educated classes) the public to which it addressed itself, and which presumably bought it, was the political and professional intelligentsia. This was 'the people' as distinct from 'the mob' (in Brougham's well-known phrase) which all governments liked to have on their side.

The State of the Nation was therefore not a mere party pamphlet; it was a government-inspired and almost certainly government-written *pièce justificative*. It was in effect a kind of primitive white paper, describing and defending the government's position on a wide range of important issues. That in itself is novelty enough; but in the immediate post-Waterloo period a special interest attaches to any considered and comprehensive ministerial view of these difficult and controversial years. There are of course obvious limitations to its value as a straight historical record. It was written for a purpose. The factual information it contains is probably reliable since it could so easily be checked. But the document as a whole is partisan. There is virtually no self-criticism or admission of error; no suggestion that some of the measures for which it claimed credit were forced on ministers by parliamentary pressure. Too much must not be expected even from honest and honourably-minded ministers when vindicating their own actions. It was not for them to supply ammunition to their political opponents. Yet no document of this kind can be produced without unconsciously revealing much about its authors. Even as a general statement of the government's view of national interests it is significant. It illuminates what the ministry thought were its most important problems; what were the criticisms against which it had to defend itself; what were the topics on which it deemed it prudent to remain vague or silent. As a revelation of the inner thinking of the Liverpool administration at a critical point in its fortunes, it has unique value. What is surprising is that it has escaped the attention of historians for so long.

The pamphlet is divided into four sections together with a brief introduction and a largely recapitulatory conclusion. The fourfold division is explained as being 'the form which the administration of the British Empire has long assumed' with public business distributed among the departments of finance, foreign affairs, home department, and the colonies. Stylistic variations suggest that the departments supplied their own material. Those on the Home Department and Colonial Department, for example, have literary touches absent elsewhere. The main work of compilation was perhaps done by under-secretaries like Harrison at the Treasury and Hobhouse at the Home Office; but it is not improbable that

[1]   11 March 1822.
[2]   The quotations from the pamphlet which appear in the text are taken from the sixth edition.

heads of departments also made contributions. Much as politicians of all classes affected to despise the trade of journalism, their covert practices were often more broad-minded than their public professions. The four departmental sections are, however, markedly unequal in length. The first and longest is Finance with 40 per cent of the total text, followed by Foreign Relations with 22 per cent. Next comes the Home Department (16 per cent), leaving Colonies and the Board of Trade, which for this purpose is clumsily annexed to it, with only 12 per cent between them. This uneven allocation of space reflects no doubt the seniority of the ministers concerned (the prime minister was then still the real as well as the nominal head of the Treasury) but perhaps also the relative importance attached to the work of their departments by the public. What is also of interest is that the pamphlet, in its praiseworthy desire to educate the public in the mysteries of government, finds it necessary to explain at the outset the actual functions and responsibilities of the principal departments of state.

In the document as a whole there is a lack of uniformity resulting possibly not only from a composite authorship but from a certain inexperience in the art of public relations. The content ranges from rational analysis and argument, and sober presentation of statistics, to warm tributes to individual ministers, frequent emphasis on the pernicious effects of the cheap press, gentle ridicule of political opponents, and almost naive pleas for greater understanding. The standpoint throughout is that of an entrenched administration facing a critical, unsympathetic and often uncomprehending public. The reference is almost invariably to 'his Majesty's ministers'. Party labels are virtually unmentioned. The talk instead is of 'political adversaries', of 'opponents of the government', or simply 'the Opposition' – as in a reference to 'that portion of country gentlemen usually voting with the Opposition'. The adjective 'whig' is employed a couple of times but seemingly only in an historical sense. There is mention of the 'former leaders of the Whigs themselves, Lord Fitzwilliam, Mr Windham, and other names', and again to 'other Whigs, still living'. Elsewhere the rare use of the word 'party' is as an adjectival equivalent to 'factious' or 'partisan'. Even if the members of Lord Liverpool's administration had long abandoned any claims to whig ancestry, they show no sign here of wanting to assume an alternative party designation.

The constant refrain of the pamphlet, the note on which it begins and ends, is the almost wistful desire of ministers to be seen by the public as working in the general interest of the community and to be fortified in their labours by public recognition of their sincerity and integrity. Ministers, it is asserted in one of the early paragraphs, were conscious of the value, in public even more than in private life, of a good name. They naturally wanted to stand well with the public. For themselves

> they must feel that they desire public confidence for a conscientious and effective discharge of their duties; for the country, they must desire, and desire most anxiously, that a general feeling for the public good, and a general persuasion that the government is industriously occupied in pursuing it, may excite such a spirit of concurrent effort between the people and their governors, as to give manners the effect and authority of laws, and may bring into disuse any statutes, if such there be, required in more turbulent times to repress public disorders. Such is the general purpose of the statement and review which follow.

This is not how later liberal historians paint Lord Liverpool and his colleagues; but there is no mistaking either the spirit of the pamphlet or the sincerity of the language.

II

In the department of finance, it is explained,

> the First Lord of the Treasury and the Chancellor of the Exchequer have it in charge to provide for the maintenance and due distribution of the public revenue, and for the integrity of all those sources of navigation, commerce, manufactures, internal trade and industry, from which such revenue must be derived; and, finally, (in cooperation with the other Boards appointed for this special purpose) they have to provide for the naval and military defence of the empire, and the maintenance of the docks, arsenals, ordnance etc. in all the means and material of future operation.

This is a surprisingly wide list of responsibilities. It illustrates among other things the extent to which the first lord of the treasury could control administratively the greater part of the working of the government quite apart from his political authority as prime minister.

The discussion of the state of the country's finances starts with the position at the close of the long and exhausting French war. The case is put clearly and trenchantly. Ministers in 1815 regarded themselves as having a twofold duty: that of dealing first with the problem of the National Debt and heavy current taxation, and next with the dismantling of the swollen army and navy establishments. (In assessing what they did, it should perhaps be parenthetically observed that the sphere of state action in the early nineteenth-century was by modern standards extremely restricted. The bulk of government spending, in peace as well as in war, went on the armed forces under the three heads of Army, Navy and Ordnance. Expenditure on everything else apart from the Civil List was lumped together under the heading of Miscellaneous.) As a basis of comparison the government in 1815 took the last 'normal peace' year of 1792, even though (as the pamphlet reminds its readers), Pitt had recognized and afterwards regretted that he had put the establishment for that year too low. The 1792 establishment for the army, for example, was only 46,000. Since those distant and frugal pre-war days nearly a quarter of a century had elapsed, most of it spent in waging a long continental war. The financial responsibilities of the state were now much heavier. Social conditions had changed; the population had grown, the authors of the pamphlet reckoned, by at least a fifth, the task of preserving domestic order had been made additionally difficult by the 'new force given to public passions' by the growth of a popular press. There were new strategic and technical considerations – the system of relieving colonial garrisons by units instead of drafts, the disturbed state of Ireland, and an increase in the number of colonies (43 in 1816 compared to 26 in 1792). The garrisoning of the enlarged colonial empire alone required at first as many troops as Pitt's total (if unrealistic) army establishment of 1792. Two particular military problems were the defence of Canada against a recently belligerent USA, and potential unrest in the new colonies which were not only unaccustomed to British rule but 'impatient, turbulent and even democratically inclined'. (In the political vocabulary of the day 'democratic' carried the same revolutionary overtones as 'communism' in the twentieth century.)

In these altered circumstances the cabinet had initially fixed an establishment of 99,000 for the army and 33,000 for the navy, enabling them to discharge more than 300,000 men from the armed forces by the end of 1816. To persist with this new level of peace establishment, however, proved politically impossible. There followed further successive ministerial reductions until by 1819 the size of the army had been brought down to 78,000. Since the armed forces constituted the chief financial liability of the government other than servicing the National Debt, this severe retrenchment resulted in a visible decrease in expenditure on the normal machinery of the state. From £20 millions in 1817 it fell to £18 millions in 1821.

This, however, was only one half of the problem facing the ministers. The reduction in expenditure was more than offset by the decrease in their revenue. This was a political and parliamentary matter. What Castlereagh in an unguarded moment called 'an ignorant impatience of taxation' characterized both the House of Commons and the nation at large. The pamphlet tactfully passes over in silence the refusal of parliament to continue the wartime income-tax in 1816, though this fiscal defeat profoundly weakened the ability of the government to finance itself from current taxation in succeeding years. In 1822 the pamphlet preferred to examine continuing consequences rather than repine over lost causes. In 1818, for instance, of a total of £21 millions needed for administrative purposes, only £7½ millions could be raised by ordinary taxation, leaving the rest to be obtained by issuing new government stock (£3 millions) and exchequer bills (£11 millions). The main reason for this gap between income and expenditure is not elaborated, perhaps because it was only too familiar to the British public. It was of course the huge burden of interest on the National Debt, amounting that year to nearly £47 millions.[1] In other words the cost of servicing the National Debt was more than twice as much as that of all the other forms of expenditure by the state put together. Of the money to pay for those 'normal' functions of government, only a third could be obtained from current revenue; the rest had to be borrowed.

No economies in manpower could bridge this enormous gap between revenue and expenditure. By 1819 ministers felt that they had already reached nearly the end of practical economies in government. By 1820, declared the pamphlet, 'every branch of the public services . . . had been cut down to the lowest possible degree consistent with their efficiency'. By 1821, after more desperate scraping of the barrel, the direct question is put

> whether in the degree of these retrenchments ministers have pared away a little too near the quick, and whether some of them have not already been found to put into peril, and assuredly to augment the difficulty of a due and prompt administration of the public service.

Pursuing this mild counter-attack, it asks its readers to consider whether in government as in private life 'present cheapness is always the best economy'.

What now, in retrospect, appears as the turning-point in the post-war financial policy of the Liverpool government is the series of measures adopted in 1819,

---

[1] *Annual Register 1819*, p. 407 (Parliamentary Accounts, Public Expenditure for year ending 5 January 1819). The figure is made up of the interest on the permanent debt (£44.6 millions) and on exchequer bills and Irish Treasury bills (£2.2 millions).

including the decision to impose new taxes as well as raid the Sinking Fund, in an attempt to bring current expenditure and current revenue more into line. This however is dealt with in circumspect language. The improved revenue of that year, exceeding the estimates by £3½ millions, enabled the ministry to repay £5 millions to the Bank of England and another £5 millions to discharge exchequer bills. The authority of the Finance Committee is invoked to take responsibility for imposing another £3 millions of taxes, though the committee in reality was little more than the government in disguise. To the vaguer force of public opinion is ascribed the diversion of £12 millions from the Sinking Fund. Two other financial reforms of that notable year (one major and one minor) are portrayed as parts of the continuing campaign for retrenchment and economy. These were a change in customs and excise which resulted in administrative savings, and the recommendation of the Currency Committee set up under Peel's chairmanship to resume cash payments. 'With his Majesty's ministers,' the pamphlet observes piously, 'economy has been a business, and reduction a duty.'

The improved state of national finances resulting in part at least from the new policy of 1819 enabled the pamphlet to sound a distinct note of hope. The state is becoming solvent at last; it is possible to set aside annually £5 millions for the Sinking Fund as an earnest of the government's intention to diminish the National Debt, this 'mortgage which undoubtedly presses heavily upon the industry of the people'. The conclusion to the long survey is almost triumphant.

It may now be confidently asserted, that the system of loans and new taxes has reached its termination; that we are now living upon our income.

It was a claim that would have seemed utopian only a few years earlier. But what fortified the ministers and justified their optimism was a conviction that the economy of the country was fundamentally sound and that the ills from which it had been suffering were transitory. National resources were unimpaired; it was only a question of liberating them. Commerce, navigation, manufacture, internal trade, and consumer demand (or what the pamphlet calls 'the national consumption') were all healthy. Imports, whether of raw materials, materials for re-export, or for home consumption, were rising steadily. Mercantile tonnage had grown. The manufacturing industry had become on average more productive than during the war and was either expanding or at least holding its position. The yield from customs and excise and from direct personal taxation was buoyant: £2 millions more in 1821 than in 1820 and likely to go on rising. In the face of these many indicators of the strength of British economy, occasional fluctuations in prosperity could be seen for what they were. 'The question is, what is our general condition, and not what is our particular suffering under a cause manifestly temporary.'

The broad picture drawn by the pamphlet is of sober and successful national housekeeping; but there are a number of points on which it was evidently felt advisable to offer a special defence or explanation. While claiming that 'under no former administration has so much been conceded to the commercial interest of the empire', ministers were (perhaps uneasily) conscious that they had said little in the pamphlet about agriculture. After three years of low farm prices and falling rents, this would certainly be seen in some quarters as a significant omission. The notorious corn law of 1815 is not mentioned, perhaps because by 1821 ministers did not regard it as either efficient or defensible. They were only too aware of the slump in agricultural prosperity since the war; but while admitting the fall in rents and prices, the only remedy they held out to the complaining landed interest was the slow operation of market forces. The current depression they attributed to over-expansion during the war and a succession of unusually good harvests since 1818. The intrinsic strength of British farming, they argued, was unimpaired. It was merely a matter of waiting for supply and demand to adjust themselves. 'It is totally impossible that the present state of the markets can continue, or that agriculture, like manufactures, should not accommodate itself to a new state of things . . . incidental irregularities will pass away, and farmers and landlords will obtain the prices to which they are entitled.' It was not perhaps a message of much comfort to the discontented.

In the opinion of many agriculturalists one of the main reasons for low food prices was the deflationary effect of the return to the gold standard under 'Mr Peel's bill' of 1819. Ministers would have none of this. 'Corn became cheap, not because money was dear, but because corn was plentiful.' While they accepted some disadvantages in a resumption of cash payments, these were outweighed by the advantages. The purpose of the measure was twofold: to restore the old value of the currency, and to provide a security against the inflationary effects of unlimited paper money. Of these the more important consideration in the eyes of the ministers (and it is an interesting admission) was the second. 'They considered the main and principal value of cash payments to be in the single circumstance, that they contained in themselves a control and security against a too extreme issue of paper, and confined such issues to the real exigences of trade and business.' For this strict monetary policy they took particular credit; the decision had been theirs alone. 'It was not one of those measures into which they were pushed, either by party contest, or popular clamor.'

On a different issue, where they had in fact been pushed into action by 'popular clamor', they were no less outspoken. The long campaign against pensions and sinecures, dear to eighteenth-century public opinion and opposition politicians, had by the post-Waterloo era largely exhausted its practical possibilities. This however did not prevent it from continuing to be a prominent plank in the radical programme. It was still a popular article of belief that much of the national distress could be attributed to the profligate granting and extravagant cost of these administrative excrescences. The retort of the pamphlet to this ancient but evergreen accusation was brisk and unrepentant. It was true that in 1817 ministers had put through a bill for the abolition of sinecures but this was simply 'a concession to public opinion, and was chiefly of public value, inasmuch as it afforded the occasion of producing before the public the real state of a question upon which they had been much deluded.' The total cost of sinecure offices did not exceed £100,000; only three of them involved substantial sums; and the money came from the income of the crown. Moreover, sinecures were 'effectively pensions with the names of offices'. Almost without exception they were granted to retired state officials in lieu of the official pension to which they otherwise would be entitled. In financial terms the savings under the 1817 bill were almost worthless since the money for pensions would now have to be found elsewhere. The pamphlet therefore bluntly disclaimed any credit for what ministers had done. 'They gave the bill because the public demanded it . . . its value was nothing.'

While dealing brutally with this sacred cow of radical belief, the government was careful to reject the imputation that it was obsessed by soulless economic dogma. In its cautious progress towards free trade, ministers clearly felt that they had enemies on two flanks – old-fashioned agricultural and mercantile protectionists on one side, inflexible academic theorists on the other. It was not, argues the pamphlet, that ministers either ignored or denied the validity of the free-trade doctrine in the abstract. The same text-books were open to them as to others. They did not need to be instructed that 'the first and best principles of commerce would be a perfect freedom of trade'. They could point in fact to what they had already done to remove restrictions on Indian and colonial trade and to break down the great monopolies. Yet as responsible politicians they were unable to go 'the full speculative length of those gentlemen who . . . have recommended the general adoption of all the theories of Smith and Turgot.'[1] There was a wide difference between theory and practice, 'between diagrams of navigation upon dry land, and practical courses rendered necessary by sea and winds'. Simple as it would be to talk by the text-book and adopt the vocabulary of the exchange and bullion market, they had been brought up in a different school. 'A nation has other interests besides those of money-making.' The first concern of the empire was national defence and the preservation of those sources of strength, particularly navigation and commerce, on which its traditional protection depended. In any case, absolute liberty of trade would only be beneficial when it was adopted as a general system by other countries.

One final argument is brought forward to justify the government's financial and commercial measures. It was aimed primarily at those farmers and manufacturers who complained of low prices; but its implications were far wider. It was in effect a theme that dominated economic policy for the rest of the century, since it was at bottom a question of the standard of living of the working classes. While attention is modestly drawn to the action of the government in 1817 of appropriating £1½ millions for creating employment for the poor, there is no pretence in the pamphlet that this was anything more than a temporary alleviation of distress in a particularly bad year. The more important point which the pamphlet emphasizes is that low prices, though diminishing profits for individuals, had a beneficial effect on the country as a whole. The prosperity of a nation, it declared forcefully, did not depend on high prices and large profits but on a state of general well-being.

> Cheapness, or in other words, the abundance, is but so much added to the comfort and substance of the people . . . it is of no inconsiderable addition to our general wealth that so large a proportion of our population is so well and so sufficiently clothed. Is it possible, indeed, to pay a weekly visit to our country churches, and yet refuse to recognize the vast superiority of our laboring poor, in the quality and cleanliness of their clothing, above those of the continental nations?

The argument ends on a high tone.

> It is the interest of a paternal government, that the largest possible proportion of its whole population should be enabled to reach the comforts and decencies of life; and

---

[1] Adam Smith (1723–90) the free-trade political economist; A. R. J. Turgot (1727–81), finance minister of Louis XVI, who supported the *laisser-faire* views of the Physiocrats.

this can never happen in any extent but under larger supplies and low prices.

It was an argument that Peel was to use over the repeal of the corn laws a quarter of a century later; a prescription that was to serve for the whole Victorian era.

III

The section of the pamphlet devoted to foreign affairs has a melancholy interest as giving the view of the Foreign Office in the last year of Castlereagh's life. Seven months later he was dead by his own hand. His successor, one imagines, while differing little in principle from his policy, would not have breathed the same eirenic spirit which pervades these pages.

As with finance, the starting-point for its survey is 1815 when, it is asserted in characteristic Castlereagh language, 'the European commonwealth was reconstructed at this period chiefly upon three principles.' These three principles were first, an adequate distribution of strength among the leading states to ensure both their general independence and their ability to withstand a French attack long enough for their allies to come to their rescue; second, the restoration (subject to the overriding claim of the first principle) of all European states to their former position; and last, some form of compensation for lost territory where full restoration was not possible. The familiar pattern of the territorial settlement worked out at Vienna, with its elaborate system of checks and balances, is then briefly described.

Current British policy on the continent is defined, again in terms which seem redolent of Castlereagh himself, as

> the maintenance of the general peace of Europe by the personal amity of the sovereigns, and by a system of mediation, which should, on the one side, recognize the perfect independence of the several states in their own internal concerns, and, upon the other, should hold forth their common interest, and therein their common obligation, to consult the general policy of Europe in all questions affecting the safety of the whole.

Conscious perhaps that this description might, to a suspicious British public, summon up the spectre of the Holy Alliance and the principle of the right of the Great Powers to intervene in the affairs of the smaller states, the pamphlet proceeds at once to deny the reality of such fears. It was 'a malicious and most unjust representation' of the system to assert that the allied powers, including England (regrettably the words Britain and British are rarely used in this context) were bound by treaty to control or arbitrate upon the interests of other countries. If the spokesmen of some of the allied powers sometimes used language which seemed to indicate this, there was no such principle enshrined in the treaties which bound the allies together, and consequently 'the king and government of England do not admit' that they are implicated in such a policy. But such apprehensions were unjustified. 'It is not perhaps too much to say, that the Holy Alliance of the present time, like the treaty of Pillnitz[1] in the French Revolution,

---

[1] Following a meeting at Pillnitz between the Emperor of Austria and the King of Prussia in August 1791 a declaration was issued on their behalf announcing their intention to restore the King of France to his throne. Though it was asserted in France that there were secret articles to the agreement, it was not in fact a treaty.

has no other existence, at least in the degree asserted, than in the factious writings of the day.'

There follows an illuminating *tour d'horizon* of British relations with the rest of the world. With Spain and Portugal the emphasis is on British neutrality and non-intervention in the internal conflicts of that unsettled peninsula. With France the chief concern of Britain is to see that country established and happy, quietly occupying its legitimate place in the European states-system. For that the right policy consisted in tactful diplomacy, avoidance of any air of national superiority, and the recognition that there existed in France, as also in Holland, a hostility of popular feeling and a spirit of commercial rivalry, which made it difficult to achieve any closer relationship. With the various states which made up Italy, the only practical and proper course for a British government was one of non-intervention in their internal politics, however much sympathy there was personally for liberal aspirations among the Italian people.

When the discussion turns to Austria, the autocratic empire of the east which, with Russia, was a standing target for British radicals, a warmer note is infused. 'No sovereign is perhaps more injuriously treated than the Emperor of Austria.' He was not the despot 'which our libellous writers represent'. On the contrary, in relation to his exposed and scattered dominions, he had too little power rather than too much. The only unity among the different lands that made up his empire was that they had a common monarch. Their national animosities and his own limited constitutional authority deprived the emperor of effective sovereignty. In Hungary he enjoyed no more than 'the feudal superiority of the supreme chief over his barons'. In Germany his power was patrimonial rather than political. In Italy he had to contend with the natural hostility of a subject race. On the larger European stage the rise of the Prussian monarchy and the expansion of Russia were developments 'which, in the vicissitudes of time, and in the varying policy of cabinets, may more seriously affect the safety of the House of Austria.' After this prophetic warning comes the moral for the British public. The position of Austria was one of great difficulty and delicacy. It was only natural that she should jealously protect the stability of the European settlement which was her main security and in the destruction of which she would be the first victim. 'The tone and conduct of the British government towards Austria, have been regulated by a knowledge of these circumstances.'

Towards Russia and Turkey, those two great non-European empires, more cautious if still sympathetic language is employed. The government was unable to share the hostility expressed by the political opposition in Britain towards the Tsar. It saw nothing in his conduct to justify such hostility. On the contrary, his public actions had been marked by sincerity and moderation. The insurrection of the Greek peoples had placed him in a situation of great embarrassment. In a simple and primitive society like Russia strong religious feeling, and an emotional identification with the Orthodox Christian Greeks, constituted a political force to which even the Tsar had to defer. As long as the Turco-Greek problem[1] remained unsolved, British mediation would have two objectives – to put an end to the

---

[1] The Greeks began their revolt against the Turks in 1821 and proclaimed their independence in January 1822. The hostilities continued until 1829 when the great powers intervened to establish an independent Greek kingdom.

fighting, and to protect the Greek population from any reprisals. Our natural sympathies were with the Greeks, but – the pamphlet argues – this should not be allowed to overrule the cardinal principle of non-intervention by the great powers. Any departure from that principle would have incalculable consequences for the peace and stability of Europe. Whatever the character of the Turkish state, it occupied a specific place in the European system and should have enough strength to carry out its rôle. Its disappearance would disturb the whole European order and it was a particularly British interest that this should not happen. 'It is our best preventive policy to maintain her in this degree of strength.' Given the internal weaknesses of the Turkish empire, and the unreliability of its army, there could be no advantage for Britain in any further reduction of Turkish power.

The last great power examined is the United States. Here too the tone is one of sympathy and understanding. Of all the nations, it is pointed out, America had suffered most from the return to peace in 1815. 'As England, during the war, manufactured for the world, America, in a very great degree, was the carrier of the world.' Since 1815 its commerce and revenue had almost halved. Inflation had been succeeded by deflation, a glut of unsold goods, and unemployment. As far as Anglo-American relations were concerned, however, there was solid ground for optimism. Since over 70 per cent of American revenue came from customs duties, its government had a material inducement to remain at peace with Britain. Nothing would be more damaging to American trade than a naval war, just as Britain herself would suffer severely from the loss of her best customer. Common interest, along with the ties of common origin, bound the two countries together. Three recent events – the renewal of the commercial convention in 1819 for another ten years, the assistance given by Britain to the American negotiations with Spain over the cession of Florida, and the loosening of the restrictions imposed by the Navigation Acts, to enable American ships to have access to the West Indies through the free port of Bermuda – had been evidence of this. Then follows a striking and eloquent passage not unworthy to be ranked as Castlereagh's last message to his countrymen.

> It will be time enough, a century hence, to think of contending interests. . . . The sea is open to both nations, and assuredly there will be no disposition in England to appropriate this highway of the world. America has a territory, and a new and virgin territory, almost as spacious as the face of the seas themselves. She is of the same stock, and has the same materials of greatness and future glory with Great Britain. Let her use the example we have set her, and run the same race.

IV

The functions of the Home Office, as defined at the start of the pamphlet, illustrates the narrowness of its departmental responsibilities before the coming of anything that could be described as a welfare state. Its duties are described as 'the maintenance and supervision of the public peace, and the due execution of the laws for the support of an internal order and tranquillity'. For these purposes, it is explained, the Home Secretary had to anticipate future as well as suppress current disorder, uphold the magistracy, involve when necessary the law officers of the crown, and superintend the police of the metropolis. While those were his duties, the restraints he had to observe receive equal emphasis. Remembering that he was a minister of a free government in a free constitution, the Home Secretary 'should execute his duties with as little cost as possible to personal liberty'. He must not apply extraordinary powers to ordinary necessities. He must use no more force than was needed to meet the observed danger.

Over the whole discussion of law and order there clearly hangs the shadow of the disturbed period from 1816 to 1820 – the age of the Luddites, the Spa Fields riots, the secret committees, Peterloo, and the Six Acts. Though there is an understandable reluctance to recall in detail these unhappy events, the eulogy pronounced on the recently-retired Home Secretary, Viscount Sidmouth, almost inevitably involved a spirited defence of government policy towards the problems of agitation and violence in these years. It is pointed out that the all-party secret committees of both houses of parliament had been convinced of the danger and that their judgement had been vindicated by the uncovering of actual seditious conspiracies and one notorious plot to assassinate the cabinet. As elsewhere in the pamphlet, a large share of blame is placed on the radical press and 'that general circulation of their cheap seditious tracts, which were the first movers of the popular turbulence'. Nevertheless, the general outlook is optimistic. The worst was over; order had been restored; the country had entered on a period of tranquillity. There is a sufficient mood of relaxation for the pamphlet to make a mild joke at the expense of Cobbett who, once 'the most perilous and malignant of these libellers', it observes in a reference to his recent publication *Cottage Economy*, 'has become a commentator on Swedish turnips and Leghorn bonnets'. Though repressive legislation remained on the statute-book, it was kept *in terrorem* rather than for perpetual employment in the courts. 'The six acts, as they have been termed from their number, exist only as so many wholesome rods, suspended over the heads of the seditious leaders'. It was a sign of the improved state of public feeling that seditous publications had greatly declined and that juries could now be trusted to bring in proper verdicts. 'In no single instance whatever, within the last four years, has government failed in its resort to juries, whether in prosecutions for treason, libel, or seditious misdemeanour'.

This note of hope as far as the scene in England is concerned disappears abruptly as soon as the discussion shifts to Ireland. It was perhaps a sign of Peel's special knowledge of Ireland that two-thirds of the section on Home Affairs is devoted to the state of that unhappy country. The language is as downright as it is depressing. First comes a recapitulation of the long list of Irish grievances: absenteeism, unreasonably high rents, no poor law, little industry, illicit manufacture of cheap whisky, lack of education, over-population, under-employment, inefficient magistracy and police, and inadequate law-enforcement legislation. The commentary which succeeds this bitter decalogue of Irish woes goes on for page after page. The absence of a resident aristocracy is compared to the effects of the dissolution of the monasteries. It left the Irish poor in the state the English poor were in at the end of Henry VIII's and beginning of Elizabeth I's reign. 'It spreads hopeless poverty, irremediable ignorance, and barbarous ferocity through the population'. Over-population had produced 'a country covered with beggars – a complete pauper warren'. Lack of proper poor relief led to 'mendicancy and vagrancy' and fostered the growth of the 'irregular brotherhoods and societies' which disturbed the peace of Ireland. As the remorseless examination continues one feels that not even a professed critic of the government could have drawn up so damning an indictment.

Yet, equally depressing in its effect on the reader, is the constant argument that it is not in the power of the government to find a cure for any of these ills. Rack-renting (though the term used is 'disproportionate rents') and absenteeism, were matters for the Irish landowners – 'they belong to manners, and not to laws'. Lack of trade, manufactures, and capital was neither the fault of the government nor within the ability of the government to supply. The debased social condition of Ireland was a product of history. It could not be cured in a day; and was not something susceptible to legislation. 'It is totally impossible to civilize a people by act of parliament.' Only the gradual influence of impartial administration, firm continuous government, and more disciplined habits could effect the necessary changes: not least a change among the Irish upper classes. When the government wished to introduce severer measures against smuggling and illicit distillation, it is pointed out, the Irish gentry themselves had objected and forced ministers to withdraw. The quality of the Irish magistracy, the pamphlet says restrainedly, was very far removed from that of the country magistracy in England. For this the chief reason was clearly absenteeism but the government was deprived in consequence of the support on which it mainly depended for efficient local administration. 'It is impossible for government to work without suitable subject-matter.' Marginal assistance had been given to Ireland in the form of protection for the linen industry and subsidies to fisheries. Essentially, however, all government could hope to do was to refrain as much as possible from measures of coercion and trust in a gradual return to a more orderly state of affairs – a policy, to use its own words, of 'amelioration by measured steps'. Only one crumb of comfort is offered at the end of this pessimistic analysis. 'None of the present distractions in Ireland can be ascribed to religious differences – Catholics and Protestants are alike sufferers and aggressors. It is but rank faction, therefore, to refer her present state to tythes, taxes, and the absence of a complete Catholic emancipation.'

It is a bleak scene which appears in this view of Ireland as seen from Westminster in 1822. There was much in what the pamphlet said, particularly of the kind of objective, balanced considerations which administrators often, and usually with little success, bring forward to counteract political and sectarian passions. It was at least part of the truth about Ireland, and perhaps the more important part. Arguably the Irish problem was as resistant to man-made solutions even in 1822 as it proved to be for the following hundred years. Yet it implies that the hopes of the government were placed on the narrowest of foundations. If law-abiding habits could only result from a long period of efficient, stable rule; and insoluble grievances made any long period of stable, efficient rule impossible, there was no escape from the cycle of disorder and agitation. When Catholic Emancipation had finally been granted in 1829, Peel reverted once more to the standpoint of 1822. 'Ten years' experience of the advantage of obedience,' he wrote to his Irish Chief Secretary, 'will induce a country to be obedient without much extraordinary compulsion.'[1] Yet when was such a decade ever vouchsafed to British administration in Ireland?

---

[1] C. S. Parker, *Sir Robert Peel* (1899), II, 122.

V

Whoever was responsible for the section of the pamphlet on colonial affairs was clearly conscious that he was dealing with a British public which had not in the past shown much interest in the subject. For example, 'it has been too much the practice of popular writers to undervalue the possession of Canada'. Yet Canada, it is argued here, was of 'primary importance'. It was an area in which we were in contact with the United States; its existence was a stimulus to the British merchant navy; it was a market for British manufactures; in time of war it would be a valuable base for operations in American waters. Jamaica again, the pamphlet maintains, was a colony scarcely inferior in importance to Canada. It was the headquarters of the sugar trade, 'the corn of the Tropical world' as it is imaginatively described, and as an article of food sugar was second in value only to the products of British agriculture. The revenue from sugar duties, in fact, exceeded the whole revenue from Ireland. Indeed, if all the combined revenue from duties on colonial goods were taken into consideration, it amounted to only slightly less than the total revenue from the land (beer, malt, hops and land-tax) in Great Britain and Ireland. In financial terms, therefore, the colonial interest was a close rival to the landed interest – a proof, as the pamphlet somewhat pointedly observes, of the absurdity of concentrating on one particular branch of the economy to the exclusion or depreciation of the others.

Canada and Jamaica are not the only colonies which are brought to the notice of the possibly indifferent or uninformed reader. The newly-acquired Cape of Good Hope, though of little immediate value, is described as having immense potentiality. It was 'a vineyard, and assuredly, at no distant period, a granary under the most favorable climate in the world'. The Cape, as 'an appendage to the British Empire' was only an infant colony but there was no limit to the extent to which 'the characteristic spirit, activity, and intelligence of British colonists' might not push its boundaries in the interior of Africa. All such expansion would benefit commerce and industry, particularly in serving as an outlet for surplus manufactured goods which periodically glutted the home market.

Though the British people in 1822 showed on the whole little imperial enthusiasm, and the radicals of the Manchester School variety were soon to be decrying colonial possessions as a costly burden on the mother-country, the Colonial Department under Lord Bathurst and his colleagues was on this evidence anxious to emphasize their present value and future prospects. The Board of Trade under Robinson and Wallace was on more solid ground in advertising the usefulness of its work to the late-Georgian public. It had the advantage of a specific programme of legislation to announce. The review of the Navigation Acts, it promised, would assist British commerce in general and remove the grievances of foreign states without sacrificing British interests. The new warehousing scheme would strengthen Britain's position as an *entrepôt* for international trade. The new timber-duties introduced the previous session aimed at reconciling the diverse claims of the North American colonies, the Baltic suppliers, the shipowners, and the home market. Mention of lower timber-duties brought up the more general question of tariff reform. Here the language is cautious and slightly defensive. 'It is always a matter of great practical difficulty to repeal a protective system.' In view of the many interests implicated ministers should be praised for what they had succeeded in doing rather than reproached for doing too little. When any alteration was made in the British commercial code, the whole structure was affected. One change always tended to lead to another. 'All amendments in our commercial system are necessarily of this nature. We have not to repair a movement, but to reconstruct a machine.' But only at one point is there a distinct note of discouragement. By a recent act the government had established direct trade between India and Europe and thrown it open to the private trader as well as the East India Company. But it warned that too much should not be expected from this ending of an historic monopoly. Because of the special nature of Indian society no rapid expansion of British exports to the sub-continent was likely. 'In fact, the main consumption in India of European manufacture is, and always must be, by her own European subjects.'

In the concluding pages, dealing with the wider field of international trade, the Board holds out hopes of a general review of the tariff system with the object of replacing prohibitory legislation by protective duties. Prohibition merely led to smuggling with all its evils and cost to the government preventive service. Protective tariffs would answer the same economic purpose with profit to 'the government and the public morals'. As stated, the objective is a limited one; but it is clear, nevertheless, that two years before Huskisson went to the Board of Trade, the department was already permeated with free-trade ideals. The virtues it preached in 1822 to the British business world were initiative and competition. 'The sole security for preference to British manufacturers is in their own superior skill, intelligence, and activity; in their vast accumulated capital; and in a magnitude and quality of machinery, the growth, like our capital, of a hundred years of successful commerce.'

VI

The pamphlet ends, as it began, on a personal, diffident, but still optimistic note. It was necessary for a government carrying out 'grave and invidious duties' not to be deterred by 'mistaken popular clamor'. It was equally necessary for it not to undervalue the support of public opinion. 'It happily belongs to the nature of a free government and an intelligent people, that public opinion is never long misled.' Parties and prejudices would pass away; but the permanent benefits of good measures would always make an 'effectual, though perhaps tardy, appeal to the gratitude of a generous nation'. The ministers were entitled to praise for the way in which they had performed their public duties; the more so since they had 'declined to vindicate or assert their just and obvious claims'. In a final peroration, in which the syntax collapses under the strain of an overloaded sentence and refuge is taken in a six-line quotation in the original Latin, one last slightly incoherent plea is made for understanding and appreciation.

> Is it unreasonable to express a confident assurance, that the future annalist, if not the passing generation, will recognize the public obligation to the ministers of George the Fourth, and will hereafter enumerate them among those wise and substantial, but unpretending and untalking benefactors, who in times of great peril and difficulty . . . is it too much to claim for his Majesty's ministers the praise of those who . . . deserve the more applause from others, as, under the most unequivocal public services, they least assume it for themselves.

So ends one of the oddest and most revealing essays in public relations attempted by any nineteenth-century administration.

4

'Cheap Government', 1815–1874[1]

'Taxation and religion have ever been the two prime movers in human revolutions.' Or so wrote John Morley in his book on *Oliver Cromwell*. If under religion we can include such secular faiths as republicanism, communism, and fascism, this eminently Victorian dictum is still true. Historians, however, are apt to spend more time on religions, both spiritual and secular, than on the mundane subject of taxation. Money is left to the economists more often than religion is to the theologians. Taxation is not usually regarded, for example, as one of the causes of the Reform Act of 1832. Yet contemporaries seem to have thought there was a connection. Lord Durham, one of the authors of the bill, in a speech to the House of Lords of 13 April 1832 argued that the question was not merely one of political representation but of government expenditure. In classic Whig style he traced the historical link between the limited parliamentary constitution set up after 1688 and the subsequent growth of the National Debt, foreign wars, subsidies to continental powers, increased state expenditure, and the increasing burden of the poor rate. 'All these proofs of an unlimited and unchecked expenditure . . . became known to the people at the conclusion of the [Napoleonic] War. Great distress followed, much discontent and loud complaints.' Nearly twenty years later another member of the committee of four which drew up the reform bill, when questioned about the motives behind the measure, replied in a similar vein. Answering Roebuck, who was collecting material for his *History of the Whig Ministry of 1830*, Sir James Graham wrote

> You are aware that for two or three years before the formation of Lord Grey's Government I had taken a line which was considered radical on questions relating to public expenditure; and when I was unexpectedly asked by Lord Grey to form part of his Administration. . . . I was admitted into his Cabinet as a Whig and something more. Reform and Retrenchment were the watchwords which led me to power.[2]

The defeat of Wellington's ministry on a hostile motion for an enquiry into the Civil List, which let in the reforming Whigs in November 1830, was perhaps more appropriate than is often realized.

There was in fact deep concern in 1830 over taxation and governmental expenditure and the roots of this feeling went back far into the eighteenth century. Its intellectual ancestry was impressive. Taught by his experience of France under Louis XV, David Hume had long ago pointed to the evil effects of despotic government on commerce and the baneful consequences of arbitrary

[1] Not previously published though the subject formed the basis for a paper read to the Institute of Historical Research in London many years ago.
[2] C. S. Parker, *Life and Letters of Sir James Graham* (1907), I, 117–18.

taxation. The great Adam Smith in his *Wealth of Nations* had stressed the beneficial results of free individual enterprise as against the dead hand of governmental regulation. Jeremy Bentham criticized the state and its institutions as corrupt, inefficient and expensive in his *Fragment on Government* in 1776 and followed the attack up in his *Principles of Morals and Legislation* in 1780. These utilitarian critiques of the traditional machinery of the state provided a respectable academic background to the periodic agitations over sinecures, pensions and administrative abuses which were a normal part of faction politics in eighteenth-century parliaments. By the start of the nineteenth century the notion that government was expensive because it was corrupt, and corrupt because it was aristocratic, was firmly planted in radical consciousness and perhaps in many others who would not have regarded themselves as political radicals. Such scandals as the alleged sale of commissions by the duke of York's mistress in 1809 which obliged him to resign from his post of commander-in-chief of the army; or the earlier impeachment of Lord Melville, the First Lord of the Admiralty, for alleged misuse of naval funds in 1806, only served to confirm this impression.

What raised the old, conventional controversy to a new plane was the unprecedented strain of the Revolutionary and Napoleonic Wars between 1793 and 1815. It has been calculated that prices in 1810 were three times as high as in 1770. On any reckoning the war brought the worst inflation the country had experienced since the early Middle Ages. If the ungrateful public of Nelson and Wellington complained, it was not without some reason. Never had there been so long and so expensive a war. The revenue extracted by the state from the British people rose from £19 millions in 1793 to £50 millions at the time of Pitt's death in 1806 and to £72 millions by the time Napoleon was finally vanquished in 1815. Actual expenditure by the government was even higher. In 1814 and 1815 it reached £117 millions, the difference being met by loans; and it was this huge government borrowing to bridge the gap between income and expenditure that was for many contemporaries the most alarming feature of the financial position at the end of the war. The National Debt in 1793 was £238 millions (£228 millions funded and £9 millions of short-term loan). By 1816 this had risen to £902 millions (£816 funded and £86 short-term). The servicing of this enormous debt was the largest single item government had to face when calculating its expenditure. In 1816 £44 millions were swallowed up by the interest on the debt, accounting for virtually the whole of the ordinary revenue of the state. Moreover, while other items of expenditure could be reduced by economies and retrenchment, the debt interest was almost immovable. It represented a fixed contractual payment which could only be reduced by paying off the capital sum borrowed or, when market conditions were favourable, by negotiating lower interest rates with existing fund-holders through an exchange of stock. Both devices had only a limited application. Otherwise the debt was, so to speak, a first charge on the government's resources. Not only the political honour but the financial credit of the state was involved in the punctual and full discharge of its legal obligations to its creditors. As late as 1827, in spite of all that had been done in the interval to lessen the burden, debt charges still amounted to over 70 per cent of the expenditure of the state. Those who are tempted to echo the conventional condemnation of Vansittart as the worst chancellor of the exchequer in modern British history ought in justice to examine the actual financial situation he had to face after

Waterloo.

The connection between the growing alarm and resentment over high taxation, and the renewed agitation for parliamentary reform, was perceptible long before the end of the war. The change in the character of the reform movement from doctrinaire ideology to emphasis on practical grievances was noted soon after Pitt's death in 1806. Tom Grenville, brother of Pitt's former foreign secretary, gave it as his opinion in 1808 that

> independent of the general spirit of reform which had been bred by the changes and revolutions of all the countries in Europe, the increased pressure of taxes in latter days has here produced, in the people at large, and in the parliament too, a very jealous and feverish suspicion of offices and emoluments.[1]

From this point of view the sensational scandals in high places which marked the early years of the century were particularly damaging since they strengthened a widespread conviction in the public that something must be done to purify the whole frame of government. A belief among practical men that corruption would be cured by a reform of parliament was a much greater threat to the existing order than abstract opinions on the virtues of widening the basis of the legislature. Even apart from flagrant examples of misuse of official power and public money, wartime taxation was a constant reminder of the rapacity of governments. This in itself was enough to turn people's thoughts towards reform. Tierney, for example, referring to the duke of York scandal and the renewed calls for a reform of the parliamentary constitution, told the House of Commons in 1809 that 'what many, he believed, understood by parliamentary reform was a relief from the weight of the taxes'. It was not, he continued, that there was a desire in the country to subvert the constitution, but people felt strongly about taxation, especially the wartime innovation of income tax; and people in consequence listened to the advocates of reform 'because the idea went to encourage the hope that by this reform they would be in some measure at least relieved from the pressure of taxation.'[2] It was in these years that corruption, extravagance, taxation and reform became linked in the mind of the British public. Patriotic pride in the British victories of the last few years of the war served to overlay their discontent; but it broke out again with the coming of peace. After Waterloo the government had to face the financial grievances of a generation of tax-payers. The revolt of the House of Commons in 1816 over the ministerial proposal to prolong the income-tax for another year was a sign of the times.

For William Cobbett, the greatest of all the post-war agitators, financial reform was the central issue in politics. It was only when he had come to the conclusion that there was no hope of achieving it in an unreformed House of Commons that he turned to parliamentary reform as its necessary preliminary. In his *Letter to Sir Francis Burdett* of September 1816 he laid down what was for him a self-evident truth that 'if the people had been fully represented in Parliament this enormous load of taxes would never have existed'. Two months later, with his famous *Address to the Journeymen and Labourers*, he began his long campaign to educate the working classes into his belief. During the next fifteen years his ceaseless attack on the fundholders and 'tax-eaters' was a powerful ingredient in the case

---

[1] Duke of Buckingham, *Memoirs of the Court and Cabinets of George III* (1853), IV, 244.

[2] *Cobbett's Parliamentary Debates*, XIV, 509–10 (11 May 1809).

for parliamentary reform. All the post-war concessions forced on the government by parliament, all the retrenchment carried out by Liverpool's laborious administration, failed to shake popular belief in this central article of the radical creed. A persuasion of the unnecessary expensiveness of government coloured the whole movement for a reform of parliament. It followed as a logical consequence that when that reform was finally accomplished, it was confidently expected by its supporters to bring about immediate relief from taxation; nor was this the only benefit anticipated as a result of 1832. 'Cheap government – cheap bread – cheap justice – and industry unfettered and productive' announced that Bible of Radicalism, *The Extraordinary Black Book*, in 1832, 'will reward our efforts in the triumph of the Reform Bill'. In his *Manchester Lectures* the previous winter Cobbett had put the matter very simply. 'We want no change in the form of the government; we want, indeed, to make this same government *a great deal cheaper* than it is.' His heroic 'Fourteen Reform Propositions' recommended to a reformed parliament included the abolition of pensions, sinecures, and half-pay allowances for retired officers; reductions in official salaries; the disbandment of the regular army; the ending of tithes; the sale of surplus ecclesiastical property and crown lands; the repeal of all internal taxes except the land-tax; and the application of the money obtained in these ways to the liquidation of the National Debt on an equitable basis. 'If the Reform Bill do not lighten the burdens of the people,' he argued, 'it is agreed, on all hands, that the bill will be of no use. . . . Unless it lead to a great taking off of taxes, it will be a mere mockery.'[1]

Similar sentiments, if not such rough remedies, were common among the radicals who came into the House of Commons after the Reform Act. The mild and learned Grote, for example, historian of Greece and parliamentary candidate for the City of London, proclaimed in his election address in October 1832 that

> The oligarchical interest hitherto predominant in our Legislature have kept up an exorbitant scale of public expenditure, fruitful in corrupt influence, and oppressive as well as demoralizing to the nation. This long-standing course of abuse it will be among my earliest endeavours to rectify.

When in the 1833 session he loyally cast a vote against Ingilby's motion to repeal the malt tax which would have wrecked Althorp's budget (had it been persisted in) and nearly caused Grey's resignation, it provoked (wrote his devoted wife and biographer) much displeasure among his City supporters 'who, in common with all the new constituencies, considered Reform as embodying relief from fiscal burdens.'[2] For the first few years after the Reform Act there was intense pressure on the Whig ministers to achieve this gratifying result. Hobhouse even felt obliged in honour to resign office when his colleagues refused to repeal the house and window taxes. Year by year the government responded (much as Lord Liverpool's government had responded between 1816 and 1822) to the inexorable public and parliamentary demands for tax-reduction. Economies in the armed forces (the only large field of government expenditure other than debt interest) brought defence costs down to less than £12 millions in 1836 – the lowest point ever reached in the nineteenth century. These hard-bought savings enabled cuts to be made in direct taxation, the most unpopular because the most visible

[1] *Cobbett's Manchester Lectures* (1832), pp. 11, 85.
[2] Mrs Grote, *The Private Life of George Grote* (1873), pp. 71, 86.

contribution made by the British public to the upkeep of the state. Between 1831 and 1836 the inland revenue was reduced by a net amount of over £4½ millions. Yet this tax-reduction in response to popular pressure had no coherent fiscal policy behind it. Althorp had made an attempt at that in his first year as chancellor of the exchequer; he did not repeat the experiment. Lowering direct taxation merely denied the Whigs scope for any significant continuation of the free-trade policy inaugurated under Liverpool's ministry in the 1820s. The less the chancellor of the exchequer received from direct taxation, the more he had to rely on indirect taxation. In turn this left him peculiarly exposed to the effects of trade depressions on the yield from customs duties.

The Whigs were therefore in a dilemma. They soon reached the point where no further reductions in direct taxation were possible. They could economize no more, even though all their tax-cutting had resulted in a net saving of only £3¾ millions in the inland-revenue account during the years 1831–41, compared with the £11 millions net savings achieved by the reviled 'tory' governments of 1820–30.[1] They were scraping the bottom of a barrel from which their predecessors had long ago removed most of what was disposable. By 1837 they had no financial reserves left. For the next six years, despite the desperate expedient of putting on a £1 million new taxes in 1840, government expenditure regularly exceeded revenue. It is not surprising that Whig reputation as administrators fell and that the classes to whom a balanced budget was important began to look to Sir Robert Peel.

The handicap for the Whigs had been the populist strain in their political outlook engendered by their long period of opposition before 1830 and their deference to the huge majority of 'reformers' returned at the 1832 election. As authors of the Reform Act, they were required to satisfy some at least of the expectations created by the act; they were prisoners of their own past. But this sensitivity to the demands of their supporters explicitly debarred them from taking up the one remedy which financial experts on both sides of the House of Commons prescribed for the endemic fiscal weakness of government. This was a return to the unpopular wartime tax on incomes (still often described misleadingly as the property tax) which had been abolished by the legislature against the will of the executive in the first full year of peace. Althorp, Poulett Thomson, and Sir Henry Parnell were income-tax supporters among the Whigs, as Peel, Herries and Goulburn were among the Conservatives. The majority of their colleagues in both parties, however, flinched from such a drastic and unpalatable expedient. Indeed Althorp in 1833 had brandished the income-tax over his recalcitrant followers in the Commons like a whip, to induce them to accept the government's unpopular malt and window taxes. Lord Liverpool had used the same tactics in 1819 to persuade the king to accept the necessity of reimposing the malt tax. It seemed that the fate of the income-tax was to lie unused, like a birch in a school cupboard, restraining the unruly by the power of imagination rather than actual application.

Peel's restoration of the income-tax in 1842 was an act not so much of fiscal originality as of political courage. The weapon existed; the question was, who would be bold enough to use it. In the event its long-delayed return – some

[1] *Report of the Commissioners of Inland Revenue for the years 1856–59* (Cd. 1870), II, 219.

twenty-six years after its defeat in 1816 – extricated the state from the financial *cul de sac* into which the Whigs had allowed themselves to be drawn between 1832 and 1841. The significance of the new source of revenue was not simply its size. Unlike the wartime income-tax at 10 per cent which in its last year had produced nearly £15 millions, the yield, from the reduced peace-time rate of 7*d.* in the pound, averaged only £5¾ millions *per annum* in the first decade of its resumed existence. The importance of the tax was that it acted as a contingency fund to meet deficits and provide cover for further tariff experiments. The flaw in the Whig free-trade budget put forward as an act of desperation in 1841 was that it reduced duties simply on the theory than an increased volume of trade resulting from lower duties would more than compensate for the lower rates. In practice, as was shown in 1842–3, it took two or three years before expanding consumption was able to balance the immediate loss to the exchequer. Peel's income-tax bridged this gap. If the tax proved, in Gladstone's words, a 'colossal engine of finance' it was because it was certain in its yield, not difficult to collect, and not counter-productive in its effects. The actual amount which was judged politically prudent to raise by it was initially very moderate. At the outset Peel asked no more than that a 7*d.* tax should be accepted for a period of three years. In 1844 he secured its renewal for another three years; and though he confessed he would have preferred that period to be five years, he indulged the House of Commons with the enticing speculation that it might still be possible to discontinue the tax even at the end of the shorter period.

The peculiar character of the income-tax as a temporary, emergency levy clung to it for another generation. Found indispensable by chancellors of the exchequer, opposed on varying grounds by MPs of all parties, popular with Chartists, Trade Unionists and the working classes who did not pay it, cordially disliked by those who did, the income-tax in the middle of the nineteenth century led a threatened existence. Those who most warmly approved it were largely unenfranchised; its opponents strongly entrenched in the middle-class electorate created by the Reform Act of 1832. Had it been left to the House of Commons alone, the tax would have gone the way of its predecessor even more swiftly. From 1848 to 1853, particularly after Peel's death in 1850, the Whigs were hard pressed to retain it. Charles Wood, their chancellor of the exchequer and a convert to Peelite finance, was in favour of putting up the rate and making it a permanent part of the revenue. But by 1848, with an economic depression and uncertain parliamentary majorities, he found this beyond his power. The old generation of radicals like Hume, and the new generation like Cobden, made retrenchment the main plank in their platform after the 1847 election. Even more ominously the Protectionist Party seemed disposed to join in the cry for cheap government. An emotional reaction against all Peel's handiwork, and a genuine anxiety over the agricultural depression of 1848–51, for a time made them almost indistinguishable from the traditional radical 'economists'. At the end of the 1849 session Henley and Newdegate moved for a 10 per cent reduction in official salaries, Drummond and Christopher for a general lowering of all taxes; and they actually beat the government with radical aid in a thin House. It was like the 1820s all over again. Early in 1851 a party meeting at Lord Stanley's decided to attack the income tax itself; and later in the year Stanley toyed with the idea of going to the country on a cry of 'Protestantism, Protection, and down with Income Tax'. As it was, with protectionist support, Hume managed to defeat the ministers on his motion to limit the income tax to one more year. There was alarm in the cabinet and Grey, the irresolute son of a resolute father, circulated a memorandum to his cabinet colleagues advocating a policy of relief to agriculture and abandonment of the income tax.

II

In the battle for cheap government which was waged with varying degrees of intensity between the Reform Act and the Crimean War, there were implications that went beyond mere financial calculation. One, perhaps the most important, was the question of national defence. By the mid 1830s it was becoming a serious question whether the post-reform House of Commons would be ready to sustain an adequate level of expenditure on the army and navy. The British public were not pacifist but they disliked paying taxes; and this was the worst combination of all. That sober periodical the *Annual Register* observed in its review of 1837 that

> we doubt whether another long war will ever be carried on by our government, subject as it will now more immediately become to the fluctuating impulse of public opinion. The consequence of the change would hardly be a matter of regret, were there not reason to fear, that the people may still be as ready to involve themselves in quarrels, as they will afterwards be unduly impatient to get out of them.

Much the same reflection occurred to politicians. Sir James Graham (in the 1820s as unreasonable an economist as any) in 1838 put the rhetorical question to his friend Stanley, 'Is the country willing to bear burdens necessary to uphold its position in the foremost Rank of Nations? . . . I have my doubts, and the popular will on this point is now all-powerful in the House of Commons.'[1] Ten years later Palmerston told his prime minister Russell that 'almost any expedient to face the temporary difficulty would be better than to proclaim to Europe that we are too poor and too much distressed to be able to defend the country'.

The facts bore out many of their fears. Despite increased *ad hoc* expenditure by both governments in the 1840s, by 1850 the amount spent on the armed forces (£13½ millions) was the lowest since 1839. The rage for economy in the late 1840s and the weakness of Russell's administration, had caused the abandonment of the ministerial proposal to raise the income tax to a 1/- in the pound and with it the abandonment of most of its rearmament programme. It was no accident that the deficiencies in manpower, administrative staff, and support systems, revealed by the Crimean campaign, had been preceded by forty years of almost uninterrupted retrenchment in the service establishments. In the bleak but honest words of Sidney Herbert in 1854, the reason why Britain at the start of every big war was only able to fight a little one, was that 'through every Government and every Parliament we have always had the same stereotyped system of economy in military affairs'.

There was another less obvious, more political consequence of the cry for cheap government. It secretly strengthened the reluctance of some politicians to contemplate a further instalment of parliamentary reform. If a more popular fran-

---

[1] Netherby Papers, 9 Dec. 1838.

chise was likely to create an electorate even more opposed to taxation, there seemed a case on national grounds for resisting the slide towards democracy. Even Russell, almost alone among senior Whigs in his hankering for another reform bill, told his cabinet in 1851 that it was essential to establish the revenue on a sound footing before creating new franchises and constituencies which were likely to return MPs capable of upsetting the whole system of taxation. Early in 1854 Palmerston told him bluntly that it was already difficult to maintain the service establishments and the difficulty would increase if future parliamentary elections depended on the votes of men incapable of forming large views of national policy and finance. It was widely agreed that a more democratic electorate would not support even the minimum level of defence expenditure unless every conceivable economy had first been made. Four years later, as part of his argument for further parliamentary reform, Bright was denouncing the whole system of diplomacy, wars and alliances since the Revolution of 1688 as 'a gigantic system of outdoor relief for the aristocracy of Great Britain'. The implications were obvious.

The dilemma for mid nineteenth-century administrations was how to resist pressure for a widening of the franchise and at the same time insist on a sufficiently high level of taxation to maintain defence preparedness and a credible foreign policy. For more than a generation after Waterloo Britain was mainly living on the credit it had gained in the Napoleonic Wars. When that credit ran out, as it did in the Crimean War, it was not long before realists in the rising state of Prussia like Bismarck and von Roon diagnosed the practical inability of Britain to intervene with any effect on the mainland of Europe. How to convey to the insular British public a knowledge of their relative impotence was another matter. A social oligarchy, conscious of its narrow political basis and conditioned by several generations of cheap government propaganda to accept a cramped view of state finance, was ill qualified to state its case. Yet in reality Britain was a wealthy society which could easily have borne a much heavier load of taxation than its aristocratic rulers thought it prudent to impose. As early as the 1820s Lord Liverpool had pointed out that direct taxation in Britain was lower than in any other state in Europe and that the growing wealth and population of the country made the current burden of taxation a light one. Thirty years later one of the leading directors of the Bank of England urged a Whig chancellor of the exchequer to bring this truth home to the nation.

> Our Finances must be ill administered and the public interest be exposed to peril, while no sufficient effort is made to combat faction and ignorance by a bold, and uncompromising, utterance of the truth. The Nation should be told that Taxation is not heavy but light – that England is far less severely taxed than other great European states, perhaps even than America . . . that the ultimate effect of the mania for reduction and the crusade against Taxation will probably be, some great misfortune connected with insufficient public establishments, or the non-payment of the Dividends. That as we are wealthy beyond all other Nations, so we ought to indulge in the luxury of a good government to an extent which they cannot afford.[1]

Such views, however, were held only by an esoteric minority. Large sections of

---

[1] *The Correspondence of Lord Overstone*, ed. D. P. O'Brien (Cambridge, 1971), II, 508, G. W. Norman to C. Wood, 11 March 1851.

the Victorian public, especially the middle classes, were still imbued with the idea that good government was cheap government, that the state was expensive enough already, and that to give it more would simply subsidize waste and inefficiency. Charles Dickens, with his satirical descriptions of the Court of Chancery and the Circumlocution Office, represented the views of the great British public more accurately than any director of the Bank of England.

The aristocracy contributed to its own difficulties. Not only were its leaders for the most part unskilled in public relations, but they were ready, when it served their personal interests, to echo popular sentiment. A standing obstacle to the 'bold and uncompromising utterance' of financial truths was the faction-fighting endemic in the British parliamentary system. The Whigs, who were the 'party of government' for most of the time between the first and second Reform Acts, had to live down their pre-1830 past. The radicals, with no ministerial responsibilities, could carry on their traditional campaigns for retrenchment and economy with a comfortable feeling of consistent rectitude. The protectionists under Stanley and Disraeli seemed to be degenerating into an old-fashioned 'country party' with all the narrowness of outlook and selfishness of interest which that implied. In this triangular conflict, which at times threatened to overwhelm the half-hearted defences of the Whigs, what saved the government was a fundamental disagreement between its opponents on commercial policy. The radicals were free-traders but did not think that this was inconsistent with a desire for further retrenchment. They wished to reduce the amount of revenue at the disposal of the government in order to force more economies at the expense of the armed services. For a variety of reasons they tended to be critical of the income-tax. Some of them opposed it on principle; others, like Cobden, believed on grounds of social justice that, if taxation there must be, direct taxes were preferable to indirect. Nearly all of them, however, disliked the income-tax in its existing form. Their main reason was that it failed to distinguish between settled income from property and the more precarious income from salaries in employment and profits from trade; and therefore, in their view, favoured the landed interest. The protectionists on the other hand, if only as a gesture to their supporters and as a vindication of their own record, wanted to see some tariffs on foodstuffs restored. By forcing the ministers to abandon the income-tax, they hoped to make them return to a policy of tariffs for revenue, among which a small duty on corn, for example, could legitimately take a modest place. Both groups showed hostility to the income-tax, therefore, but for different reasons; and it was this difference which put any long-term alliance out of the question. The parliamentary debates of 1848 had gone far to demonstrate that there was an indissoluble link between the retention of free-trade and the retention of the income-tax. This in the end was the argument which swayed the majority in the House of Commons and probably in the country also. It was the one breakwater against the general tide in favour of a cheap and ever-cheaper government; and to it, more than anything else, was due the survival of the income-tax in these critical years.

It was a close-run thing. In 1848, despite Russell's decision as prime minister to introduce the budget himself, he failed to carry his bold – in the circumstances perhaps rash – proposal to renew the income-tax for another five years and simultaneously raise the rate to a 1/– in the pound. The universal outcry forced him to make an humiliating retreat and (as Peel had warned the Whigs in 1847) defeat jeopardized the tax itself. The issue whether the income-tax should be retained at all, and if so, for how short a period, was publicly debated between 1848 and 1853 in a way in which it had not been since 1816. Hume's success in 1851 (whatever his motives) in limiting the tax to one more year, was widely taken as signifying its approaching demise. After Peel's death in 1850 there were few unequivocal champions of the income-tax among the leading men in parliament. Those who in practice wished to keep it a little longer were apt to agree with its opponents that it was in principle a regrettable fiscal imposition. Wood, as chancellor of the exchequer in 1851, told the Commons that he disliked the tax as much as ever and denied that the government's proposal to renew it for another term of three years implied any intention to make it permanent. Aberdeen, as prime minister in 1853, when introducing Gladstone's income-tax bill in the House of Lords, admitted that it was an objectionable tax only to be justified on the grounds that its discontinuance would necessitate even more objectionable taxes to fill the gap. Gladstone himself, when presenting his bill, freely discussed the defects of the income-tax as a method of raising revenue: its inquisitorial character, the encouragement it gave to fraud, the injustices of its incidence. 'It is not well adapted,' he told the Commons, 'for a permanent portion of your ordinary financial system.' With such friends, critics of the income-tax were almost superfluous.

III

Gladstone's success in gaining a renewal of the income-tax in his 1853 budget is commonly taken as consolidating its position in the state financial system. His brilliant exposition enabled him to secure from parliament a seven-year extension of the tax, a longer period than Peel had ever asked for or any other previous chancellor had obtained. Yet it is only in retrospect that this event can be seen as the end of five years of crisis and a decade of uncertainty. In fact, for another twenty years the income-tax was still classified as falling outside 'normal revenue'. At the time Gladstone's achievement was explicable only in terms of his elaborate plan to extinguish the tax by instalments until in 1860 it ceased altogether. As late as 1857 the two ex-chancellors of the exchequer, Gladstone and Disraeli, both in opposition, were pressing the Palmerston administration to adhere to that time-table. By then however it was too late.

The real turning-point in the history of the income tax, and of the whole era in which 'cheap government' was the fashionable cry, is the Crimean War. No doubt more could have been done to finance the war from current revenue rather than borrowing; and the war itself ended more abruptly than was expected. Nevertheless, the income tax came into its own again as a sheet-anchor of state finance. The rate was immediately doubled to 1s. 2d. in the pound in 1854 and in 1855 raised again to 1s. 4d., which yielded an unprecedented sum of £16 millions in 1856–7. It was a sign of the opulence of Victorian society that this record feat was accomplished without recourse to the full precedent of Pitt's 2/– rate in the Napoleonic Wars. In the inevitable debate over the best method of financing the war, the historical analogies with Pitt, Perceval and Liverpool were in many people's mind; and there was a genuine fear of imposing too crippling a burden of direct taxation on the public. If the Crimean War demonstrated once again the versatility and effectiveness of the income tax, it did not remove at once its traditional unpopularity. Even so, unlike previous wars, more than half the cost of the Crimean War was met from current revenue and income-tax alone paid for a third of the total.

Equally important, perhaps, was the financial optimism which paradoxically was engendered by the war. A nation which had braced itself for a long and costly struggle with the greatest military empire in the world, found itself in the event able to bear the expense without immediate hardship or ultimate ill-effect. The heavy reliance on borrowing, particularly in the early stages of the war, and the raising of the duties on articles of popular consumption, which both Gladstone and his successor as chancellor of the exchequer G. C. Lewis adopted as a means of spreading the burden, were accepted with remarkable equanimity by the public. While the financial classes seemed to be losing their old fear of a large National Debt, the British people as a whole seemed more concerned to win the war than argue about ways and means. Either the popular mood had changed or the editor of the *Annual Register* in 1837 misjudged his countrymen in suggesting that they would soon lose their zeal for war once they had experienced its financial realities. More than one observer noted that among the consequences of the war was a tolerance of high spending which in its own way was just as significant in marking the end of the 'cheap government' era as the rehabilitation of the income tax. Stafford Northcote, a future Conservative chancellor of the exchequer, wrote in his book on financial policy published in 1862 that

> the Russian war, in its direct and still more in its indirect consequences, put an end to the policy of 1853. It was that war which . . . not only rendered large expenditure necessary, but infected the whole nation . . . with ideas of extravagance.

Though by 1857–8 expenditure was showing a sharp reduction from the £86 millions it had reached in the last war-year, it never returned to the parsimonious levels of the long period from 1816 to 1853. As an opposition Whig Palmerston in 1842 had opposed the return of the income tax. As prime minister in the 1860s he was one of its stoutest champions in the cabinet. If the British people wished to spend large sums on education and other social purposes, he reasoned, as well as keeping up a proper scale of defence, they must be prepared to pay for that luxury. Gladstone as chancellor of the exchequer found little support even from his fellow Peelites for his increasingly Manchester School outlook on public finance. For the rest of his career in fact the cost of government rose steadily until by 1890, with an even larger and wealthier society, state expenditure was comparable in its amount to the last costly wartime years of 1810–15.

The vocabulary and habits of the 'cheap government' era did not vanish overnight. As late as 1868, in words that Cobbett might have written and would certainly have approved, the Reform League advised the working classes enfranchised by the reform act of the previous year not to vote for classes or parties but for individual candidates who would benefit 'not only yourselves but the whole nation . . . [by] reducing the enormous expenditure and taxation'.[1] Gladstone, as is well known, sought to restore the fading political reputation of the Liberal party by fighting the 1874 general election on a proposal to abolish the income tax.

---

[1] Quoted in F. B. Smith, *The Making of the Second Reform Bill* (Cambridge, 1966), p. 235.

He was defeated and to the end of his life he remained perplexed that the cry had failed to make an impression on an electorate which contained a larger proportion of income-tax payers than was the case after the third Reform Act of 1884. His retrospective explanation was that the mere notion of getting rid of the income tax was by then so strange that the country 'got no effective grip of the idea'. If he was correct, it signalled a notable shift in public opinion since 1853. Whatever the reason, it was a decisive event; and to Gladstone's aged and sombre mind the moral was clear. 'With this facile and classic instrument in their hands every government disposed to enlarge expenditure for whatever purpose had a sure and easy road opened to them.'[1]

The last word, like the first, may be allowed to Morley, Gladstone's biographer as well as Oliver Cromwell's. He shared the sentiments of his Victorian hero. The failure in 1874 to get a mandate to abolish the income tax

> marked the decision of the electorate that the income-tax – introduced in time of peace by Peel and continued by Mr Gladstone for the purpose of simplifying the tariff and expanding trade – should be retained for general objects of government and should be a permanent element of our finance. It marked at the same time the prospect of a new era of indefinitely enlarged expenditure with the income-tax as a main engine for raising ways and means.

Yet though the era of cheap government had come to an end, its effects had been more pervasive than commonly realized. It was only by the cheese-paring standards of the 1816–53 period that late-Victorian governments could be regarded as spendthrift. In reality, when allowance is made for the bigger population and greater national productivity of British society in the latter part of the century, the administration of the state was still remarkably cheap. The proportion of national income taken by the state was in fact lower in 1870 than it had been in 1780. Though *per capita* taxation was nominally twice as high as before the French war, that taxation represented a smaller proportion of the total national wealth.[2] Britain remained a very wealthy country that was very lightly taxed. Whether the growth of that wealth had been accelerated by the insistence on cheap government in the earlier part of the century is another question.

---

[1] *Prime Ministers Papers* (H.M.C. 1971) *W. E. Gladstone I, Autobiographica*, p. 101.
[2] Sir Norman Chester, *The English Administrative System 1780–1870* (Oxford, 1981), pp. 72–3.

5

Parliament and Democracy in Britain: The Three Nineteenth-Century Reform Acts[1]

It could be said with reasonable assurance that the three British nineteenth-century parliamentary reform acts established the broad principle of political democracy, leaving the finer details and the separate problem of female suffrage to be solved in the twentieth century by the legislation of 1918, 1928, and 1948.

What this generalization obscures, however, is the odd circumstance that the acts of 1832, 1867 and 1884 were passed by men who had no belief in the kind of political democracy implicit in universal suffrage and equality of electoral districts and who feared that the introduction of such a system would lead to the tyranny of the illiterate many over the cultured few and of a numerical majority over the interests of minorities. For the greater part of the century the view of most politicians, and indeed of most educated people, was that the parliamentary vote was a trust and that the proper exercise of that trust called for a certain degree of education and social responsibility. Direct advocates of democracy – the radical reformers of the early part of the century, the Chartists of the 1840s, and the extreme radicals of the age of Gladstone and Chamberlain – never found much substantial support in the House of Commons.

There is another difficulty in accepting parliamentary reform as a smooth evolutionary process moving in successive stages towards a clearly defined goal. It is this. The three acts were carried by sharply contrasting methods and with sharply contrasting motives. The lack of symmetry between the three acts is quite startling, particularly in the political methods employed to obtain for them parliamentary approval. In 1831 reform was for the new and untried ministry of Lord Grey virtually a condition of retaining office. In 1867 reform came as the outcome of what might be not unfairly described as a kind of parliamentary Dutch auction (one in which the price becomes progressively lower) between a weak Conservative minority administration and a majority but divided Liberal opposition. In 1884 it was the product of a conspiracy between the two party leaders over which the House of Commons had virtually no influence. If we ask ourselves why it was that these three parliamentary reform acts passed in such different ways at different times, it is difficult to avoid the answer that at certain dates they suited the tactics and were to the advantage of one or other of the great political parties.

This rather mundane reflection if it is to be persuasive, needs to be established in a wider context. In 1831 it was clear that Lord Grey's ministry (the first in which the Whigs as a party had held office for a quarter of a century) would have

[1] A paper read to the Coburg Seminar of the Prince Albert Society on 'British and German Parliamentarism' in September 1984. Subsequently published (with a slightly different title) in *Prince Albert Studies* vol. III (Munich, 1985).

to bring forward a parliamentary reform measure if it was to survive. It had no guaranteed majority in either House of parliament and whatever it did, reform was certain to be raised early in the first session as one of the more important political issues. That the country generally had expectations of reform in the winter of 1830–1 is a commonplace. Yet it is worth noting that these expectations did not amount to a large degree of popular pressure until the cabinet had actually put their proposals before parliament. The contemporary charge that Grey first created public excitement by his bill and then used that excitement to justify the bill had an element of truth.

The excitement was caused by the radical nature of Grey's proposals compared with all previous attempts at reform in parliament, particularly the more recent plans urged by the Whigs when in opposition. Grey, of course, had been identified with the cause of parliamentary reform ever since the 1790s. The boldness of the 1831 bill, however, arose from his conviction that the reform question could only be settled for his generation if the public was offered as full and generous a measure as possible. Grey did not miscalculate the degree of public fervour he was able to rouse on behalf of his bill. What he underestimated was the degree of opposition he would encounter in parliament and from the king.

It would be wrong, on the other hand, to assume that the parliamentary reform movement, which after all had existed with varying degrees of popular support for some fifty years, constituted a direct demand for political power on the part of a large section of the British public. What it represented was more a widespread feeling in the country that only by changes in the electoral system could abuses and defects in government be eliminated and beneficial legislation be secured. It was the ends in view and not the means thought necessary to secure those ends that were important. Though Britain had not gone untouched by the ideological conflict raised by the French Revolution, the domestic parliamentary reform movement was mainly nourished by practical grievances – the disasters of the American War of Independence, the high taxation and inflation which had financed the Napoleonic Wars, the frequent scandals in government and Court circles which marked the first twenty years of the century, the unpopularity of the Church of England, the resentment of Dissenters at their continued legal inferiority and the aftermath of war in the form of economic depression and social distress after 1815.

What was expected of parliamentary reform was it would lead to a series of consequential reforms in both State and Church. As the great middle-class radical agitator William Cobbett argued in his Manchester lectures in the winter of 1831–2, 'a great many people mistake the Reform Bill for reform itself, and a very great mistake it is. The Reform Bill furnishes the means of the reform.' It was the failure of the Whig cabinet to grasp this truth which led to so many of their difficulties and internal divisions after 1832 and to Grey's disillusioned retirement after only a couple of years. Instead of being able to live on the gratitude of the electorate for what they had done in 1832, ministers found themselves under constant pressure from their supporters in the country for further legislation of a kind they had never envisaged when they framed the reform bill.

Nevertheless, before reality had soured expectation, it was the great mass of public feeling which sustained the cabinet in their long and painful struggle in 1831–2 which involved a premature dissolution of parliament, a general election, an attempt by the king to find an alternative ministry, and the coercion of the House of Lords. The fierce contest over this first great reform of the electoral system not surprisingly produced a debate on fundamentals unmatched by any of its successors. It was, if one may use the phrase, the most 'principled' of the three nineteenth-century reform acts. It was fought out by a determined but unhappy cabinet which had gone too far to withdraw and a determined but often despairing opposition which was never able to offer a satisfactory alternative reform of their own. A paradox of the whole reform process was that the violence of the party battles was in inverse proportion to the extent of the actual changes proposed. Though no precise statistical calculation is possible, the probable result of the first Reform Act was to add about 300,000 to the existing electorate of about 500,000. Some estimates make the increase even smaller. In any case it was substantially less than in 1867 or 1884.

What caused the bitter debate in 1831–2 was, of course, the fact that this was the first successful attempt by any British government to carry out a major change in the electoral system. It was a crucial event because it set a precedent. Even so, what was intended by the cabinet was no more than a pruning, purification and enlargement of the existing electoral structure. The motive behind the measure was to strengthen the aristocratic constitution by widening its political basis. It was emphatically *not* a democratic measure. It was, as Lord Grey insisted, a conservative measure in the truest sense. The new franchise qualifications in both county and borough were in all cases higher than the lowest of the existing qualifications: a circumstance rarely remarked on though it makes the act unique among the six acts passed between 1830 and 1948. It was a rationalization of the old untidy electoral machinery rather than a downward extension.

The reform crisis of 1866–7 offers an almost total contrast to that of 1831–2. In the first place the great precedent had been set; the principle that it was proper for the legislature to review the system by which it was elected had been given respectability. Since 1832 in fact there had been many discussions in parliament on the need for further reform, if only to remove the imperfections left or even created by the act of 1832. Bills had been introduced by successive ministries of opposed political complexion in 1859 and 1860, only to founder on opposition or apathy. There did not, however, seem any strong feeling in the country on the question. The failure of Chartism, the social and economic reforms of the 1830s and 1840s, the growing prosperity of Victorian society, the diversion of the energies of the more sophisticated working-class leaders into trade unionism and other economic activities – all this made it difficult to stir up popular demand for a wider franchise. Though particular pressure-groups and specific reform societies existed, they did not have a mass following. What decided the timing of the next instalment of parliamentary reform were personal and party considerations. Of these the most important were the death in 1865 of the veteran Liberal prime minister Lord Palmerston who had been a consistently conservative influence in domestic politics; the desire of the elderly Lord John Russell, who had personally introduced the 1831 reform bill (the only political triumph he had ever enjoyed), to atone for the frustrations of his subsequent career; and Gladstone's somnambulistic intuition that parliamentary reform was a popular cause he ought to take up.

The bill these two Liberal leaders produced, though moderate, split their party and brought about the entry to office of a Conservative ministry which lacked a majority in the House of Commons – as indeed it had lacked one in that chamber for the previous twenty years. Though the defeat of the Liberal bill and the offensive language of some of its critics, notably the old-fashioned Whig, Robert Lowe, stimulated the activity of reform organizations in the country, the initiative still lay with the cabinet. It was not clear at first what they wished to do. Importance has sometimes been attached to the so-called Hyde Park riots of July 1866 when a ban on the use of the park for a reform demonstration led to scuffles with the police, the overthrow of sections of park railings, and the trampling-down of flowerbeds. Except for the effect on the career of the Home Secretary concerned, however, it is difficult to take this episode very seriously. What is often forgotten is that the following year another meeting organized by the Reform League in Hyde Park passed off quietly without damage to a single flowerbed, let alone railings and policemen. This second, peaceful, demonstration has in fact been claimed by one historian as an event that did more to assist the passage of the bill than the mild disorders of 1866. It is hard to attach much importance to either episode.

The ultimate determination of the Conservative cabinet to pass a reform bill of their own was based less on what was happening in the country than on a calculation of party advantage. Three motives seem to have been operating. First, to settle the reform question now that it had been inconveniently raised by their opponents. Next, to remain in office as long as possible – a natural desire in a party which had been almost uniformly in opposition since 1846. Lastly, to demonstrate to the public that parliamentary reform was not a party issue and that the Conservatives as well as the Liberals were entitled to take up the question. To this must be added a determination, particularly strong in Disraeli (the ministerial leader in the Commons) to discredit his personal rival Gladstone and keep the Liberal party divided. There was, on reflection, little to be lost and perhaps something to be gained by changing an electoral system which only once since 1832 had returned a Conservative majority – and that perhaps in exceptional circumstances.

Nevertheless, to embark on legislation without control of the legislature is a hazardous business. The cabinet's policy involved them in abrupt and sometimes contradictory changes in their detailed proposals and a steady surrender to chance majorities in the House of Commons. The end result was an act more extensive than had ever been intended by either party and one whose precise effects could only be a matter of guesswork. It resulted from a process of constant and extraordinary improvisation on the part of a few ministers. Their bemused followers scarcely knew to what they were committing themselves other than it was a measure recommended by their own leaders rather than one introduced by the hated Gladstone.

Much of the early discussions had revolved round the need to ensure a certain level of knowledge and responsibility in any new class of voters to be enfranchised. In the later stages such considerations, along with the principle of lateral rather than vertical extension of the electorate, were cast aside. In its final form a genuine household suffrage, freed from any restrictions such as the payment of rates, became the basis of the new borough franchise. The practical results were startling. Over a million new voters were added to the electorate, representing for the whole United Kingdom an increase of 80 per cent and for England and Wales an increase of 88 per cent. The increase was all the more dramatic for being concentrated in the boroughs, where the electorate more than doubled. It is hardly surprising that the great, if gloomy, publicist Thomas Carlyle, called it 'Shooting Niagara' and that even the prime minister Lord Derby admitted cheerfully that it was a 'leap in the dark'. The future Lord Salisbury, then Viscount Cranborne, had even harsher words for the recklessness of his own leaders. Never, he wrote in the *Quarterly Review*, had there been such an example of political perfidy in the whole period since parliamentary government had been in existence.

The character of the 1867 act, at once drastic and lopsided, made a further adjustment within the foreseeable future almost inevitable. The exclusion of the country dweller from the household franchise was logically indefensible; and the inadequacy of the 1867 redistribution of seats threw into sharper relief the steady growth of urban and industrial population outside the parliamentary boundaries of the borough constituencies. Round London, for example, in the western districts of Yorkshire, in south Lancashire, and in central Scotland, the historic distinction between borough and county was being rapidly obliterated. It would be a misconception to regard the 1884/5 legislation as merely bestowing on the agricultural labourer what had been granted seventeen years earlier to his urban, industrial, counterpart. Had this been so, it would have been in the interest of the Conservative rather than the Liberal party to make the change. In reality, lowering the county franchise was bound to produce a large increase in a class of elector who traditionally voted Liberal. After the Liberal defeat in the general election of 1874 there was clear official encouragement from the Liberal leadership for the idea of a further extension of the franchise and a bill for that purpose was expected to be brought forward at the start of Gladstone's second ministry in 1880. In the event the introduction of another parliamentary reform measure was delayed for three and a half years.

The third Reform Act has in general received far less scrutiny from historians than its two predecessors. Yet it was in many ways a remarkable measure. The delay in bringing it forward was its first curious feature. Certainly there was no great demand in the country for yet another instalment of electoral reform. What organized agitation occurred, came after the defeat of Gladstone's first bill in the upper House and took the form of an agitation against the House of Lords rather than one in favour of democracy for its own sake. The justification for Gladstone's bill lay in wider considerations – the unbalanced state of the franchise and the changed attitude of Victorian public opinion towards another downward extension of the electorate. Whatever their private misgivings, politicians now had to show a proper deference to the fashionable view that the mass of the British people had shown themselves worthy of political responsibility. What Gladstone called 'the enfranchisement of capable citizens' became a piece of conventional wisdom against which it was morally indecent and politically dangerous to argue – a political cliché elevated above rational criticism. Even the Conservative peers in the House of Lords only threw out Gladstone's first bill on the argument that it should have been accompanied by a suitable measure for redistributing the constituencies. The real parliamentary struggle did not come therefore over the extension of the franchise, even though the bill as eventually passed added another 80 per cent to the already enlarged electorate created by the 1867 act. It came over what was to the parliamentary parties the more important tactical issue of the new parliamentary constituencies.

A second oddity about the act was that the whole inter-party dispute was settled rapidly, secretly, and authoritatively by the two party leaders, Gladstone and Lord Salisbury. They then pushed the bill through parliament in a quite astonishing demonstration of party discipline – or, as some might unkindly say, party subservience. The House of Commons, which had debated at such length the 1831–2 bills, and almost dictated the form of the 1867 act, was in 1884–5 little more than a rubber-stamp. What counted were the decisions arrived at privately by six men, of whom only three really mattered – Gladstone, Lord Salisbury, and the Liberal electoral expert Dilke.

This extraordinary episode, and the motives which lay behind it, is still a matter of some speculation. To elucidate the serpentine mind of Mr Gladstone or the astute intelligence of Lord Salisbury, who was able to combine a detached and pessimistic Conservative philosophy with a sharp practical appreciation of political tactics, is a task that must be entered upon with some caution. Circumstantial evidence suggests, however, a number of considerations which probably weighed with them. Though Gladstone was not a democrat, he was undoubtedly a populist politician and adept at raising public issues (even to the extent of persuading himself that he had supported them all along), where it was to his immediate advantage to do so. A Liberal reform bill in 1884, followed by a redistribution bill in the following session, would round off his term of office on a creditable reforming note and offset to some extent the growing unpopularity of his government's Egyptian policy.

Even more important perhaps in Gladstone's mind was the connection between parliamentary reform and the Irish question. Ireland and the emergence of Parnell as leader of the Irish Home Rule Party had dominated Gladstone's second ministry. Once the issue of a third Reform Act was raised, the prime minister made up his mind that it must include Ireland in its operation. Tactically this would be essential to ensure Parnell's agreement or at least neutrality. But there were other more subtle considerations. For the Liberals, indeed for any British government, the Irish electoral situation could scarcely be worse than it was already. An enlargement of the Irish electorate at least offered the chance of testing Parnell's apparently iron grip on the parliamentary representation of Ireland. If a popular Irish electorate continued to support him, then this would provide a firm political justification for a new Irish policy based on Home Rule and enable the government to disentangle itself from its controversial Irish land legislation proposals.

Certainly Gladstone's insistence, against all precedent, on a unified reform measure for the whole United Kingdom, was in sharp contrast to the tepid and conventional remarks he made about the 'peasantry' of England and Wales (whereby he meant the landless rural labourers) as 'capable citizens' who should now be admitted to the franchise. It was precisely the inclusion of Ireland in the government's bill which aroused greatest unease in the Liberal ranks. There had been no mandate for it at any of the party conferences and it produced the most powerful and prophetic passages of the reform debates in parliament. There are clear indications, however, that even before Christmas 1884 and long before the general election of 1885, which saw the triumphant return of Parnell with some ninety Home Rulers elected under the enlarged franchise, Gladstone had made up his mind in favour of some form of devolved government for Ireland. It does not seem unreasonable to regard Gladstone's 1884 reform bill as the opening shot in his long Home Rule campaign.

As for Lord Salisbury, the considerations which governed his actions were almost entirely tactical. Though he did not like the extension of the suffrage, he knew it could not be prevented and as party leader he declined to tie his followers to a losing cause. What Gladstone had oratorically described in 1866 as 'the great social forces which move onward in their might and majesty' could not be stopped in 1884 if the Liberal government of the day was determined to advance their progress. Nor did Salisbury want to bring on a Lords *versus* Commons conflict. The initial battle in parliament was therefore only a skirmish. Salisbury's main object was to keep his hands free and to manoeuvre for position. Linked with this, however, was a larger consideration. Among the other social forces making themselves felt in late-Victorian society was one which favoured Salisbury's party rather than the Liberals. This was the unmistakable growth of conservative feeling among the urban middle-classes – 'Villa Toryism' as it was nicknamed with reference to its strength in the well-to-do suburbs of the larger towns. Any rearrangement and sub-division of constituencies which increased the number of urban seats capable of being won by the Conservative party was a prize worth winning. Redistribution and not the franchise, therefore, became the real issue in 1884; and it was here that a further advantage presented itself to the shrewd, realistic mind of Lord Salisbury.

At the start of the reform crisis the leadership of the Conservative party was still in the indecisive state in which it had been left in 1881 by the death of Disraeli. Salisbury was leader of the party in the House of Lords; Northcote in the House of Commons. In turn Northcote's position in the lower house was undermined by the ambitions of Randolph Churchill and the activities of the Fourth Party. The reform crisis of 1884 was an opportunity for Salisbury to assert his authority in the party at large, not only over Northcote but indirectly over the more dangerous pretensions of Churchill. In exactly the same way Gladstone took care during the crisis to keep out of the limelight the younger and equally dangerous figure of Joseph Chamberlain. Both party leaders had a common interest in agreeing with each other and presenting their respective party followers with a *fait accompli*.

The moral to be drawn from these three reform episodes is not perhaps an elevated one. In all three crises party and personal advantages played a considerable part: an underlying one in 1831–2, a dominant one in 1866–7, and a large one in 1884–5. Yet one must distinguish between motives and consequences. British political evolution in the nineteenth century has incurred the reproach that democratic reform came too slowly and lagged behind social progress. There is much to support this view. Large as the additions to the electorate had been between 1832 and 1884, they still left Britain with something perceptibly short of full democracy. Only two adult males in three in England and Wales, three out of five in Scotland, five out of ten in Ireland, had the vote. It was the second, third and fifth decades of the present century, within the lifetime of many still living, which saw the establishment of the principle of one man, one vote, together with the admission of women to the franchise on equal terms with men, which is commonly held to mark the perfected political democracy.

The first three reform acts now regarded as milestones along the road to that achievement were then no more than – and were intended by their authors to be no more than – modifications of the traditional pre-1832 system. Even at the end of the nineteenth century the traces of the historical unreformed structure were still visible in the absence of any legislative principle of manhood suffrage, in the retention of old and largely obsolete historic franchises, in plural voting, in the separate representation of the universities, and in the still discernible though now tenuous link between ownership or occupation of property and the qualifications for voting in parliamentary elections.

Yet there is a case also for the contrary view: that this slow and piecemeal approach towards democracy proceeded at least as fast as, if not faster than, social development. Much of the conventional justification among late-Victorian politicians for extensions of the franchise rested on little more than a string of comfortable assumptions. They talked of 'the respectable working-man' (to mention the disrespectable 'residuum' soon became unfashionable), of 'capable citizens' (with little attempt to define 'capability'), of 'trusting the people' (though they did not say with what). This vocabulary was based on not much evidence other than the absence of violent popular disorders after the middle of the century (with Ireland always the admitted exception) and on the practical continuation in power of an aristocratically dominated ruling class. It was this apparently remarkable social stability, even more striking when contrasted with the continent of Europe, which made it possible for each of the two great political parties in turn to propose, or at least not vociferously oppose, substantial additions to the electorate on which they both depended for parliamentary office.

At the same time they were able to ease their intellectual consciences by repudiating any theoretical principle of democracy and continuing to pay lip-service to the old Whig doctrine of 1831 that only those classes which had shown themselves worthy of the trust should be admitted within the pale of the constitution. The comfortable conviction was accepted that there existed, in Bagehot's famous phrase, a powerful 'deferential' element in the British people. It was possible for Disraeli, for example, in 1867 to make a plausible but ultimately untenable distinction between 'popular privileges' and 'democratic rights', and for Gladstone the previous year to talk approvingly of 'the growing capacity and intelligence of the working classes, and of their admirable performance at least of their duties towards their superiors'. It was this optimism again, to quote from the same speech by Gladstone (March 1866), which made it not altogether absurd to ask the gentry in the House of Commons to welcome the new electors 'as you would welcome recruits to your army or children to your family'.

The confidence was not, however, based on any very informed knowledge or at any rate critical consideration of British society. As the studies of Booth and Rowntree towards the end of the century demonstrated, there was still a vast amount of poverty and social degradation in the larger towns. As for electoral morality, violence and corruption were standing features of parliamentary elections for most of the Victorian period, as the passage of an important Corrupt and Illegal Practices Act in 1883 amply demonstrated. The decline of the once common practice of bribing the poorer voters came about as a result not so much of greater moral sensitivity as of the sheer impossibility of using these time-honoured methods with any effect in the mass electorates created by the second and third reform acts. In the countryside, which on the whole had been more free of the traditional electoral malpractices, though not of strong social pressures exerted from above by farmers and landowners, the irony was that the rural labourer was enfranchised just at the time when the great agricultural depression and large-scale migration to the towns robbed the concession of any particular value.

It would in fact be difficult to show that the newly enfranchised masses had either exhibited their fitness for the vote or were qualified for its exercise on any previously accepted critieria. Nor did the rise of a cheap, sensational national newspaper press under such new-style proprietors as Harmsworth and Northcliffe hold out much encouragement for the future. Robert Lowe's famous remark after the 1867 legislation, that 'we must educate our masters' (more accurately 'compel our future masters to learn their letters') applied with even more force to the 1884 act. The first compulsory education act was passed in 1870, three years *after* the second Reform Act had created a working-class majority in the boroughs. In the rural areas the early inefficiencies of the educational system and the notorious difficulties of enforcing attendance of country children needed for small jobs on farms, made it unlikely that the new electorate was much affected by formal state education until the generation after 1900. One of the more reflective British prime ministers, Stanley Baldwin, who had been born in the year of the second Reform Act and had watched all this process as he grew up, said in 1928 that 'democracy has arrived at a gallop in England and I feel all the time that it is a race for life. Can we educate them before the crash comes?'

Even so, there was probably some advantage in the course taken by parliamentary reform in Victorian Britain, narrow, selfish, short-sighted and muddled though the process had been. It is often a charge against aristocratic or oligarchic societies that they rarely surrender power until they are forced and that then it is too late for the concession to produce any benefits. In an oblique fashion the British reform acts, specially those of 1867 and 1884, had the merit of coming when there was no particular demand for them by those who stood to be enfranchised. As Professor Norman McCord has suggested in one of the more perceptive articles on the nineteenth-century reform acts which have appeared in recent years, not only were those acts typically English in their untidy 'muddling-through', on no discernible basis of principle, but *because* of that, they avoided any direct class conflict of the kind which has damaged the stable evolution of democracy in other countries.

If that point is accepted, one further comment may be allowed. Political parties do not as a rule earn much praise from political theorists. Yet in their pursuit of self-regarding ends, it may be that the Liberal and Conservative parties of the Victorian age contributed more than they intended to the general good.

Part II

Elections and Electioneering

6

Peel and the Oxford University Election of 1829[1]

The emancipation of the Catholics in 1829 was a decisive point in the history of many human affairs. For the Irish it meant the renewal with redoubled strength of the long campaign that led by way of O'Connell and Parnell to rebellion and ultimate independence. In Peel's career it was the first of the great 'betrayals' which divided his party in 1830 and shattered it in 1846. To Peel personally it brought a permanent estrangement from his own university which a second rebuff in 1834 only made more bitter and decisive. All three sequels hung together on a single line of development.

The penal laws against Catholics, inherited from the sixteenth and seventeenth centuries and maintained in the eighteenth century by public prejudice and the corporate interest of the Anglican church, were first seriously threatened by the national revival of Catholic Ireland. In 1793 the Irish Catholics were enfranchised and by the beginning of the nineteenth century the policy of complete emancipation had entered English domestic politics. Pitt's act of 1800 created a parliamentary union of the two islands but his promised concessions to the Catholics were abandoned in the face of royal opposition. Ireland felt herself betrayed and for the next thirty years Englishmen disagreed over Catholic emancipation even when they agreed on all other political issues. Consequently in 1817, when a seat for Oxford University fell vacant, this cherished reward of high-church Toryism went not to Canning, who in all respects except one was the obvious candidate, but to the young Peel whose work in Ireland showed the promise of a great future and whose religious orthodoxy had gained for him the nickname of 'Orange' Peel from Irish nationalists. Canning died in 1827 and his liberal coalition was soon succeeded by the more conservative Wellington ministry. One result of the ministerial changes involved was a bye-election in the Irish constituency of county Clare. The Irish peasantry, obeying their priests rather than their landlords, elected the great agitator, O'Connell, although as a Catholic he was legally incapable of sitting in parliament, and thus created a precedent for future Irish action that had incalculable potentialities. It was a crisis in Anglo-Irish relations and it was met with surrender on the part of the government. At the beginning of the parliamentary session of 1829, the ministry of Peel and Wellington announced its intention of introducing a bill for the removal of Catholic disabilities. To the country at large the news came as a sensation; to many Tory Anglicans it seemed infamy. Not only was the measure revolutionary in itself but it was brought forward by men who had consistently opposed its principle. Few realized how grave was the situation in Ireland which had inspired the government's resolve

[1] First published in *Oxoniensia*, vol. IV (1939).

and few could comprehend or endorse the motives which induced Peel, in spite of twenty years uncompromising Protestantism, to take upon himself the task of conducting the bill through the House of Commons. To the charge of inconsistency from the general public Peel could affect indifference; to his constituents of Oxford University, however, he felt almost an official obligation. The predominantly clerical electorate had chosen him largely because of his steady support of the established church and he held it incumbent on him to give them an opportunity of reconsidering their choice.[1] Such deference to the prejudices of the electorate were rare among contemporary members of parliament and he encountered some critism for his view of the representative function. It was, Croker told him, 'a democratical and unconstitutional proceeding and a precedent dangerous to the independence of the house of commons.'[2] But the university was not an ordinary constituency and Peel no ordinary politician.

Scrupulous as he was determined to be, nevertheless it appeared to him only prudent to discover at the outset whether there would be any need for his scruples. The fittest channel for ascertaining the feeling of the university seemed his old college, Christ Church. Dr Lloyd,[3] the bishop of Oxford and his former tutor, was a close friend who had taken an important part in securing Peel's first election for the university in 1817 and had remained in confidential communication with him ever since. As early as the middle of January 1829 he had been privately informed by Peel of the government's decision and although he had been greatly distressed by the news, his attachment to and belief in the younger man stayed unbroken. Peel could be confident therefore of obtaining from the college both assistance and secrecy in the delicate matter he was about to lay before them.[4] On 31 January, nearly a week before the assembly of parliament and the publication of the general intention of the ministers, he wrote to Smith, the dean of Christ Church, announcing his determination to bring in a bill for Catholic emancipation and offering, or at least suggesting, his resignation if the feeling of the university desired it. At the same time, as though anxious not to be judged unheard, he enclosed a memorandum explaining and justifying his line of conduct in some detail. The receipt of this odd communication naturally put the dean in considerable embarrassment. He was afraid to show it to many members of the university or put it officially before the board of heads of houses because either action might make the confidential information contained in it a matter of general knowledge and discussion at Oxford before the rest of the country had heard anything of it. He consulted Dr Lloyd and the two men decided to confide in only one other person, Gaisford, the regius professor of Greek.[5] The triumvirate agreed immediately on one point; that it was impossible to carry out the task

---

[1] Parker, *Peel*, II, chh. III and IV; Mahon and Cardwell, *Peel's Memoirs* I, esp. pp. 312–41. Part of the correspondence in the Peel MSS, on which this article is chiefly based, is published in the Memoirs. But many important letters were not included and from some of the printed letters passages of a personal or indiscreet nature were omitted. References will only be to sources not given in the Memoirs.

[2] Jennings, *Croker Papers*, II, 7.

[3] Charles Lloyd 1784–1829; lecturer, tutor and censor of Christ Church; regius professor of divinity 1822; bishop of Oxford 1827. He supported the Roman Catholic emancipation bill in the House of Lords.

[4] Brit. Mus. Add. MS 40343 f. 329.

[5] Thomas Gaisford 1779–1855, later dean of Christ Church 1831–55.

with which Peel apparently wished to commission them. By themselves they could not discover the feeling of the whole university and even if they consulted the heads of houses, the opinions so obtained could not be regarded as truly representative. Gaisford thought that Peel ought to resign at once;.the dean, foreseeing the awkward position in which the college would then be placed, was unwilling to advise such a hasty and positive step; and Lloyd, already deeply anxious at the government's surrender to the Catholics, wavered tiredly between the two. He saw objections both to an outright and to a conditional offer of resignation. The one might seem a brusque repudiation of the university connection; the other might cause resentment by appearing to put the onus of decision on the resident members. 'My fear is,' he confessed subsequently to Peel, 'that if your letter to the vice-chancellor (written with the same intention as that to the dean) be laid before the heads of houses, some hot men among them . . . will say, "What have we to do with this? He knows we cannot call upon him to resign" and so, they may send you an answer, not in good humour, leaving you to act as you please.' The question of the memorandum created another difficulty. To the little committee of three at Christ Church, Peel's punctilious explanations seemed unnecessary. The motives which had led to his action were part of his public policy and the only fit place for their discussion was the floor of the House of Commons. As far as the university was concerned it was quite sufficient to state that he had been compelled by his view of the interests of the country to the course he had taken. The only concession to university feeling which they thought he might profitably make was to state that his original opinions on the Catholic question remained unchanged although he was now obliged by circumstance to follow a different line of action. A phrase of that nature inserted in the letter would enable the memorandum to be dispensed with altogether. Finally therefore it was agreed to send all the papers back to Peel so that he could reconsider the whole matter. If he still wished to keep to his original plan, the dean would personally lay the papers before the vice-chancellor. But their advice was to write directly to the vice-chancellor and make him, as by virtue of his office he would naturally expect, the instrument for sounding the feeling of the university. In a long and troubled letter, the first of an almost daily series during the next two weeks, Lloyd made the further suggestion that Peel should delay communicating with the university until parliament had met and the government's decision was publicly known. 'I cannot disguise from you,' he added, 'that both the dean and Gaisford were thunderstruck and very sad, when the contents of the letter first burst upon them. Both immediately said, "Why not try to carry strong measures and then, if you are defeated, give way?" And this, I fear, is the course of action which could alone have satisfied this country.'[1]

Peel's sensitive temperament was hurt by the return of his letters but it did at least convince him that to ask individual members of the university whether he ought to resign was useless and embarrassing. He therefore altered his letter from a conditional to a formal and positive resignation and sent it to the vice-chancellor so that it reached him on 5 February, the day of the opening of parliament. All he requested in it was to be informed when it would be most convenient to the university for his resignation to take effect. On receiving this letter the vice-

[1] *Ibid.*, f. 334; Add. MS 40398 f. 116.

chancellor, J. C. Jones, the rector of Exeter, at once summoned a meeting of the board of heads of houses and proctors. It met at noon the same day and authorized the publication of the letter at the meeting of convocation in the afternoon. An ironical and unfortunate coincidence resulted. The intention of the government to grant emancipation was known in London on 2 February.[1] The meeting of convocation at Oxford on the 5th had been called to discuss petitions to parliament against the concession. Peel's letter was read out immediately after the petitions had been overwhelmingly approved by 164 votes to 48; and the vice-chancellor's acknowledgement of the letter was accompanied by another communication requesting him in the absence of the other university member, T. G. Estcourt, who was kept away from the opening of the session by family trouble, to present the petitions to the House of Commons. On the following day a formal reply from the board was sent to Peel, regretting his decision to resign and begging him to use his own discretion as to the date. This official courtesy was given more point by a private letter from the dean of Christ Church, written with the knowledge and approval of the vice-chancellor, earnestly advising him to delay his resignation until the measure for Catholic emancipation had been introduced and discussed in parliament as until then a cool judgement on the issue could not be expected at Oxford.[2] For the moment, certainly, the university was too confused for a considered opinion to assert itself. No details were known of the proposed bill and it was not clear whether Peel intended or wished to stand for re-election. There was considerable support for his action but on the other hand Protestant feeling was undoubtedly strong and the voting in convocation on the petitions against emancipation made some hasty people conclude that a similar majority would be found against Peel in an election. The moderate Tories could be relied on to champion their man even if his measure was not altogether palatable and it was certain that the Whigs, too few and uninfluential to put up a separate candidate, would offer no resistance. But there were two other parties in the university whose attitude was more important and less predictable. The Ultra-Tories would take no part in electing Peel again but they might not oppose him; in any case, following university precedent, they would not force a contest unless they could find a candidate with a reasonable chance of success. Finally Christ Church, Peel's own college, might decide to support him as a body. If they did so, the weight of numbers and influence they could exercise might be decisive; but if the general temper of Oxford proved to be against Peel, it was unlikely that the college would risk its unity and prestige in a contest with the rest of the university.[3]

It appeared at first that there would be no serious opposition to Peel's return. 'Well, Mr Dean, I suppose you will propose him again immediately,' said Dr Landon, the Tory head of Worcester, to Smith after the meeting of convocation; and the remark seemed typical of the common feeling. Christ Church, at least, displayed a favourable attitude. Lloyd had travelled up to London on the 5th to see Peel but he had read the letter of resignation before he left and strongly approved it. The dean, though not enthusiastic, was prepared to propose Peel for

---

[1] Jennings, *Croker Papers*, II, 12.
[2] Add. MS 40398 fos. 174, 205.
[3] Add. MS 40343 fos. 340, 343.

re-election. He refused personally to urge Peel to allow himself to be nominated or even to enquire from him whether he desired to be returned but he allowed the senior censor, T. V. Short,[1] to write to Lloyd in order to discover what Peel's real feelings were.[2] Short himself was a warm Peelite and told Lloyd that he had no doubt that it was the wish of the Common Room that Peel should be brought forward and that he would unhesitatingly advise the college to do all they could in his support. The only difficulty was the rumour current in Oxford that Peel would refuse to stand. Provided, however, that he would consent to be nominated, Short expressed his confidence that there would be no opposition to his return if the college came forward to support him. 'It is very right in him to expose himself to our votes,' he concluded, 'but I should despise Oxford if they suffered him or any other man to suffer for honestly doing what they knew that he deemed his duty.'[3] Short, however, was notorious for his ultra-liberal opinions and Lloyd privately thought that he did more harm than good by his zeal. More influence was wielded by Marsham, the warden of Merton, who came to Lloyd on his return from London to enquire whether Peel would accept re-election. Lloyd expressed a fear, which he had already discussed with Peel, as to the propriety of his standing again and the danger of aspersions on his character if he was re-elected; but Marsham dismissed these scruples as hyper-quixotism and gave his opinion that Peel's re-election was a duty which the university, if permitted, would certainly fulfil. Lloyd, who was probably the only man in Oxford with a knowledge of Peel's inmost feelings on the matter, thereupon decided to allow Peel's supporters to follow their strong inclination. He thus added his own not inconsiderable name and influence to the growing movement for Peel's return. As far as Christ Church was concerned, his action was decisive. On 9 February the Common Room met and unanimously resolved to support Peel's candidature. A circular letter to the members of other college Common Rooms was drawn up, announcing their intention, to which was subjoined a copy of Peel's letter to the vice-chancellor; but it was decided not to issue this before Wednesday, 11 February.[4] The delay may have been due to a desire on Lloyd's part to ensure that Peel would definitely accept nomination at the hands of the college. No positive decision had yet been reached between them and the most that Lloyd had permitted himself to say at Oxford was that he had no reason to think that Peel would decline re-election. It was not until 8 February that Lloyd himself had decided in favour of nomination and although he had immediately written to Peel, no answer could be expected to arrive before 10 February. In the interval thus created, events occurred which completely changed his attitude. Lloyd, whose death four months later was ascribed to the painful anxiety he suffered during these weeks, was still nervous and irresolute. Fears for the effect of the Emancipation Act, fears for Peel's reputation, fears for the welfare of the college and for the animosities of a bitter contest within the university, all conspired to make him shrink at the first threat of danger. The day after the meeting of the Christ Church Common Room he received information of a meeting of heads of houses for the express purpose of

[1] Thomas Vowler Short 1790–1872; censor of Christ Church 1816–29; later bishop of Sodor and Man 1841–46, and of St Asaph 1846–70.
[2] *Ibid.*, f. 345.
[3] *Ibid.*, f. 347.
[4] *Ibid.*, f. 353.

opposing Peel. He was thrown into a fit of agitation and determined to forbid the censors to take any further steps in the matter of Peel's nomination. The opposition meeting took place on 11 February and in consequence of the hostility to Peel which was exhibited, Lloyd made up his mind to withdraw the college entirely from the position which they had privately, and he now felt unwisely, taken up. Peel had written to him the day before, giving him considerable latitude in deciding according to the chances of success whether his name should be put in nomination. Interpreting this commission in its widest sense, Lloyd informed the censors that Peel had requested him to put a stop to the activities of the college on his behalf. 'So there,' he wrote to Peel with something like relief, 'is an end of it.'[1]

The opposition to Peel which had caused Lloyd's precipitate retreat had been formed before a candidate had been found to replace him. There had at first been some mention of the attorney-general, Sir Charles Wetherell,[2] a violent opponent of reform and Catholic relief, who was subsequently dismissed by Wellington for his extravagant attacks on the Emancipation Bill. Later there was talk of Lord Chandos,[3] Sir Robert Inglis,[4] and Lord Encombe.[5] But as late as 13 February there was still no definite candidature and with the moderates proposing to put up Hobhouse[6] or Marsham himself, in default of Peel it seemed that the ultras would after all be deprived of a sectarian triumph.[7] But if they lacked a candidate, they did not lack the strength in the university to support one. The list of those who on 13 February announced their intention of electing a more fitting representative than Peel, included the nine heads with other members of Magdalen, Worcester, Jesus, St Mary's Hall, University, Trinity, Queen's, St Edmund Hall and St John's, together with other names from Balliol, Oriel, Lincoln, BNC and Corpus.[8] The formidable influence of this body was difficult to obscure. Dr Lloyd could write with a renewal of partisan spirit that apart from Routh of Magdalen, there was not a name in it known outside the precincts of the university;[9] and Granville Vernon urged Peel not to submit passively to 'the doctrine that the resident members of the university are entitled to meet in their cells and dictate in their darkness to the collective body.'[10] But it was patent that the ultra party represented a powerful body in Oxford and that they would exercise a great influence on the country voters who cared little for Peel's intellectual qualities and political connections and much for the example and persuasion of their old colleges. All that was needed was a candidate; and a candidate was eventually found in Sir Robert Inglis. His merit had not previously been conspicuous and his claims to the university seat not immediately obvious;

[1] *Ibid.*, fos. 355, 356, 357.
[2] He had been a demy of Magdalen, 1786–91.
[3] Oriel; MP for Buckinghamshire, 1818–39; son of the 1st duke of Buckingham and Chandos, whom he succeeded in 1839.
[4] 2nd bart; Christ Church; MP for Dundalk, 1824–6; Ripon, 1828–9; Oxford University, 1829–54.
[5] John Scott, grandson and heir of Lord Eldon, the famous Tory lawyer and politician.
[6] Henry Hobhouse, 1776–1854; BNC; DCL Oxford, 1827; Tory lawyer and politician; keeper of State Papers, 1826–54.
[7] *Ibid.*, fos. 355, 357, 368.
[8] Add. MS 40398 f. 258.
[9] Add. MS 40343 f. 368.
[10] Add. MS 40398 f. 244.

but he had two qualifications to recommend him to his sponsors. Like Peel he was a member of Christ Church and so could be expected to draw part at least of the big Christ Church vote from his rival. Secondly his support of the established church had been staunch and orthodox enough to satisfy even the most distrustful clerical elector. It is not unlikely that the more Tory members of Christ Church played a part in his selection. After Lloyd had prevented Peel's nomination by the college, it was soon deeply and apparently irrevocably divided. Even if he had wished to do so, Lloyd would have found it difficult to secure unity a second time on Peel's behalf. He had been criticized for his withdrawal but criticism was soon useless to reverse the development of opinions. 'Independently of the considerations which actuated me at first,' he wrote defensively to Peel on 18 February, 'considerations in which I thought and think still that your honor was involved, look at the state of our chapter; the dean neutral but rather against than for; Dr Hay a violent antagonist; Dr Woodcock neutral; Dr Buckland and Pusey[1] for; Dr Barnes and Pett doubtful. Under these circumstances, could I have insisted on the dean coming forward and proposing you to the chapter? It was far better to leave the expression of feeling to come from the university.'[2]

The idea of nominating Peel had no sooner been abandoned by Christ Church, however, than it was taken up in another quarter of the university. Although the support for him was apparent from the first, nothing had been done to give a lead to that opinion. Even the heads of houses known to be in sympathy with Peel had seemed to be 'sunk in hopeless apathy,' as Whately[3] later described to Peel. Ultimately the vice-principal of St Alban Hall, Mr Hinds, fearing that the body of Peelite support might prove ineffective through mere lack of initiative, persuaded Whately, who was his principal, to start active measures for putting Peel in nomination.[4] Encouraged by the example of one who in his day was perhaps the best known character in the university, Peel's supporters met at Merton on 12 February and decided to form a committee to secure his re-election. The list of adherents included the heads of seven houses (Merton, Oriel, New College, All Souls, Pembroke, Magdalen Hall and St Alban Hall), a strong body from Christ Church, and a few members of other colleges. Marsham, the warden of Merton, was made chairman of the committee and an election room taken in High Street. From here on the following day a manifesto was issued, explaining (since some explanation seemed neecessary) that Peel's 'characteristic sincerity and total absence of reservation have imposed a restraint on his own college and precluded them collectively from putting him again in nomination,' and appealing for support 'lest under the excitement of the moment, the interests of the university should be committed to some less able or less tried representative.'[5] Meanwhile Marsham wrote confidently to Peel informing him of what had been done but begging him not to acknowledge or reply to the letter. Peel, however, unwilling to allow an issue he had thought dropped to be taken up once more, yet finding it

---

[1] The future leaders of the Oxford movement were divided on this issue; Keble and Newman were against Peel; Pusey, probably because of Lloyd's influence, supported him.
[2] Add. MS 40343 f. 374.
[3] Richard Whately 1787–1863; fellow of Oriel; appointed principal of St Alban Hall 1825 and archbishop of Dublin 1831.
[4] Add. MS 40399 f. 9.
[5] Add. MS 40398 f. 246; 40343 f. 369.

difficult to decide in London on points that demanded a close knowledge of politics in Oxford, thought it best to express his general attitude to his new supporters. He therefore sent a letter for Marsham through Lloyd, pointing out that public business made it necessary for him to return to parliament as soon after his resignation as possible; that the date of the university election rested with the vice-chancellor who might decide to postpone it until after the Oxford assizes at the beginning of March; and that taking everything into consideration, it might prove most convenient to all if no effort was made to re-elect him as the university member. Lloyd forwarded the letter to Marsham who proposed to his committee to lay it before them. They refused to see it and took up the attitude that they had proceeded so far on their own initiative and responsibility and even Peel could not be allowed to interfere with the course of a university election. Lloyd, who moved restlessly from one mood to another, was now inclined to let them continue their work. Optimistic reports on the strength of the Peel party were coming in and there was a widespread impression that many who disagreed with Peel's policy would not actually vote against him in an election.[1] Certainly the formation of Marsham's committee had given a great impetus to the movement for Peel's return. Within forty-eight hours a committee had been set up in London to cooperate with that in Oxford. Granville Somerset, one of the government's parliamentary managers, was appointed chairman; a number of well-known politicians signed the manifesto on Peel's behalf; an industrious canvass was started and several offers of support and influence came from outside the capital. Lord Londonderry promised to send his son's tutor to Oxford on polling day and wrote a card of recommendation on Peel's behalf while Granville Vernon offered to influence the clergy in his district. It was said that most of London and all the lawyers were on Peel's side and even the civic authorities took part in the campaign. The Lord Mayor of London proposed to give Peel the freedom of the city in the hope that it might prove useful in preventing some of the London clergy from acting against him.[2] On 22 February Granville Somerset was able to send Peel an encouraging account of the campaign in the capital. 'I cannot help,' he wrote, 'entertaining the most confident expectation of the successful issue of the election; at the same time it is so utterly impossible to know the intentions of a very large proportion of the members of convocation, that I will not pretend to anticipate what sort of majority is likely to be the result of our exertions. There is certainly a very strong feeling of Protestantism against which we have to contend, and my individual canvass has been the most unfortunate of any; at the same time we have obtained support in quarters where I little expected it.'[3]

But the real centre of events was Oxford; and the work of Peel's committee there was hampered by two doubts. The first was whether Peel would really consent to serve again as member; the second, whether there would be sufficient time for the university election to take place before he was returned to parliament for some other constituency. On the first point Peel's attitude was clear if also unsatisfying. In private, though this was perhaps the affectation of a proud and sensitive man, he professed complete indifference to the events at Oxford. All he

---

[1] Add. MS 40343 fos. 361, 374, 383.
[2] The distinction was accepted by Peel but not until after the election.
[3] Add. MS 40398 fos. 244, 313, 319, 320. See the printed account in the Brit. Lib. (731.m. 14/7) of the meeting of Peel's supporters in London at the British Coffee House on 14 February, 1829.

wished was to do what was best calculated to save his college and university from embarrassment. He expressed no desire to be nominated and an extreme reluctance to fight an election. 'For God's sake,' he had written to Lloyd on 11 February, 'take no step directly or indirectly that would appear to intimate a wish on my part to be returned. I have no such wish and I think a protracted contest even if it ended successfully would be very embarrassing and painful to me.' On the other hand he was unwilling to do anything that would appear 'peevish and ill-humoured or disrespectful' and if his supporters chose to put him in nomination, he would not repudiate their action or vacate the seat if elected. But he would do nothing to assist them and would proceed with the business of resignation and re-election as though the university did not exist. All this was not encouraging. Yet it is at least possible that the committee at Oxford interpreted Peel's mind in a truer sense than his own words would convey. It is hard to doubt that he would have welcomed an honour which his pride and scrupulousness prevented him from soliciting. In any case the committee decided to persist with his nomination. The only problem was that of time. The vice-chancellor's reply to Peel's letter of resignation had left him free to select his own date for his retirement so long as the university received ample notice. Peel then named 20 February and this date proved acceptable to the authorities. To Peel's committee, however, who were under the impression that he would at once take steps to be returned to parliament elsewhere, it seemed useless to continue, as the university election was not expected to come on until several days after the 20th. Marsham, seeking a way out of the difficulty, enquired from Peel whether it would be possible for him to be returned for parliament at once and subsequently apply for the Chiltern Hundreds a second time in order to stand for the university election. But there was no need for these dramatic gestures. Peel, in spite of his earlier declarations, was prepared to remain out of parliament until 2 March and promised Marsham to put no obstacle in the way of his nomination for the university provided the election could be held before that date.[1] The last complication was now removed and Peel's committee moved confidently towards the election.

On 26 February, the first day of polling, Oxford was crowded with voters and onlookers and 'party, religious and political feeling . . . wound up to the highest pitch.' The animosity against Peel was made unpleasantly evident. Marsham proposed Peel in a speech that had to contend with a running clamour from the crowd, and Dr Ingram, the president of Trinity, who proposed Sir Robert Inglis, had to stop short his speech because of the impatience of the crowd to poll. 'During these speeches,' reported George Dawson, Peel's brother-in-law and, though an eye-witness, perhaps a partial observer, 'the clamour, violence and insulting language used by your opponents was almost beyond endurance. The common courtesy, every decency of life was forgotten, and I assure you without exaggeration that I should have fancied myself on the hustings at Westminster – indeed I think Westminster has the advantage. I never felt less proud of having been a member of the university and cannot but think the honor of representing it, most over-rated. I did not think it possible that a large assembly, composed entirely of educated men, would have shown themselves so devoid of decency and

---

[1] Add. MS 40398 fos. 261, 269.

so utterly deficient in everything that constitutes a liberal and enlightened audience. To you I may say the truth with respect to the conduct of the masters of arts and I regret to be obliged to add that their inveteracy against you, and their coarse and base remarks upon your conduct were almost enough to make the blood of your friends boil in their veins.'[1] By the end of the following afternoon the battle was seen to be lost; Peel was 126 votes behind with no hope of making up the deficiency. The final figures were Inglis 755, Peel 609. A few days later Peel returned to parliament as member for the little Wiltshire town of Westbury, a pocket borough held by Sir Manasseh Lopez.

There were of course the usual recriminations. Peel's committee had been a poor one; Marsham's speech had been protracted, injudicious and ineffective; the enemy had resorted to such ungentlemanly devices as sending out an appeal in the name of a college when the college was in fact divided.[2] At this interval of time, other criticisms occur; a different result might have been obtained if Peel had delayed his resignation until the end of the session instead of challenging opinion from an over-strained sense of honour while it was still in the first shock of astonishment and dismay; and Lloyd's failure to preserve the unity of Christ Church on Peel's behalf and timidity in not naming him at the first possible occasion was a source of weakness which need not have been present. The opposition at least made capital out of it:

> Such is Peel – so much honoured,
>   his college, d'ye see,
> Will not bring the man forward but
>   leave him to me.'[3]

But Peel, whatever his private feelings, professed satisfaction. No reproach could be levelled at his conduct and the strong support in the university for his policy had been revealed to the world. Meanwhile his friends could pride themselves on the composition of Peel's defeated but respectable minority. He had secured twice as many first class men as Inglis; fourteen out of twenty professors; twenty-four out of twenty-eight prizemen; all the noblemen who voted; and, crowning triumph, three hundred and thirty-three clergymen.

[1] *Ibid.*, f. 323, Dawson to Peel. See also the printed speeches and pamphlets on the Oxford election of 1829 in the Brit. Lib. (731.m. 14). Mr J. N. L. Myres reminded me that a permanent mark was left on Christ Church, illustrative of the bitter feeling aroused in the college at this election: the words 'NO PEEL,' branded on a door at the bottom of Hall staircase with red-hot pokers, and still to be seen there.
[2] Add. MS 40398 fos. 323, 325.
[3] B.L. 731.m 14/10.

7

Brougham and the Yorkshire Election of 1830[1]

The representation of Yorkshire in the unreformed parliamentary system was the 'blue ribband' of the county seats just as the representation of Oxford or Cambridge University was the supreme moral and academic distinction. Yet it was only occasionally that the political weight of a Yorkshire member matched his social prestige or that any special national significance could be attached to a Yorkshire election. There were several reasons for this. The Yorkshire gentry, like those in other counties, preferred as a rule to send average rather than exceptional men to represent them in parliament; they did not look beyond their own broad acres for candidates; and they regarded a contested election as a desperate and objectionable remedy for political differences. In the last ninety years of its history as an undivided constituency, Yorkshire witnessed only three contested elections and only on the rare occasions when a Yorkshire political figure came forward on some great national issue, such as Wyvill and Savile at the time of the American Revolution or Wilberforce in the age of Pitt, did the representation of Yorkshire assume a real as well as titular leadership. The election of Henry Brougham in 1830, though an outstanding event in Yorkshire parliamentary history, was not of this kind, however; and the circumstances under which he was returned were as peculiar as the man himself.

Brougham was the first candidate not a Yorkshireman to be elected for the county since the Reformation; the first lawyer since the Commonwealth. His return for Yorkshire was the one sensation of the general election of 1830; yet in less than a month after the meeting of the new parliament he had vacated his seat to take a peerage as Lord Chancellor. Rarely can a parliamentary seat held for so brief a time have made more impact on the contemporary political scene. It was in the flush of his Yorkshire victory that Brougham tabled his motion of parliamentary reform at the opening of the new session; it was to avoid a debate on that motion that the Wellington ministry resigned after their civil list defeat in November 1830; and it was that resignation which led to the accession to power of Lord Grey and the great reform ministry of 1830–2. That, of course, in the summer of 1830 could scarcely be foreseen. But even at the time, Brougham's election was hailed as an omen and an example by observers on both sides. 'Of all the portentous signs for the present ministry,' announced the *Edinburgh Review* complacently, on receiving a stop-press message with the intelligence from the victorious candidate himself, 'the most appalling is the nearly unanimous choice

[1] A paper read to the Thoresby Society in 1954 and subsequently published in the *Transactions of the Leeds Philosophical Society*, vol. viii (1956). I incorporated some of the material in my essay on 'English Reform and French Revolution in the General Election of 1830' in *Essays Presented to Sir Lewis Namier*, ed. R. Pares and A. J. P. Taylor (1956).

of Mr Brougham to be member for Yorkshire. This is assuredly the most extraordinary event in the history of party politics.'[1] Yet, though the election for Yorkshire in 1830 of a national figure was to have national consequences, there were more characteristically local and personal elements in Brougham's return for the county than even now have generally been recognized; and behind what the *Edinburgh Review* was pleased to call his nearly unanimous choice was a tangle of different and far from unanimous interests in which the unrepresented town of Leeds played in the end the decisive role.

The key to the Yorkshire election of 1830 was money. The great contest of 1807, which cost the Fitzwilliam and Lascelles families over £100,000 each, had been the first since the fall of Walpole and might well have been regarded as earning Lord Milton a seat for the remainder of his House of Commons career. At the general election of 1826, however, the intensity of public feeling on the question of Catholic Emancipation threatened to produce another contest. It was the first election at which four members were to be returned for the county[2] and five candidates came forward to claim the vacancies. Stuart Wortley, a moderate Tory who had liberal views on the Catholic issue, was deserted by many of his party and was spared the necessity of defending his seat by his elevation to the House of Lords as Baron Wharncliffe. Two Tories of stiffer opinions, William Duncombe and Richard Fountayne Wilson, were put up in his place and were eventually joined by a 'Liberal Tory' in the person of Richard Bethell of Rise. On the Liberal side efforts were made to induce Lord Morpeth, the son and heir of the Earl of Carlisle, to join Lord Milton. But he declined to run the risk of a contest and another colleague was found for Milton in John Marshall, the wealthy Leeds flax-spinner. For some time Marshall had been anxious to enter parliament and had in fact, through the agency of James Brougham, successfully negotiated with Mr Jolliffe of Petersfield a return for that borough at the cost of 5,000 guineas. Though not unattracted by the greater prestige of a seat for Yorkshire, Marshall was apprehensive of the strain of a contested election. In the end, however, he was persuaded to stand and the seat at Petersfield was given to his son. William Marshall's courage and the assurances of his backers were vindicated and, as had been expected, in the end Bethell shrank from an outright contest in order, as he said later, not to ruin himself.[3] But his retirement was only announced on the eve of the poll, and by that time the expenses of the election had already mounted to a total of £150,000. The Fitzwilliams alone spent £26,000 and if what Marshall subsequently wrote in his *Memoir* was true, that the joint expenses on the Liberal side amounted to £53,000, he spent at least as much as his aristocratic colleague in merely preparing for a contest which in the event did not take place.[4] This was more than most candidates would care to face a second time

---

[1] *Edinburgh Review*, July 1830, quoted by A. Aspinall, *Brougham and the Whig Party*, p. 177. For the unusual precedents of Brougham's candidature for Yorkshire, see *Parl. Representation of Yorkshire*, ed. A. Gooder, vol. II, vi (*Yorks. Arch. Soc. Record Series* XCVI).

[2] Two seats having been transferred from Grampound in 1821.

[3] Speech on the hustings at York, 1830.

[4] For the Fitzwilliam expenses at this election see 'Earl Fitzwilliam and the Corn Laws', by David Spring (*American Hist. Review*, LIX, 301). Marshall's *Memoir*, privately printed (N.D.) was written at various times. The last section, covering the 1826 election, is dated 1828. Brougham, in his *Life and Times* (III, 38), says that Marshall's son stated that his father had spent nearly £20,000 on this occasion. But Brougham, writing at the end of his life, is not likely to be a more trustworthy witness

and in 1830 there was a noticeable disinclination among the four sitting members to risk a repetition of their earlier outlay. Marshall, who was old and ill-fitted for public life, had reasons other than financial to justify his retirement. But simultaneously, Milton, who had sat for the county for nearly a quarter of a century, also announced his withdrawal. The reason he gave was the advanced age of his father, the Earl Fitzwilliam, and the consequent likelihood that he himself would be called to the upper house sometime during the life of the new parliament. Yet there are private indications that the fear of expense was an equal deterrent. T. W. Tottie, who as Liberal agent had served the Fitzwilliam interest for many years, wrote to Milton at the beginning of July, expressing with a proper mixture of sympathy and respect his regret that after the great victory of 1807 Milton had been involved in a second heavy expenditure in 1826. It was, he continued, unworthy of the Yorkshire freeholders to permit it, and a justification for his lordship's determination to avoid the risk of having to encounter similar treatment now.[1]

On the Tory side the wealthy and eccentric Fountayne Wilson, who had been one of the No-Popery candidates of 1826, also retired from parliamentary life. Of the four sitting members, therefore, only Duncombe was still left in the field at the beginning of July. There was no lack of suitable candidates to fill the three vacancies; the difficulty was the lack of money. It was not a question of apathy as regards the election, wrote George Strickland[2] to Milton on 11 July, but 'every name being coupled with a determination not to spend any money, no person knows how to act'. On this score there was no difference between Tories and Whigs. There was a rumour that Fountayne Wilson would start one of his cousins, Edmund Beckett Denison or William Beckett,[3] in his place and support them from his apparently bottomless purse; but it was clear that no one of ordinary prudence would commit himself to the expense of a contest even for the prospect of a permanent seat. Bethell, the retiring candidate of 1826, was in many respects an obvious claimant for the second Tory seat; but Bethell held prudent views on the matter of finance and through Lord Wharncliffe his attitude was made clear to the Whigs. Indeed, Wharncliffe urged on Milton the need for all the leading figures of the county to set their faces against a system of expense which could only deter the better candidates and present the seats to men rich enough to purchase them.[4] While names were being doubtfully canvassed on both sides, a

---

than Marshall writing two years after the event. Perhaps the figure quoted to Brougham was 'nearly £30,000' and the error was in editing and transcribing. I have since been informed by the City Librarian of Sheffield that there is a final account book for the 1826 election (Wentworth Woodhouse Muniments – E. 215) signed by the Fitzwilliam auditor, Francis Maude, in which the total figure is given as £54,347, to which is added in a different hand below, 'Lord Milton's moiety, £27,173; Mr Marshall's moiety, £27,173'. The total figure of the final account for the 1807 election is £98,614.

[1] Tottie to Milton, 3 July 1830, in the Corr. of 3rd Fitzwilliam (Wentworth Woodhouse Muniments, Sheffield Library). I am indebted to the Earl Fitzwilliam and the Trustees of the Fitzwilliam Settled Estates for permission to use this and other extracts from the same source in this paper.

[2] *Ibid.* Strickland was the son of Sir William Strickland of Boynton, co. Yorks, and a friend of Brougham. He succeeded to his father's title in 1834.

[3] Edmund Beckett, assumed additional surname of Denison in 1810, later MP for W.R. of Yorks; William Beckett, banker of Leeds. Both were sons of Sir John Beckett of Leeds, 1st Bt.

[4] *Ibid.* Wharncliffe to Milton (undated but written in late June or early July, 1830). See also, Chas. Wood to Milton, 27 June 1830.

fresh complication was introduced by the emergence of a freak candidate who, though nominally a reformer, threatened to embarrass both the orthodox parties. This was Martin Stapylton of Myton Hall, who in the middle of July publicly announced his intention to stand for the county on the sole issue of purity of election, and in private made it known that he would stand a poll as long as any freeholder was ready to vote for him free of expense.[1]

There were still, however, two vacancies to be filled and at this stage it was evident that Morpeth for the Whigs and Bethell for the Tories were becoming the respective choices of their parties and only needed sufficiently authoritative invitations to declare themselves. On 14 July there was a Tory meeting at Bradford attended by delegates from several towns, including the two Mr Gotts from Leeds, and presided over by Col. J. P. Tempest. It was agreed to obtain signatures for a formal requisition to Bethell and though after discussion it was decided not to include any public statement that he should not be put to any expense, it was understood that he was to be supported on that principle.[2] A deputation accordingly waited on him two days later and though he did not agree absolutely to stand, his attitude was not discouraging. More requisitions followed, including one from Leeds and another from a meeting of East Riding freeholders at Beverley. This sustained political courtship had its accustomed reward and on 21 July Bethell consented to stand. With that the Tory preparations for the election were completed and they nourished the hope that by confining themselves to only two candidates they would ensure a quiet and inexpensive election. Indeed it was probably only the financial consideration that had been responsible for Bethell's long delay in announcing himself.

Meanwhile the opposite camp was still in considerable confusion. From the start it had been feared that the withdrawal of both the Liberal sitting members would have unfortunate effects, and it had been hoped that at least Marshall could be persuaded to stand again. Even if that were impossible, it was strongly felt that it would be unwise to expose a single Liberal candidate to the joint opposition of his rivals and that two regular Whigs should therefore be brought forward to meet the challenge. Lord Morpeth was the obvious successor to Milton and with the backing of the great Fitzwilliam influence was almost certain of election. The problem was to find him a colleague. In the early stages of the election campaign the name most frequently mentioned in this connection was J. C. Ramsden, the son of Sir John Ramsden of Byrom Hall and through his wife related both to Lord Dundas and Lord Milton. The Ramsdens were good orthodox Whigs and J. C. Ramsden was in fact already one of the sitting members for Malton, a Fitzwilliam nomination borough. But he was not anxious to exchange so pleasant a seat for the rigours of a county election; and his father was, probably on financial grounds, strongly adverse to the suggestion. The negotiations reached a point at which the younger Ramsden entrusted his kinsman, Thomas Dundas, with an election address to the county to be used in certain eventualities; but it was clear that only strong pressure from their patrons, the Fitzwilliams, would overcome Sir John Ramsden's opposition to his son's candidature. By 9 July therefore, Dundas was

---

[1] See his election notice, *Leeds Intelligencer*, 5 June, and also Strickland to Milton, 14 July 1830 (Fitzwm. Corr.).
[2] *Ibid.* Strickland to Milton, 14 July 1830.

advising Lord Milton to abandon the idea.[1] There were various other possible, and even respectable, candidates – Sir J. V. B. Johnstone of Hackness Hall, Sir George Cayley, Charles Wood, George Strickland.[2] But none were of outstanding quality and almost certainly not one of them could afford to meet the cost of a contest from his own resources. This was in fact the Whig dilemma. What was done in 1830 might well decide the balance of the county representation for many years ahead. If the Whigs were not prepared to acquiesce in the possession of only one seat, they would have to find ways and means of meeting a contest. With the obtrusion of Stapylton on the ordered pattern of county politics, a pacific division of the four seats between Tory and Whig had been made impossible. It was true that Stapylton might in the end be frightened off the scene. As one of Milton's correspondents truly observed, 'the representation of our county is like a game at Brag, and many who bray loudest and earliest will win it.[3] But as sensible an observer as Althorp expressed the fear that Stapylton's intervention might prevent the Whigs from running two candidates.[4] In any case, however, the possibility of a contest had to be faced.

In the middle of July, Strickland, Johnstone, and a few other Whig gentlemen met at Northallerton for the summer sessions. They discussed the still unsolved problem of filling the vacancy in the Whig representation; and their tempers were probably not improved by meeting there Martin Stapylton, in a wilder state than usual and loudly declaring that he would go unflinchingly to the polls. The upshot was that Strickland and Johnstone went on to Leeds in order to consult with the West Riding Liberals on the choice of two popular candidates. If agreement could be reached, they hoped to be able to call a general meeting of Liberal supporters who would invite the two candidates to stand free of expense and would individually pledge themselves to bring a certain number of freeholders to the polls. In that way, it was calculated, some 10,000 electors could be brought up without cost to the candidates or the party. At Leeds they called on Tottie, the Liberal agent, to explain their plan and then went on to meet the same day (14 July) a number of leading Leeds Liberals, including Marshall, Samuel Clapham, and Edward Baines, the influential editor of the *Leeds Mercury*. The encounter was not a cordial one. Strickland explained that Milton could not come forward again and Marshall said that his own decision to retire was unchanged. The two Whig representatives then put forward their proposal to invite two popular candidates to stand with a pledge of support free of expense. It was here that the difficulties arose. It was agreed that Morpeth would be eligible as one of the candidates, though there was a perceptible coolness in the attitude of the Leeds Liberals towards him; but the various suggestions for his colleague met with distinct hostility. Some half a dozen names of Whig squires were put forward by Strickland and Johnstone; but to each the response was that he was not a man for whom

---

[1] *Ibid.* Dundas to Milton, 9 July; Ramsden to Milton, 10 July 1830. Thomas Dundas was the eld. son of the 2nd Baron Dundas (cr. Earl of Zetland 1838) whom he succeeded in 1839.

[2] Sir John Vanden Bempde Johnstone, b. 1789, succ. as 2nd Bt. 1807; Sir George Cayley of Brompton, co. York, b. 1773, succ. as 6th Bt. 1792; Chas. Wood, eld. son of Sir Francis Wood, of Barnsley, whom he succ. in 1846. later Whig chancellor of the exchequer, 1846–52.

[3] *Ibid.* Sykes to Milton, 9 July 1830.

[4] *Ibid.* Althorp to Milton, 22 July 1830. Althorp thought it possible that Stapylton and Brougham would drive off Morpeth, and perhaps others.

the freeholders of the West Riding would journey to York to vote, without being paid for their trouble. In the end all that was decided was that a general meeting should be called at York on 23 July to choose two Liberal candidates and that the West Riding Liberals should be entitled if they wished to make a nomination.[1]

The problem of finding a second Whig was now more difficult than ever. No county gentleman would come to the hustings under the shadow, as George Cayley had gloomily expressed it to Milton the previous month, of a £100,000 contest. Yet the West Riding freeholders, who constituted the bulk of the Liberal electorate, could not be induced to go to York at their own expense to vote for any of the candidates whom the Whigs had in mind as second string to Morpeth. 'Under these circumstances,' wrote Tottie to Milton, 'and with the experience recently afforded of the taste for Expense among Yorkshire Freeholders, it becomes rather a serious matter to invite any Independent Gentleman to come forward on Whig principles. I do not find that any one is seriously thought of here by our Friends and I cannot name an Individual in the County that they would be likely to invite with a pledge of support free of expense.'[2] It was precisely when matters had reached this deadlock that Baines, with admirable timing, made his dramatic public proposal to invite Henry Brougham to stand for Yorkshire.

It was not a new idea of Baines. In 1812 he had suggested Whitbread or Brougham to succeed Wilberforce. But outside the small but powerful Baines circle at Leeds it is unlikely that Brougham was in anybody's mind as a possible candidate for the county until the *Leeds Mercury*, in a carefully prepared editorial, came out with the suggestion on 17 July. How the proposal originated and how long it had been maturing is not known. Too late Strickland remembered that as he was going off after the Leeds meeting on 14 July, Samuel Clapham had said something to him about the Anti-Slavery Societies being in favour of an invitation to Henry Brougham. Strickland had replied at the time that not being a Yorkshireman, Brougham would not do and such an attempt would only create jealousies. But he thought so little of the remark that he did not mention it in his account of the meeting written to Milton the same day.[3] Indeed it was probably not until just before the York meeting on 23 July that the Whig gentry as a whole realized how deeply the idea had taken root and how effectively the West Riding Liberals had organized themselves to carry it through. Nevertheless, the intense activity on Brougham's behalf shown by the Baines party in the interval between the two meetings made it evident that the West Riding Liberals had irrevocably committed themselves to the support of his candidature. Lord Milton, at least, who was kept well informed of what was passing in Leeds by Tottie, the Liberal agent, and by John Nussey, the chairman of the Coloured Cloth Hall Trustees, could have had no illusions on the subject.

Milton, in fact, was now in a position of considerable embarrassment. The Fitzwilliam interest was still undeclared and a great deal attached to Lord Milton's attitude to the Brougham candidature. But there were many considerations involved. He did not need to be told that Brougham was not a candidate that

---

[1] For accounts of the Leeds meeting of 14 July, see *ibid*. Tottie to Milton, 14 July; Strickland to Milton, 14 and 31 July; *Leeds Intelligencer*, 29 July 1831.

[2] Tottie to Milton, 14 July (Fitzwm. Corr.).

[3] *Ibid*. Strickland to Milton, 14 and 31 July.

would be easily stomached by the Yorkshire squires. Whigs as well as Tories must have echoed the litany of objections to Brougham published by the Tory *Leeds Intelligencer*[1]: that he was not a native; not a resident; with no property in, and no knowledge of, the county; and as a lawyer too engrossed in professional pursuits to attend to county interests. To which might have been added an unspoken but widespread conviction that his whole professional career had been marked as much by reckless egotism as by parliamentary brilliance. Yet Brougham, for all that, was one of the leading members of the organized Whig opposition to which Lord Milton belonged and would undoubtedly be a member of the government if ever they secured office. There was, too, a purely local consideration. Brougham was the choice of the industrial towns of the West Riding and Milton could not be indifferent to the prospect of an open breach between the Liberal middle classes of the west and the Whig gentry of the north and east. For the time being, therefore, he made no overt move and profiting by his inaction the Baines party in Leeds boldly claimed that the Fitzwilliam interest was on their side.

Milton's two chief adherents in Leeds were thus left in complete uncertainty as to the course they should follow. Tottie, as a good servant of the party, set off for York on 23 July with the simple determination to support whichever two candidates were approved by the meeting. Nussey was anxious for something more definite. He was not one of those enamoured of Brougham, though he could see that some of his fellow-trustees at the Coloured Cloth Hall were considerably impressed by the proposal to bring him forward, and he endeavoured to counteract the growing momentum of the Brougham movement by recommending to the Trustees the name of Sir J. V. B. Johnstone. But though his name was formally moved and seconded, nothing effective could be done until the general meeting at York. Anxious, however, to test opinion outside Leeds, Nussey went over to York the day before the meeting to discover how much support Brougham would be likely to obtain and whether another suitable person belonging to the county could be brought forward. Outside the smoke of the industrial area, he found a more congenial political atmosphere. Brougham, he learned, would not be acceptable; Sir J. V. B. Johnstone would be. Nevertheless, there remained the question of the Fitzwilliam influence, still aloof and undeclared. Nussey therefore wrote to Milton from York on 22 July, asking discreetly but urgently whether he intended to support Brougham; whether, if not, he wished the report denied; and whether he approved the Johnstone candidature. To have ignored this appeal would have argued not neutrality but indifference. Even so, Milton preserved a careful and flexible attitude. His reply, written apparently in the small hours of the morning of 23 July, was probably intended to be shown by Nussey at his discretion to other persons at the meeting due to be held that day. It mentioned, cautiously and approvingly, Mr Ramsden and Sir J. V. B. Johnstone, as good Liberals and possible candidates; and while not actively opposing Brougham, made it clear that Milton's preference would lie elsewhere.

> The report you have heard at Leeds and again at York, that I intend to support Mr Brougham, must have originated with, and have been circulated by persons, who had not the slightest ground for circulating it. I cannot, of course, say whether,

[1] 22 July.

under certain circumstances, I might not be disposed to support Mr Brougham, but those circumstances do not appear to me to have arisen as yet. . . . My notion is that if *proper* persons can be found in the County, we ought to bring them forward before we have recourse to a Stranger, however brilliant his talents may be.[1]

By the time this message reached Nussey at York, the party meeting was only a few hours off and members were already assembling at Etridge's Hotel.

Before the general proceedings began, the Whig gentry gathered for preliminary discussions in a separate room. A number of suggestions were made for the choice of second candidate. Indeed, so many gentlemen now seemed ready to come forward – Charles Wood, Sir J. V. B. Johnstone, Wrightson, Strickland – that Nussey, watching their deliberations, was filled with apprehension at the disunity of the gentry compared with the resolution of the Leeds delegation which had arrived to support the nomination of Brougham. This party, which also conferred privately beforehand in another room, included Messrs Baines, Clapham, Rawson, Pease, and other well-known West Riding Liberals, together with the Rev. Thomas Scales, a Leeds presbyterian minister and a leading abolitionist, all clearly determined to carry Brougham's candidature. Among the squires, however, there was no mention of the interloper until the arrival of Daniel Sykes, the brother-in-law of Henry Thornton, the philanthropist, and himself a warm supporter of negro emancipation. But even so, no real agreement on their action was reached before they went into the general meeting shortly after midday.

The proceedings opened quietly with the unanimous adoption of Morpeth as prospective Liberal candidate. John Marshall than rose to address the meeting. He stated that the great commercial and manufacturing interests of the West Riding, not being represented in parliament except through the county, were desirous of returning a man of business to look after their affairs, and in the absence of any outstanding person in Yorkshire, on whom they could agree, had decided to put forward Henry Brougham. This motion was seconded by Sykes, who answered various theoretical objections that might be levelled against Brougham's candidature; referred to his efforts against slavery; and said it was not too much to allow the commercial interests of the county one of the four county members to represent them. Taken aback by this firm line, the first Whig speakers did little more than make various disjointed criticisms of Brougham's suitability; and though Thomas Dundas mentioned J. C. Ramsden as a possible candidate, no specific counter-proposal was made. Marshall and Baines came to Brougham's defence and the discussion grew more heated. Charles Wood told the Liberals that there was a stronger feeling against Brougham than they cared to admit; and Mr Cayley, son of Sir George Cayley, in the strongest anti-Brougham speech of the meeting, said that it would be an insult to the county to propose him. This called up the Rev. Thomas Scales, who said that not politics but religion and humanity had brought him to the meeting, that no one could equal Brougham in carrying on the great work of freeing the slaves; and told the meeting flatly that

[1] *Ibid.* Copy by Nussey of letter from Milton to Nussey, dated Wentworth, Friday morning, half-past four. The presumption is that Milton sent Nussey the first letter to use at York but had not time to make a copy of it himself. Nussey therefore made a copy on arrival and sent it to Milton with his own letter giving an account of the meeting.

whatever they decided now, Brougham would certainly be proposed as a candidate on the hustings.

This intransigent speech brought matters to a crisis. The leading Whigs, in an effort to save the day, conferred in a group clustered at the bow window behind the chairman, and eventually Sir J. V. B. Johnstone announced that for the sake of unity the various Whig pretenders to the second seat had agreed to sink their claims in a common support of Mr J. C. Ramsden. His name was then formally proposed as candidate by Charles Wood. There was now a complete deadlock and some angry recriminations ensued. Clapham reminded the Whigs that it had been agreed at the Leeds meeting on 14 July that the West Riding Liberals would have the right to propose one member. Johnstone could not deny this but he said that he had no idea that they were going to put forward Brougham; and in this he was supported by Strickland. Nevertheless, in view of the uncompromising stand of the Leeds delegation, it was obvious that there could never be any united support for Ramsden and that to persist with his candidature would probably precipitate a bitter and expensive struggle at the election. Some of the moderate Whigs, including Strickland and Dundas, realized that Wood's motion would have to be withdrawn; and even the chairman, Marmaduke Wyvill,[1] threw his weight into the scale by observing that 'it was evident that Mr Brougham must be nominated'. Strickland explained afterwards[2] that what decided his action was the conviction that if a second candidate was put forward besides Brougham, it might entail the defeat of Morpeth, which was his chief concern, or that of Bethell or Duncombe, which he also did not think desirable. In the face of these doubts, Wood finally gave way and withdrew his motion, though he did it with ill grace and explicitly reserved the right of himself and his friends to exercise their freedom of action. The chairman then put Brougham's name to the meeting and on a show of hands[3] it was decided to support him as the second Liberal candidate for the county.

It had taken nearly three hours discussion to reach this conclusion but with it the real decision of the 1830 Yorkshire election had been taken. If it owed much to the purposefulness of the West Riding delegation, and in particular to the leading Liberals of Leeds, it was also facilitated by the disunity and unpreparedness of the county Whigs. Even Nussey, who had no love for Brougham, was moved to criticize their aloofness and lack of political tact in a private letter to Lord Milton, written immediately after the meeting –

> It appears to me to be for the interest of the landed gentlemen to make themselves better acquainted with the views, feelings and interests of the trading part of the County. So small an identification of feeling or attention to the interests of the dense population is really necessary to obtain the necessary popularity that I feel astonished so little is done to consult the feelings and obtain the favour of such an important and encreasing multitude of their fellow citizens . . . , I felt adverse to Mr Brougham from the wish to draw the landed interest into a close connection with the

[1] Son of the famous Rev. Christopher Wyvill.

[2] *Ibid*. Strickland to Milton, 31 July.

[3] The Tory *Leeds Intelligencer*, whose editor was present at the meeting(see *Leeds Mercury*, 21 August), said that it was a small and doubtful majority. Charles Wood told Milton that it was 'very nearly divided'. The *Leeds Mercury* said that it was two to one; and this estimate was confirmed privately to Milton by Thomas Dundas.

trading interests of the County and if possible to produce an approximation to a reciprocity of good offices and relations between them.[1]

As it was, the Whig gentry had walked blindly into the net. Some, it is clear, remained irreconcilable; the more prudent accepted the situation and drew what comfort they could from it. Indeed, there was no real alternative. The York meeting had been called to choose two Liberal candidates, to be returned free of expense; and that object could only be achieved if Brougham were allowed to be one of the candidates. If the generality of the country gentry would have preferred, as Dundas wrote to Milton, 'a regular game preserving Yorkshire squire to Brougham', the Whig leaders were not entirely dissatisfied. There was every prospect now that two Liberal seats would be secured and all their information suggested that the supporters of Duncombe in the North Riding and Bethell in the East, would not risk danger to their own men by starting a third Tory candidate.[2]

From Brougham's point of view, the decision of the York meeting virtually gave him the return for the county. On Saturday, 24 July, he had arrived at York for the county assizes and was at once informed of what had passed at the meeting on the previous day. On the following Monday a deputation arrived from Leeds, including Tottie, Clapham, Baines and T. B. Pease, with a requisition to Brougham and Morpeth to stand as candidates signed by over 200 freeholders and reinforced by an assurance that every endeavour would be made to return them free of expense. Though such private advice as Brougham was able to take locally was far from being unanimously encouraging, he made up his mind without delay and in a flamboyant letter dated from York on 26 July he publicly accepted the invitation to stand. Yet the interest of his election rested not only in the political faction fight that preceded it, but also in the motives of his backers and his own views on the use to be made of his new position in the political firmament. Among the proximate causes for the choice of Brougham by the West Riding Liberals was the brilliant speech he had made in the Commons on 13 July when introducing a motion on the subject of colonial slavery. The powerful dissenting interest in Yorkshire, in fact nearly all the old Wilberforce party except the Anglicans, were prepared to put out their strength on behalf of an anti-slavery candidate of such national eminence. It was the Rev. Thomas Scales who had been the most militant of the Leeds delegation at York on 23 July; and once Brougham's candidature had been assumed, the dissenting churches took an active part in the election campaign. It was no doubt with justice that the Whigs protested, as they did at the York meeting, against the tactics of the West Riding delegation in making negro emancipation the peculiar test of eligibility for Brougham, as though anybody with liberal principles could be in favour of slavery; and there was point in the remark by the *Leeds Intelligencer* that the great trick of the hour was to make the success of the anti-slavery movement appear to depend on Brougham's election for Yorkshire. Nevertheless the narrow and perfervid imagination of the abolitionists was engaged on behalf of Brougham as on behalf of no other

[1] Nussey to Milton, undated, written 23 July (Fitzwn. Corr.). For other accounts of the York meeting, see letters to Milton from Dundas, 23 July; Tottie, 24 July; Wood, undated. Also *Leeds Intelligencer*, 29 July; *Leeds Mercury*, 24 July.

[2] Dundas to Milton, 27 July (Fitzwm. Corr.).

candidate. At the time of the election the annual national conference of the Wesleyan Methodists was taking place at Leeds and on 30 July the conference passed a series of resolutions condemning slavery and urging all Methodists with the vote to use it on behalf of those candidates who pledged themselves to the entire abolition of slavery within the empire. Earlier still, the Yorkshire Protestant Dissenters' Association for the Abolition of Slavery, meeting at Leeds on 21 July, pledged itself to support Brougham and appealed to all its members to vote for abolitionist candidates.[1] 'There is enthusiasm in the Cause', reported Tottie to Milton on 24 July, using the word perhaps in its eighteenth rather than its nineteenth century sense, 'and anti-Colonial Slavery is the basis of it.' In rather more unscrupulous vein the Baines party launched an attack on Duncombe for being at best only concerned with an 'amelioration' of the condition of the slaves, and a couple of days before the election Leeds was placarded with notices advising the electors as freemen and Christians not to vote for him. To all this Brougham was careful to pay proper attention both in his canvass and on the hustings.

Yet he himself could scarcely have regarded slavery as the dominant issue of the election. As the 1830 session had drawn to a close, he had become convinced of the need for pulling down a government which showed no signs of admitting the Whigs to a share of office. For that purpose a more direct attack would be required. There was no need to ponder deeply on the form it should take. The Leeds Liberals had secured his nomination and it could not be forgotten that Leeds was, along with Manchester and Birmingham, one of the great unrepresented trinity that all reformers quoted as an example of the absurdity of the parliamentary system. As recently as March 1830, a public meeting in Leeds had sent up to London the largest petition in the history of the town praying for retrenchment and parliamentary reform.[2] Baines himself, the chief promoter of Brougham's candidature, had been a parliamentary reformer from his early days. Even before Brougham's name was publicly mentioned as a possible candidate, the *Leeds Mercury* had raised the issue of reform in an election leader devoted to 'this most important of all subjects' and urged all reformers to unite in continuous agitation.[3] And at the York meeting it had been Baines who reminded his hearers that besides his advocacy of the slavery question, Brougham had been a consistent and zealous supporter of reform and retrenchment, subjects that were very near to the hearts of the Yorkshire freeholders. When electioneering started in earnest, it became apparent that if the dissenting churches were inspired by the slavery question, the merchants and manufacturers were mainly concerned with parliamentary and economical reform. Brougham from the start made parliamentary reform one of his chief topics. On 27 July, in company with Morpeth, he visited Leeds to begin the Liberal election campaign, and dwelt at length on the subject in an opening speech addressed to an audience reckoned at 10,000. After defining his aim as the extension of the franchise to all inhabitant freeholders and of representation to all great towns, he told his hearers that the parliamentary weakness of the government offered an immense opportunity to reformers and that the 1830 election would carry the great questions of parliamentary reform,

[1] *Leeds Intelligencer*, 5 and 12 August; *Leeds Mercury*, 24 July.
[2] A. S. Turberville and F. Beckwith, 'Leeds and Parliamentary Reform, 1820–1832' (Thoresby Society, *Miscellany*, XLI).
[3] *Leeds Mercury*, 12 June.

revision of the Corn Laws, and extinction of colonial slavery, just as surely as the county Clare election had carried Catholic Emancipation.[1]

The same theme was continued in his canvass of the other industrial areas and echoed though more cautiously by his colleague Morpeth. Indeed, any parliamentary candidate venturing into the West Riding had to encounter a lively discussion of this topic. Duncombe, who did not lack courage or persistency in his politics, made an election tour of the industrial towns between 20 and 28 July, visiting Leeds, Bradford, Wakefield, Halifax, Huddersfield and Barnsley and found almost everywhere a marked interest in the question of reform. In answer to a questioner at Leeds he said he was against a wide and general measure of parliamentary reform but would not object to the transfer of seats from corrupt boroughs to large towns; and at Barnsley he said he would promote any reform that would promote purity of election. Stapylton, who also came to Leeds, was similarly called upon to express his views on the general question of parliamentary reform; though his reply, in which he expressed the desire to see the people of Britain represented in parliament and not a borough-mongering faction, lacked something of Duncombe's straightforwardness. It was clear that the events of the previous session, which had seen no less than three separate proposals for parliamentary reform put forward from different parts of the House, had left their mark on the public mind; and if Duncombe was reminded by a heckler of the Leeds petition for parliamentary reform, Brougham was challenged by Foster, the editor of the radical *Leeds Patriot,* for his vote against O'Connell's reform motion[2] in May.

Election day was 5 August, and the scene on the hustings at York was more than customarily crowded and excited. There was a host of reporters, and among Brougham's platform party was a conspicuous contingent from Leeds, including Baines with his two sons, the Rev. T. Scales (the hero of the York meeting), the Rev. R. W. Hamilton, a Leeds Independent minister and a close friend of Baines, and a Unitarian, the Rev. J. Hutton. After the usual preliminaries of proposers and seconders, the candidates in turn addressed the crowd gathered in the Castle Yard. Duncombe, in a brief and restrained speech, stressed his independence and denied that he was opposed to the abolition of colonial slavery. Morpeth made the need for parliamentary reform the principal topic of his speech. Stapylton announced that the principle of reform for which he stood was the reformation of the candidates themselves; and repeated his pledge to keep the poll open as long as a single elector was ready to vote for him. Bethell said he was in favour of enfranchising such large industrial towns as Leeds, Halifax and Manchester, though opposed to any general reconstruction of the representative system. Brougham, in the advantageous position of last speaker, touched on a variety of subjects, including corn laws, slavery, and unemployment, but devoted his eloquent peroration to a recall of the great Yorkshire reform tradition of Wyvill and Savile, and a confident expression of hope that when they met again all blemishes and abuses of the electoral system would have been swept away. The

---

[1] See the full reports of the speech in the *Leeds Mercury* and *Leeds Patriot,* 31 July; and *Leeds Intelligencer,* 29 July.
[2] *Leeds Intelligencer,* 22 and 29 July.

election itself turned out a farce. Stapylton, who appeared alone on the hustings and had no formal proposer, insisted on a poll and at the end of the day the figures of the voting were – Morpeth 1281, Brougham 1150, Bethell 893, Duncombe 876, Stapylton 63. Next day it was announced that Stapylton had left York for London and had withdrawn all personal interest from the election although he would honour his pledge to keep the poll open for any elector who wished to vote for him. In this absurd situation the other candidates endeavoured to boycott any further proceedings by withholding their own voters. A trickle of electors continued to come to the hustings, however, until at three o'clock in the afternoon the sheriff, with the consent of the remaining candidates but otherwise with doubtful legality, arbitrarily declared the poll closed.[1]

The supreme gratification of heading the poll in the largest county in Britain was thus denied to Brougham. But at least he was knight of the shire for Yorkshire and his elation was evident. He was conscious, moreover, of the quarter to which – barring some personal merits of which he might have been aware – he owed that elevation. At the end of September a grand election dinner was held at Leeds in honour of the election of Morpeth and Brougham. Tottie, under whose direction 18 unpaid attorneys had laboured on behalf of the party, was in the chair and in an introductory speech affirmed that the Yorkshire election had in itself begun a practical reform in the House of Commons. When his turn came to speak, Brougham took up Tottie's point and declared that the work had started not merely in Yorkshire, but in Leeds. This was true enough, as far as Brougham's own election was concerned, and it was with a proper sense of obligation that he went on to say that a state of affairs in which Leeds was not represented in parliament was a monstrous abuse calling for instant redress. 'I will leave in no man's hand, now that I am member for Yorkshire, the great cause of parliamentary reform,' he declared in a celebrated passage; and proceeded to outline to the assembled company the scheme of amending the representative system that he would bring forward in parliament as soon as it met.[2]

Baines might rightly be proud of the formidable cuckoo he had introduced into the Yorkshire nest; and as the autumn wore on, with no sign that the government would be able to strengthen its parliamentary position, the *Leeds Mercury* expressed a growing hope that Brougham's plan of reform would meet with success. There was, however, one shadow, faint but persistent, that lay across this brilliant scene. From the time when Brougham had first been proposed for Yorkshire, his enemies had said that he was only interested in a seat for the county as a stepping stone for his own career. These reports were duly contradicted in the faithful *Mercury*. His opponents said he was seeking power, remarked the newspaper after his election, 'they are mistaken – he has obtained it. To accept a judgeship or a peerage would be to descend, not to rise.'[3] Admittedly Brougham's public language on first receiving the invitation to stand – his ecstatic mention of a seat for Yorkshire as the highest summit to which an Englishman could aspire – in

---

[1] For full accounts of the proceedings at York, 5–6 August, see *Leeds Intelligencer*, 5 and 12 August; *Leeds Mercury*, 7 and 14 August. The final figures for the poll were – Morpeth, 1464; Brougham, 1295; Duncombe, 1123; Bethell, 1064; and Stapylton, 94.

[2] *Leeds Intelligencer*, 30 September; *Leeds Mercury*, 2 October.

[3] *Leeds Mercury*, 14 August.

some measure explained if it did not justify the *Mercury*'s high tone. Yet Baines would have been less comfortable had he seen other passages of Brougham's correspondence at this time.

As soon as his candidature had been settled, Brougham had gone to great pains to conciliate, in private, the powerful Fitzwilliam interest which even at the eleventh hour might still turn the scales against him. To Lord Milton he posed as a friend of the land-owning classes and an honest broker between the two wings of the Liberal party. Indeed he even claimed that he had strained his influence with the men of the West Riding to prevent them from abandoning Morpeth and running Strickland as well as himself as their candidates. 'I preach everywhere,' he wrote,[1] 'a close union of the landed and commercial interest. But between you and me the squires of Yorkshire will get into such a scrape as no preaching . . . can get them out of, if they do not give up their silly jealousies of the W. Riding.' In another letter to Milton, undated but of the same period, he went further and gave a curious but significant assurance that the interests of the Fitzwilliam family would not be harmed by his possession of a seat for Yorkshire, since the crisis that had recommended Brougham to the county was unlikely to recur. If every one were wise and discreet, he concluded, only good could come of his election. 'My interest in the matter can neither be great nor long.'[2] The reason for this attitude of detachment was clear enough. From the end of the parliamentary session in July, Brougham had convinced himself that the fall of the Wellington ministry was only a matter of months and that it would be replaced by a Whig government in which he himself would hold high office. Appointment to office would involve re-election and that would mean the early severance of his newly created tie with Yorkshire, since he would be unable to stand a contested bye-election in such an expensive constituency. Even before he accepted the requisition to stand for the county, therefore, he began to look about for a cheap seat which could be held in reserve for him against such an emergency. He wrote first to Lord Fitzwilliam but the Whig lawyer Scarlett had just taken the last nomination seat (at Malton) at the family's disposal. Brougham then applied, on 24 July, to another Whig peer, the duke of Devonshire, with a proposal that Knaresborough, for which Brougham had sat in the previous parliament, should be kept for him in the new, the vacancy to be filled meanwhile by his brother, William Brougham, or by Zachary Macaulay, either of whom could easily retire into private life as soon as Brougham needed the seat.[3] Nothing came of this proposal though in fact Brougham retained his seat for Knaresborough on a double return and did not abandon it until he was elevated to the upper house in November.

It must have been therefore with some reservation that Brougham accepted his triumphant election as member for Yorkshire on 6 August. In the event his judicious preparations were vindicated. In the middle of November Wellington's ministry resigned and Lord Grey was asked to form a new government. After nearly a quarter of a century the Whigs were in power once more. For Brougham it was the supreme opportunity of his personal career and he played his hand with audacity and skill. What he wanted above all was the Mastership of the Rolls, a

[1] Brougham to Milton, dated Friday evening. A (defective) postmark indicates that it was stamped at York, 31 July 1830 (Fitzwm. Corr.).
[2] *Ibid.* Brougham to Milton, undated.
[3] A. Aspinall, *Brougham and the Whig Party*, p. 176.

permanent judicial appointment which was compatible with a seat in the Commons. But too many influential persons were opposed to this and Brougham had to make up his mind either to accept another office or stay out of the government altogether. The offer of the Attorney Generalship made to him by Grey on 16 November was contemptuously declined and he announced that he would proceed with his motion for parliamentary reform undeterred by mere considerations of party. The next day he declared in court that the representation of Yorkshire was the only place he would have, and on the 18th he wrote to the duke of Devonshire that 'I cannot think of giving up Yorkshire after the kind way it behaved to me, and no other place than the Chancellor is any temptation to me.'[1] The implication of this was evident, but by that time Brougham had worked himself into a contrary and angry mood in which it almost seemed he wished the Chancellorship to be offered to him so that he might have the pleasure of refusing it. But in the end, when the fate of the ministry almost appeared to turn on his decision, he allowed himself to be persuaded; and on 22 November he took his place as Lord Chancellor on the woolsack.

The shock to his adherents in Yorkshire was profound. On the day after Brougham had agreed to go to the House of Lords as Chancellor, the *Leeds Mercury* inopportunely published a declaration that he would not take office in any new ministry and that the only post he desired was to be member for Yorkshire. Fortunately, another week elapsed before the *Mercury* had to appear again. When it did so, it could not refrain from expressing its disappointment at Brougham's decision, though it allowed on second thoughts that there was some comfort to be drawn from the prospect of the beneficial influence on reform which he would exercise from his seat in the cabinet. Nevertheless it was clear that the West Riding Liberals had been staggered by this blow from their own champion. The *Mercury* urged the Yorkshire freeholders not to think that they had wasted their energies in getting Brougham into the House of Commons. But such logic was too refined for the simplicities of electoral politics; and when the time came to fill the vacancy left by Brougham's elevation, only a half-hearted effort was made in the West Riding to claim a voice in the choice of his successor. Four months earlier the Tory *Leeds Intelligencer* had described Brougham's candidature as a victory secured by Baines, the *Mercury*, a small train of Presbyterian and Unitarian ministers, and some stray sheep of the radical party, over the Whig aristocracy of the county. But it had added the warning that this sudden appearance of power had only been made possible by the withdrawal of the Fitzwilliam interest and the sudden weakness of the official Whig cause; and clearly implied that this could not be regarded as a permanent disposition of forces.[2] This sharp but searching diagnosis was borne out by the bye-election of December 1830. The Whig gentry, returning with relief to traditional ways, promptly nominated Sir J. V. B. Johnstone as Liberal candidate. The Tories refused to disturb the peace of the county; and though at the end of November a meeting of the former Marshall and Brougham supporters in Leeds called on the liberal-minded Daniel Sykes to come forward, he wisely declined throwing up his seat for Beverley to contest the

---

[1] *Ibid.* pp. 184–7.
[2] *Leeds Intelligencer*, 29 July, 12 August.

county on such disadvantageous terms.[1] There was nothing in fact to be done. Brougham's own behaviour had made it certain that there could not be another Brougham in Yorkshire for many years to come. At the general election of 1831, fought on the direct issue of reform, Bethell and Duncombe retired and the two Liberal sitting members, Morpeth and Johnstone, were joined in a peaceful return by the orthodox and familiar figures of Strickland and J. C. Ramsden. When next the Liberals of Leeds went to the polls, it was to elect a representative not for Yorkshire but for their own newly enfranchised borough. But in one sense they had had their first parliamentary election two years earlier.

[1] *Leeds Mercury*, 27 November.

8

Oxford Politics in the Chancellor's Election of 1834[1]

The election of the duke of Wellington as Chancellor of the University in 1834 was one of the infrequent occasions in the nineteenth century when university politics came into direct contact with national affairs. Both Peel and Wellington, the leaders of the Conservative party in the House of Commons and in the House of Lords, had been favoured as candidates, and although Wellington was finally elected without opposition, the incident reacted badly on the relations of the two men. Peel felt that the duke had treated him with some discourtesy in allowing himself to be nominated before ascertaining whether Peel also wished to stand for the election. His attitude of wounded sensibility was perhaps pardonable, for the connection with Oxford which might have been renewed in 1834, had been broken in 1829, as he himself expressed it, 'through fidelity at a trying time to the Duke of Wellington.' Although member for Oxford University and thus a representative of the purest strain of Tory Anglicanism, Peel at that date had taken a leading part in the passing of the Catholic Emancipation Act by Wellington's ministry. Out of deference to the susceptibilities of his constituents he subsequently resigned and in the bye-election was defeated by Sir Robert Inglis. The rejection by the university in 1829 rankled too deeply for Peel to solicit its favours in 1834, but Wellington's lack of tact towards his sensitive colleague materially increased the coldness between them, which lasted until the beginning of 1836.

All this is sufficiently established. What may still be further elucidated is the history of the negotiations which preceded Wellington's triumphant and unanimous election. Behind the solid front which the university presented to the public eye was a tangle of college and party rivalry which the knowledgeable politicians of the day anxiously analysed and discussed. In political matters there were at the time four main parties in Oxford. The smallest numerically were the Whigs, but at the moment they could not safely be disregarded. In 1834 a Whig ministry was in office, and their followers in the university had therefore the backing of government patronage. Of more importance were the liberal Tories, strong in Merton and Oriel, who comprised the core of Peel's party of 1829, although lacking now the governmental influence which they then enjoyed. The third, and by far the dominant group, were the ultra-Tories, headed by one of the most energetic university politicians of the period, Thomas Wintle, then Vice-President of St John's, and finding their centre of organization in Laud's old college. It was this party which had been responsible for the defeat of Peel and the election of Sir Robert Inglis in 1829. Finally and provisionally there was Christ Church,

[1] First published in *The Oxford Magazine* April–May, 1938.

large enough to act as a unit, and, if united, of considerable influence.

In the late autumn of 1833 Lord Grenville, the chancellor of the university, became so seriously ill that not only was there no hope of an eventual recovery but every prospect of his immediate decease. The ultra-Tories, who since 1829 had the advantage of greater cohesion than any other party, at once assembled to devise a plan of action. A committee was appointed to meet at St John's, and it was decided to approach Christ Church with a view to securing a Conservative candidate with the best chance of success irrespective of any minor party or college connections. A delegation waited on the dean of Christ Church and informed him that their party would be prepared to support any member of his college who should be proposed, provided he possessed the indispensable Tory qualifications. The overture was welcomed, and the alliance proceeded in search of a candidate. An offer was made to old Lord Eldon, the ancient survivor of an almost forgotten school of Tory statesmen, but it was refused. Lord Mansfield was then approached, but he, to the surprise of many, also declined the honour. After these two successive failures of Christ Church diplomacy, the coalition began to weaken. The St John's Committee turned their thoughts to Stratfield Saye, where the ground had already been broken and found not entirely sterile. Lord Sidmouth, apparently early in November, had mentioned to Wellington the desire of some Conservatives in Oxford that he should stand for the chancellorship; the duke had replied that he did not consider himself a satisfactory candidate and suggested other names, the duke of Beaufort, Lord Mansfield, Lord Sidmouth himself, and Lord Talbot. Before St John's could act, however, Christ Church proposed Lord Talbot, and it was finally agreed that an application should be made first to him, and then, if he refused, to the duke. Christ Church duly applied to Lord Talbot, but were soon obliged to announce to their allies that he too declined to stand.

The Wintle party, now wearied of these fruitless negotiations, determined to bring forward their candidate without further delay. A deputation was chosen and arrived at Stratfield Saye on 28 November. Wellington told them the substance of what he had said to Sidmouth; that he was not well qualified to be chancellor; that it was desirable that the university should choose one of its own members; and that they should look for other candidates. He added, however, characteristically that in view of the difficulty which he had heard was being experienced in finding an eligible candidate, he would consult with others and in the meantime they should reflect on the objections which he had made. This expression of Wellington's incorrigible sense of duty was interpreted by the deputation as a conditional assent.

Meanwhile, Christ Church had met with an unexpected and unmerited success. Lord Talbot retracted his earlier refusal and announced that he would after all be ready to stand as candidate. This change of front had been effected by his relatives, who had suffered a natural disappointment at the prospect of so high an honour slipping without a struggle from the family. Mr John Talbot, as soon as he heard of his father's first decision, went to Oxford and let it be known that he was on his way to Ingestre to persuade him to reconsider the offer. The Talbot candidature was thus still kept open, and shortly afterwards Lord Talbot yielded to the persuasion of his son, and of his son's father-in-law, Lord Wharncliffe, and gave his definite consent.

The alliance between the Wintle party and Christ Church had already collapsed. Following on this an open breach occurred. The St John's Committee considered the renewal of the Talbot candidature after the preliminary refusal an offence both to themselves and to the duke of Wellington, and were not prepared to withdraw their man. The Christ Church party alleged that Mr Talbot had arrived in Oxford before the St John's delegation left for Stratfield Saye; that they were perfectly aware of his intention and had deliberately kept the knowledge from the duke. Feeling on that score that they had not been fairly treated, they in turn refused to withdraw. The result was a deadlock so complete that the Tory politicians outside Oxford, more concerned with the party than the man, began to grow apprehensive of a victory for a Whig governmental candidate if the election came on before it was ended. The new year arrived with a settlement of the dispute still nowhere in sight. The principals on either side had committed themselves too deeply to their supporters to retire on their own initiative; both expressed their willingness to give way to the other; both were prepared to be nominated if the other withdrew. Their supporters, however, would not come to any agreement. Each party pointed out the objections to the other's candidate and refused to give up their own. 'A Result less satisfactory of the proceedings of Persons in such a station,' wrote Hobhouse, 'cannot well have been imagined.'

Objections, indeed, were easy to discover, and many people outside the circle of the rival Juntas, as Hobhouse termed them, were impartially aware of the disadvantages of the proposed candidates. The duke was not a university man, and Lord Talbot's tastes and pursuits were not, as Peel dryly remarked, 'of a literary or academical character'. There was, too, a further inconsistency which struck the contemporary observer. Christ Church, which might have been expected to choose a Peelite Conservative, were supporting an extreme Tory, while the moderate Peelite candidate was the nominee of the ultra-Tory party. 'It is singular,' said Lord Eldon, voicing a common feeling, 'that the warmest supporters of the author of the Roman Catholic bill seem to be those who, on account of that anti-Protestant measure, threw out Peel from his situation of MP.' The general dissatisfaction with the Tory deadlock and the Tory candidates produced attempts in other quarters to find a third candidate who would reconcile all differences. Lord Malmesbury was favoured by some; the duke of Newcastle was suggested by others; while outside the university endeavours were made to persuade Lord Eldon that old age was not in itself a disqualification. One of the candidates himself took a hand in the game. Hardinge, who was at Stratfield Saye about 10 December, met Wintle there, who told him that the duke had been recommending a junction of all parties to elect Peel. 'How complaisant,' observed Hobhouse satirically, 'is Lord Grenville under these Circumstances to live on.'

Peel, however, was the name that was being increasingly mentioned among the moderate Tories at Oxford. He was eminently qualified for the chancellorship in every respect save one, his rank, and though lack of title was a disadvantage, it was not insuperable. As for the candidates already in the field, it was felt that Wellington, who had hardly shown himself enthusiastic for the honour, would readily give way to his colleague, and the mere announcement of Peel's candidature would prevent other nominations. Peel's sister Mary and her husband George Dawson were approached to discover whether Peel would consent to stand, and Mary Dawson eventually decided to communicate these overtures to

Peel himself. Before doing so, however, they sought counsel from F. R. Bonham, one of the most reliable and experienced officials in the Conservative party. Bonham, who had his own sources of information on Oxford politics, was not encouraging. He put his knowledge at Dawson's disposal, but he pointed out that everything depended on the attitude of the Wintle party. If they and the Christ Church party united in Peel's favour, he would 'carry it in a canter.' If Christ Church as a body remained neutral, and the liberal Tories combined with the St John's party, Peel's prospects would still be good, although the Whigs would probably bring up a candidate to oppose him. But if Christ Church, relying on the liberal Tories, were to start Peel, opposed or even unsupported by the Wintle faction, 'that man must have stronger nerves than mine . . . who . . . would advise Sir R. Peel to venture the doubtful issue of an election.' Undeterred by this exact and unflattering analysis, Mary Dawson wrote to Peel on 16 December, enclosing Bonham's correspondence and urging him to accept nomination. 'It would be a complete atonement for the disappointment we all experienced at Oxford in the year 1829 and would . . . be the most desirable honor and testimony of public approbation which could be conferred upon you.' She added, a trifle redundantly, that 'the Candidate who has the support of Christ Church and the St John's Committee (united) will be certain of success.' But that was the crux of the matter. Peel could hardly count on the support in 1833 of the party that had been the organizers of his defeat in 1829. Yet, if Bonham was right, and his professional calculations must have weighed more heavily than Mary Dawson's sisterly enthusiasm, without that support it was hopeless to enter on a contest; and Peel needed nobody to tell him that a defeat would be more damaging to himself and his party than mere abstention. There were ample reasons for his ultimate refusal.

Meanwhile the complaisance of Lord Grenville proved to be not inexhaustible, and on 13 January, 1834, the news of his death reached London. Events were now hastened. The Whigs, who had so far played little part in the preliminary manoeuvring for candidates, openly declared for Peel. There had been earlier rumours that Lord Harrowby would be started, but on Grenville's death it was decided not to make a Whig nomination, but to coalesce with the liberal Tories in supporting the most moderate of the opposition candidates. But this accession of strength to Peel was more than out-weighed by the rapid and decisive action of the Wintle party. Their strength was at once assembled and a requisition to Wellington, dated 14 January, was drawn up with a formidable list of signatures. The whole weight of St John's, Queen's, and Magdalen, the heads of six other colleges (Worcester, Balliol, BNC, St Edmund Hall, Trinity and Wadham), and in all some seventy names were arrayed in support of the duke's nomination. Armed with this a deputation called upon Wellington on 16 January, and in the face of this renewed and considered application, he finally consented to become a candidate. Action by the Talbot party now seemed futile, and the presence of Lord Talbot's son at a meeting of Wellington's supporters held in London on 18 January was taken as a sign of acquiescence in the blighting of the family hopes. For a few days after Grenville's death, however, the Christ Church Junta still preserved its unity. No resident there took any active part in the requisition to Wellington, and there was even some faint talk of the duke of Sutherland being started. But the only possible candidates now were Peel and the duke of Wellington, and the unity of the college could not be secured for either. Accordingly, on

17 January, the Censors wrote to inform Peel of 'the determination of the Chapter and Common Room to take no part as a body in the Election of a Chancellor.'

Apart from individual adhesions from the broken ranks of Christ Church, Peel's supporters were thus reduced to the Whigs and the liberal Tories. By Bonham's calculations it was not a combination that could hope for success, and the attempt to obtain Peel's candidature failed not for lack of support in the university, but on Peel's own well-considered refusal to stand. His party did not abandon the struggle until they found that they lacked a leader. On 15 January they held a meeting in the Warden's lodgings at Merton and resolved to make a formal address to Peel. A requisition was drawn up and signed by a respectable array of names, notably from Merton, Oriel and Christ Church. The Provost of Oriel and the Principal of Magdalen Hall subsequently added their names to the list. One copy was sent off to Peel, another to London, where the Whig lawyers were its chief promoters, and a third to Wellington asking him to reconsider his position. The duke, however, replied that the appeal had come too late, and on 17 January all activities were arrested by Peel's refusal. Three days later a printed notice was given out from Merton announcing that Peel had declined to stand.

The way was at last clear, and the duke of Wellington proceeded to an undisputed election. His installation as Chancellor in June, 1834, was made, singularly enough, the occasion for an impressive demonstration of Tory solidarity.

9

The Historical Significance of the Tamworth Manifesto[1]

On the evening of 25 November 1834 Sir Robert Peel, then on holiday in Rome, returned to his hotel from a ball given by the Duchess of Torlonia, to find a messenger from England with urgent despatches. The principal missive was a summons from the king, William IV, to return to London and 'put himself at the head of the administration of the country'. Among the other letters were two from the duke of Wellington explaining that on 14 November the king had dismissed his Whig ministry and that for the moment the duke was acting as caretaker head of a new government in the double role of first lord of the Treasury and secretary of state. The only other unavoidable ministerial appointment had been that of Lyndhurst as Lord Chancellor, a post which required legal qualifications.

Travelling as rapidly as wintry conditions in central Europe permitted in a pre-railway age, Peel reached London fourteen days later on 9 December. He found that there was a general anticipation in his immediate political circle that he would advise the king to dissolve parliament; and preparations for that event had already started. Since the total strength of the Conservative opposition in the House of Commons was only about 150 members, it is probable that Peel in any case would have thought it useless to meet parliament in its existing state. But in fact the decision to hold an immediate general election was virtually made for him. Accordingly, on 30 December parliament was formally dissolved and writs sent out for the election of a new House of Commons to meet on 19 February 1835. Twelve days earlier on 18 December Peel, having automatically forfeited his seat at Tamworth by taking office, issued an address to his constituents as a preliminary to seeking re-election.

Such a practice was a customary feature of parliamentary elections. This, however, was no ordinary address. If its form was orthodox, the circumstances in which it was issued were highly unorthodox. Peel's appointment as prime minister in December 1834 came as a climax to one of the most dramatic changes of government in modern British history. Little was known of the motives behind the king's action beyond the bare fact that the Whigs were out and the Tories – or at least the duke of Wellington – were in. Though the resignation of five members of the cabinet, including the prime minister, in the course of the previous summer had indicated the strains within Grey's reforming administration, his successor Lord Melbourne had taken over without any apparent difficulty. The recent death of Earl Spencer and consequent removal of his heir Lord Althorp from the leadership of the House of Commons to the House of Lords, though it meant the

[1] Originally delivered as a lecture as part of the 150 years anniversary celebrations of the Tamworth Manifesto organized by the Peel Society in Tamworth in December 1984 and subsequently published in a commemorative pamphlet by the Peel Society.

loss of a popular politician, did not seem enough in itself to undermine the position of the government. The large reform majority elected in 1833 still dominated the House of Commons and the Whig cabinet, however reluctantly reforming, appeared to be the only possible administration.

The need for some explanation of the king's action, and for some indication of his new ministers' intentions, was apparent to most observers. Normally such an explanation would be made in parliament. If, however, a general election was to take place before ministers could make any statement to the legislature, some other mode of communication seemed advisable. Without it the prospect of securing much additional strength through a general election seemed remote; the Liberal majority in the electorate would see little reason to change sides and potential Conservative candidates would be deterred from coming forward. The position had been made worse by Wellington's provisional appointment as head of government. Paradoxically William IV's impulsive action had seriously damaged his new administration's chances of survival even before Peel arrived back in England. The sight of the duke riding around Whitehall giving directions to the different departments might arouse amusement in some, but in others it created resentment and alarm. Wellington in 1834 was far from being the venerated public figure, almost a public institution, that he became toward the end of his life. In the 1830s there was still a residue of hostility against him as a professional soldier out of place in civilian politics. Among extreme radicals and extreme Tories there had even been an exaggerated suspicion that his 1828–30 administration had posed a threat to constitutional liberty from the sinister combination of a general at 10 Downing Street and a new, allegedly military-style, police in London formed by his Home Secretary Robert Peel. Politically the duke had angered Tories by conceding Catholic Emancipation and Liberals by denouncing parliamentary reform. His attempt to form a second administration in May 1832 had been wrongly but widely believed to have been a desperate attempt by the king to block the passage of a reform bill.

The remarkable one-man rule of the duke in November–December 1834 revived all these fears and prejudices. At the very least, his initial appointment seemed to indicate that the tone of the new government would be old-fashioned and reactionary. 'This circumstance alone,' Stanley wrote to Peel when refusing office, 'must stamp upon the administration about to be formed the impress of his name and principles.' Hostility to Wellington was in fact one of the main reasons why Stanley and his followers did not join Peel. Nor was it only the moderate Whig politicians who were prejudiced against him. Reports from different parts of the country made it clear that the duke was identified in many people's minds with the cry of 'NO REFORM'. Walter, the proprietor of *The Times* newspaper, in a letter which found its way to Peel, directly linked what he called 'the unreasonably angry hostility to the duke of Wellington' and the feeling against 'the return of the Tories to office' with the need to offer 'some fresh explanation, some popular declaration, *previous* to a Dissolution of Parliament.' Not the least of the motives which prompted the *Tamworth Manifesto*, therefore, was a desire on Peel's part to efface the unfortunate Wellingtonian image given to the new government before he himself had time to return to England.

The problem was now to effect this in a manner which would be constitutionally proper and yet attract maximum publicity. Clearly the explanation of his reasons for accepting office and any further exposition of his intended policy could only come from the prime minister himself. But even during the anxious days of waiting before he appeared in London, his colleagues – or some of them – were turning over the various possibilities that would be open to him. Ellenborough, who became the President of the Board of Control in the new ministry, thought he should use the occasion of the traditional Lord Mayor's banquet to make a speech outlining his policy. Peel mentioned the suggestion at his first cabinet and it was agreed that an approach should be made to the Lord Mayor. The dinner, however, was not due to be held until 23 December. To keep official silence for such a long period would hardly be in the interests of the government. Ellenborough on 14 December proposed that in the interval Peel should send a letter to his parliamentary supporters which could be published in advance. This would whet public appetite and provide a suitable overture for his speech at the dinner. The perennial difficulty with all such circular letters was, of course, the selection of the list of recipients. Some MPs on the list might resent the assumption that Peel had a claim on their allegiance. Others, not on the list, would resent their omission. In the rudimentary state of party organization, no reliable means existed for deciding the party affiliations of every MP; party 'membership' indeed was not an intelligible expression.

Another suggestion came from the office of *The Times* whose editor, Barnes, had been increasingly dissatisfied with the Whig administration during 1834 and had been guardedly negotiating for a better understanding with the new ministry. His chief intermediary was the newspaper's legal adviser, Scarlett, who was promoted by Peel to the House of Lords at this time and might had he wished become attorney-general. The new plan was that an address to Peel, drafted probably by Walter and revised among others by Barnes, should be signed by a number of MPs, to which the prime minister could then make an extended reply. The objection felt to this was that if the list of signatures was small, the address would not seem important enough to warrant anything more than a formal answer. Scarlett himself doubted whether Walter, who sat in the Commons as member for Berkshire, had enough influence in the House of Commons to muster the important signatories that would be needed to make it a significant document. Since Walter had won election to the House in 1833 as a moderate Liberal and supporter of Lord Grey, his doubts were probably well founded.

Peel by that time had come to a different decision. What he now favoured was a more orthodox, less complicated procedure which would avoid the embarrassments with which the earlier proposals had been attended. 'I think,' he replied to Scarlett, 'every object will be answered and in the best mode by an Address from me to my Constituents and which I can issue on any day, on the ground that my seat is now vacant.' That was written on 16 December and time was running short. The document was drafted at once, read to the Cabinet on 17 December, approved, copied out and sent to *The Times* and the two leading Conservative newspapers, the *Morning Herald* and the *Morning Post* in the small hours of the morning of 18 December. The editors had been warned of its coming, the presses were waiting and only a few hours later the contents was being eagerly absorbed by the metropolitan public.

It was four years before the opening of the London to Birmingham railway. Even by fast mail-coach newspapers took at least twelve hours to reach Birmingham. In all probability *The Times* and the other two newspapers bearing the text of the *Manifesto* were not available in Tamworth until 19 December. On that day it was widely known and being excitedly discussed all over the town. By tradition it was read aloud to a waiting crowd at the Town Hall. Mr Stevens, probably the well-known local solicitor of that name, wrote off the same day to the prime. minister.

> The Address which you have done us the Honour to transmit to Tamworth has pleased all ranks. Everybody is talking of it. We consider it a very high compliment that you should give us the first public intimation of the measures of Government.

Such were the circumstances in which the *Tamworth Manifesto* appeared before the public.

The word 'Manifesto' does not, however, appear anywhere in the document. The term was well known and had been part of political vocabulary at least since the seventeenth century. A generation earlier it had acquired notoriety from its application to the famous proclamation of the duke of Brunswick to the French people in 1792. As defined in a contemporary work of reference (*Craig's Dictionary*, published 1848), a manifesto was 'a declaration issued from a prince or sovereign, proclaiming his opinions or motives in reference to some public question'. Peel was not a sovereign ruler (though perhaps a British prime minister did not fall far short of his monarch in terms of real power); but except for that, his *Address* met the definition exactly. It was in this sense that the term was used by the leading Liberal newspaper, the *Morning Chronicle*, when discussing the document on the 19th.

> Sir Robert Peel, having ruined his Cabinet by the selection of its members, and the dubious appearance of its policy, has published a Manifesto in the form of an 'Address to the Electors of the Borough of Tamworth'.

Peel, a great student of newspapers, had probably already read this when writing the same day to Princess Lieven that he had 'had to travel from Rome, form a Government, and publish a Manifesto in less than three weeks'. In sending a copy to Talleyrand he described it more formally as a 'Declaration of the General Principles and views of the Government which I have been called upon to form'. It was as the *Tamworth Manifesto*, however, that the *Address* became generally known. Already on 20 December Greville, the political diarist, recorded that 'Peel's letter to his constituents has appeared as his manifesto to the country'. Under that title it has enshrined itself in British political history.

It made, as Greville further noted, 'a prodigious sensation, and nobody talks of anything else.' Reading the text of the *Manifesto* today, it is not easy to detect anything very sensational. But this is a common historical experience. Few things have a more dead appearance than the details of political controversies examined several generations later. In the opening paragraphs Peel obviously thought it necessary to explain why he was issuing the address at all. He said he felt it 'incumbent' on him to give an explanation of his views on public policy when asking his constituents to re-elect him; and he added, more significantly, that he was also availing himself 'of this, a legitimate opportunity, of making a more public appeal' with a 'frank exposition of general principles and views which appears to be anxiously expected and which it ought not to be the inclination, and cannot be in the interest, of a Minister of this country to withhold.' In accepting office, he continued, he hoped that his opinions were sufficiently in unison with those of the electorate to enable him to carry on the government; but he was conscious that public confidence could only be secured by 'a frank and explicit declaration of principle'.

Having justified the issue of the document, he then launched on the exposition of political principles which was its central feature. He was not, he asserted, either a defender of abuses or an opponent of judicious reform. He regarded the Reform Act of 1832 as the settlement of a great constitutional question which he had no wish to disturb. He was ready to govern in the spirit of the Reform Act provided that this meant, not perpetual change and agitation, reform for reform's sake, but a careful review of institutions, the correction of proved abuses and the redress of real grievances. Turning to specific current issues he promised to continue the Whig-instituted enquiry into municipal corporations, to meet Dissenting griev-ances over church rates, civil marriage and entry to the learned professions, to look into the pension list, to examine the position of the Church of Ireland, and to set up a commission of enquiry into the Church of England. To these primary themes he added a coda of conventional pledges in favour of peace, public credit, retrenchment, and equality of treatment for the great economic interests of the country. He ended by appealing to the electorate to give, not necessarily their complete confidence, but at least a fair trial, to his administration. It was, from start to finish, a studiously conciliatory document.

For something which can justly be claimed as signalling the birth of the Conservative party, it had this further singularity. Nowhere in it is there any use of the term 'Conservative'; nowhere is there any reference to party. The nearest Peel came to such matters is in two phrases: one when he said that the effect of the Reform Act should not be to limit the Crown's choice of ministers to 'one section, and one section only, of public men'; the other when he spoke of 'those with whom I am about to act'. But both expressions clearly relate not to a political party in the broad sense but to a more restricted group of parliamentary politicians; in this case men who had been opposed to Grey's administration, or at least were independent of it, and who by their presence in parliament had provided a possible alternative government. It was for his colleagues, rather than for a party at large, that Peel was speaking in the *Tamworth Manifesto*.

Whether this avoidance of party phraseology was instinctive or deliberate is another matter. There were good reasons why it was inadvisable to emphasize the party nature of the new administration. Not only the forms but to a large extent the actual practice of the constitution made the appointment of chief minister the personal act of the monarch in which he was deemed to have complete freedom of choice. It would have been improper by contemporary conventions to have said anything which appeared to ascribe to the influence of a political party what was owed to the confidence of the crown. This was not just the gap which frequently exists between the actual working and the inherited theory of the constitution. Naturally politicians derived prestige and power from the possession of a recog-nized following in parliament and this in turn powerfully influenced the choice of the crown. But party organization was still rudimentary and political allegiances were still too unreliable to make party the openly accepted basis of government. Not until 1841, seven years later, was the crown faced for the first time with the necessity of appointing as prime minister a man who owed everything to the victory of his party at a general election and nothing to the favour of his monarch. Even then it was to be another generation before the last remnants of royal discretion in the choice of chief minister, and the residual feeling of politicians in high office that they were still in a personal sense 'ministers of the crown', disappeared from political life. It was proper and prudent therefore for Peel in his *Manifesto* to ignore party and speak solely as the king's chief minister.

There was also the inescapable circumstance that at the time when he issued the *Manifesto* a 'Conservative party' in any organized sense could hardly be said to exist. The expression, of course, was not unknown. As early as 1827 Wellington had spoken of the '*parti conservateur*' in the country. By that he clearly meant all those who opposed radical reforms and wished to conserve the ancient institutions of the state. It did not signify that a political party formed from those elements actually was in existence. The use of the French phrase itself suggested a certain artificiality in the concept. A more solid and practical use of the word came in the *Quarterly Review* for January 1830 when an anonymous journalist wrote of 'what is called the Tory and which might with more propriety be called the Conservative Party'. The implication of his remark was that it would be better to abandon the old, narrow and slightly discredited term 'Tory' in favour of the more recent, wider and more respectable appellation 'Conservative'. In that sense it could be said that there was between 1832 and 1834 a Conservative opposition, even though it lacked unity and undisputed leadership, and had only an exiguous organization.

Nevertheless, between the 'Conservatism' of the *Quarterly*'s article in 1830 and the 'Conservatism' implicit, though not named, in the *Tamworth Manifesto*, there was a crucial difference. If 'Conservatism' was no more than a long word of continental origin to indicate the same principles as were associated with the short, vernacular epithet 'Tory', it merely described a party of resistance to the spirit of reform. To such a principle and such a party Peel was not prepared to subscribe, either during the Reform Act debates or subsequently in the reformed parliament. It was for precisely that reason that his parliamentary position in the 1833 and 1834 sessions had been largely one of isolation. He did not join in the indiscrimate ultra-Tory attacks on the government and was even ready on occasion to join ministers in resisting the demands of their radical supporters. Since for the immediate future he saw no alternative to the Whig administration, he avoided any action that might bring about their downfall. At the same time he made it clear that his own version of conservatism included a readiness to reform. A disciple of Burke, he knew that a state which is without the means of change is without the means of its own conservation. It annoyed him particularly that the many changes and reforms of the Liverpool and Wellington administrations in which he had served before 1830 had been opposed and in some cases were still being condemned by the same ultra-Tories who now expected him to lead an all-out attack on the Whigs. He made it his business therefore in his first speech in the reformed parliament to outline the central message of what later was to become known as Tamworth Conservatism: the acceptance of the Reform Act as a final settlement and a readiness to reform any institution which needed reform, specifying only that it should be done gradually, dispassionately and deliberately so that it should be permanent.

At that time, however, he was speaking not as a leader of a party but simply as an individual politician laying down the principles on which he intended to act. His declaration attracted a good deal of interest and Greville thought that by that one speech he had contrived to 'transfer to himself personally much of the weight and authority which he had previously held as the organ and head of a great and powerful party'. At the same time he had set up a standard to which a party might rally in the future. The unsatisfactory nature of an opposition which was both leaderless and divided was obvious even to the ultras. During the 1833 session, in fact, efforts were made by the more moderate members of the opposition to bring about some form of formal reunification under Peel's leadership. All attempts foundered on the persistence of men like Knatchbull and Vyvyan in demanding pledges both on policy and on future appointments which Peel had no intention of giving. When he was summoned home by the king in November 1834 to form a government, he was still simply an eminent member of the House of Commons rather than the recogized head of an organized party.

It is not surprising therefore that Peel accepted office in 1834 with considerable misgiving. He had neither anticipated nor welcomed the abrupt dismissal of the Whigs by William IV. The fact that the crisis occurred at a time when he was further away from London than he had ever been in his life, or was ever to be again, is proof of the unexpectedness of the event. What seemed clear to him as he ruminated on the situation – and he had ample time to ruminate as he travelled back from Italy – was that unless he could win over many electors and some members of parliament who previously had been on the side of the Reform Act, his administration had little chance of survival. The shrunken Conservative opposition left after 1832, even allowing for more candidates in the field and a probable recovery of seats in 1835, was scarcely in a position to overturn the vast reform majority at one stroke.

That he would be able to make some conversions was not an unreasonable supposition. Before 1832 all parliaments had possessed a substantial floating element which with proper encouragement tended to drift over to the ministers in office if they appeared to have some prospect of permanence. The disruption of the Whig cabinet in the 1834 session and the emergence of what looked like a dissident conservative Whig group under Stanley suggested that a realignment of forces was not an improbable development, even though Peel's immediate overtures met with a refusal. It was this hope that lay behind Peel's plea for his administration to be given a fair trial and his direct appeal in the opening paragraphs of the *Tamworth Manifesto* to 'that class which is much less interested in the contentions of party, than in the maintenance of order and the cause of good government.' This call to the uncommitted and the less committed was basic to Peel's whole approach to the 1834 crisis. It was an attempt to win back some of the middle ground of politics lost during Wellington's administration; and though it failed in the House of Commons (though having more success with the electorate) it was another reason why the *Tamworth Manifesto* could not be framed in explicit party terms.

Nevertheless, the circumstances in which the *Manifesto* appeared made it – and could hardly have failed to make it – a party document. Appointment as prime minister gave Peel a status and authority he had not enjoyed before. With power now, as well as prestige, he was the only figure round which the loose forces of the opposition could gather; round which they had to gather if they were to have any chance of halting the progress of the radical movement. If anyone made Peel leader of the Conservative party, it was William IV. Though in the *Manifesto* Peel spoke as prime minister and not as head of the Conservative party, the implications for party development were inescapable. The royal action had placed him in a position to make his version of Conservatism, now embodied in the *Manifesto*, the banner under which his followers must fight if they were to fight at all. By accepting his principles, and repeating them from innumerable hustings, the Conservative candidates at the general election came as near as possible in the conditions of the time to acknowledging him as leader and enlisting in his cause. The events of November–December 1834 marked the birth of the modern Conservative Party; and the *Tamworth Manifesto* was designed to assist its delivery. When Croker sent him a draft review of the *Manifesto* intended for publication in the *Quarterly Review*, Peel demurred at his argument that the Reform Act had imposed new necessities on government policy. For himself, at any rate, he could not accept that there had been any sudden change of attitude. He was saying nothing in the *Tamworth Manifesto* that he had not said earlier or that was in conflict with his public record before 1830. The necessities which had prompted the *Manifesto*, he replied to Croker, 'rather arose from the abruptness of the change in the Government, and, to say the truth, from the policy of aiding our friends at the election.'

The *Manifesto*, therefore, was both a party document and an electioneering document. This in itself made it a noteworthy event since there was no precedent for such a publication by an administration as part of its preparation for a general election. It was unusual for a ministry to issue a collective statement on its own behalf at all. The only recent instances that were in any way comparable had been justifications and explanations of what had been done in the past rather than statements of principles and intentions for the future. At the end of the 1833 session, for example, the Whig ministry had put out a pamphlet *The Reform Ministry and the Reformed Parliament* to describe its policy and list its achievements since the passage of the Reform Act. Its editor was Brougham's private secretary, Le Marchant, and contributions came from cabinet ministers like Althorp, Stanley, Graham and Palmerston, on the work of their departments. There had been a similar production in 1822 on behalf of Lord Liverpool's government under the title of *The State of the Nation*. The only important difference between the two productions was that where the Whig pamphlet confined itself to a review of the single session of 1833, its 1822 predecessor analysed the government's policies, attitudes and achievements over the whole period since the conclusion of the war in 1815.

Even so, such direct efforts by governments to improve public relations were novel. It was a mark of a certain shyness on the part of ministers of the crown to appear openly in such partisan productions that both pamphlets appeared without official ascription; though in fact their authorship was well known and ensured for them a wide circulation. Each was a conscious attempt to win over public opinion at a time when both ministries were experiencing a degree of unpopularity. Except in that one respect, neither was a true precedent for the *Tamworth Manifesto*. Since he had only just formed his administration, all Peel could do was to offer principles and promises. In the peculiar circumstances surrounding the general election of 1835, he was compelled to make the *Tamworth Manifesto* at once more general and more personal than either of the two ministerial pamphlets of 1822 and 1833.

Unique as it was at the time, the *Manifesto* has remained unique. Though a landmark in British party history, it stands as an isolated feature, there have been no imitations. In the following general elections of 1837 and 1841 Peel made no attempt to repeat the performance. The 1841 election which brought him to power was fought primarily on the issue of the defeated Whig budget and Peel took office as uncommitted as any prime minister can ever hope to be with regard to future policy. The nearest he came to a repetition of the 1834 *Manifesto* was, ironically, at the general election of 1847 when he was neither prime minister nor party leader. In his election address at Tamworth Peel defended his conciliatory policy towards the Roman Catholics of Ireland and his recent repeal of the Corn Laws. It received – as indeed Peel had intended it to receive – considerable attention in the country and many Peelite candidates used it in their own election campaigns. But since Peel also used the *Tamworth Letter* of 1847 to indicate that he did not wish either to return to office or lead a party, it can hardly be regarded as a parallel to the *Manifesto* of thirteen years earlier.

Nor has there been one since Peel's time. One reason for this is simply that the circumstances of 1834 never recurred. It was the last time a British monarch had dismissed his ministers and called on others to take their place. This alone, however, does not account for the absence of imitation. The larger explanation is that the rapid development of party politics in this period made general statements of principle unnecessary. Debates in parliament, election speeches, pamphlets and newspapers were enough to make the public conversant with the attitudes of different parties. Indeed the growth of the press made pamphlets themselves increasingly an old-fashioned form of political instruction. On the other hand, it was still too early for the development of party programmes in the modern style. Until well after the second Reform Act party leaders in the main preferred to be as uncommitted as possible. They regarded themselves more as administrators than as legislators, and their instinct was to deal with issues as they arose rather than pledge themselves to specific courses of action in advance. Only when particular issues emerged of unusual personal or public interest did prospective prime ministers on occasions indicate at elections how they would deal with them. It was with the late-Victorian proliferation of constituency organizations, in particular the holding of annual conferences of party delegates, that the idea of a party 'programme' become an established feature of British politics.

That, however, was a long way in the future. The mid-Victorian decades from 1847 to 1865 saw in fact a temporary decline in the intensity of party organizations, a blurring of party differences, and a return to something more resembling the politics of the pre-reform days. After 1847 collective statements of policy by either ministries or parties would have brought embarrassment rather than profit. The *Tamworth Manifesto*, therefore, remained an isolated event born of unusual circumstances; not something that lent itself to imitation or repetition. Its significance was not in its form, but in its content. It was not that it set a precedent or started a practice but that, with politics still in the fluid state in which they had been ever since 1827, it redefined party lines in a manner which could never have been anticipated only two years earlier. The general expectation after the passage of the Reform Act was that the battle of the future would be between an aristocratic party led by the Whigs and a Radical party pressing for fundamental changes. This never happened. The Whigs fragmented and the Radicals, unable to form a coherent party, were obliged to operate as a wing of the Liberal party. In effect two aristocratic parties emerged from the uncertain post-Reform world, both reforming, both looking to public opinion, both competing for the favour of the electorate. Instead of a damaging polarization of politics between aristocracy and a radical middle-class movement came a more stable and evolutionary party system. The *Tamworth Manifesto* was an important signpost along the road.

For the party of Peel and Wellington the winter of 1834–5 signalled a new departure. But it was not only the Conservatives who altered course. The curious mirror-image relationship of a two-party system ensured that their opponents were equally affected. The shock of a Conservative ministry in office, only two years after the Reform Act had threatened to keep them in opposition for a generation, had a galvanizing effect on the disjointed ranks of the reformers. In the first reformed parliament they had proved quarrelsome and divided, unable to agree on legislation or leadership. After the general election of 1835, which added about a hundred seats to the existing Conservative strength in the House of Commons, the Liberal opposition recovered some sense of unity and discipline. The Lichfield House Compact of February 1835 was in its inception no more than a tactical agreement between Whigs, Radicals and Irish nationalists to work together for the sole purpose of evicting Peel's ministry. But, like the *Tamworth Manifesto*, its effects were more pervasive and lasting. In its own way it was as much the starting-point for the Victorian Liberal party as the *Manifesto* was for the Victorian Conservative party.

Yet even here there was a difference. For the Liberals the lesson of the 1834 crisis was the need for unity. For the Conservatives it was the need for adaptation. The message of the *Tamworth Manifesto* was that the party must be ready not only to accept but to initiate change. Though the lesson had to be painfully relearnt in the barren years of opposition between 1846 and 1866, it never lost its validity.

10

Bonham and the Conservative Party, 1830–1857[1]

In October 1835 the *Edinburgh Review* published an account of the reorganization of the Conservative party after 1832 which included the statement that 'a political secretary was appointed with assistant committees for correspondence and the management of registration and future elections'. The person holding the position was not named. Sixteen years later Disraeli made an equally tantalizing if more flamboyantly expressed reference in his *Lord George Bentinck*.

> Sir Robert, [he wrote] had always been well served in the unseen management of his party. The great Conservative party that destroyed everything was the creation of individuals who did not figure in senates or cabinet councils; above all, of one gentleman who by his knowledge of human nature, fine observation of opinion, indefatigable activity, universal correspondence, and fertility of resource, mainly contributed to the triumph of '42, though he was spoken of only in a whisper and moved only behind the scenes.

Disraeli, like the Whig reviewer, omitted to give a name to this figure and no subsequent suggestion of his identity appears to have been made. Yet the passage cannot be disregarded as a mere rhetorical flourish. The life of Bentinck appeared in 1851 when the events it described were still fresh in the public mind; it was a book on politics for politicians by one who knew well the workings of the Conservative party in the 1840s. It is inconceivable that even Disraeli in these circumstances would invent such a character.

There is now no room for doubt that both allusions were based on fact and both related to the same man. The two volumes of the correspondence of F. R. Bonham in the Peel Papers are concerned with exactly these activities and all the indications scattered among the general mass of Peel's letters make it clear that Bonham occupied a unique place in the management of the Conservative party during Peel's period of leadership. It is noteworthy that the Bonham correspondence is included at all in the Peel Papers. It was the result, not of any chance, but of the deliberate action of Peel's literary executors; though it calls for nice judgement to decide whether their well-intended action did more harm than good.

Bonham died in April 1863 at the little suburban house to which he had retired in 1846. By his will, dated 10 March 1862, he left all his property to his sister, Susan Bonham, with whom he had lived for many years. A few months later the

[1] An enlarged version of the article 'F. R. Bonham: Conservative "Political Secretary", 1832–47' published in *Eng. Hist. Review*, LXIII (October 1948). Source references are given here only for material which did not appear in the original article. All the five figure references refer to Additional Manuscripts in the British Library.

trustees of the Peel Papers, Edward Cardwell and Earl Stanhope, offered to purchase her brother's correspondence. Their motives were perhaps compounded of human charity and political caution. Bonham died a poor man. The official valuation of his effects was under £600 and though his sister was not left destitute, it is probable that she was in straitened circumstances. At all events, she gratefully accepted the terms proposed to her by Cardwell in June – an annuity of £40. Since she was already eighty-two, the actuarial calculation was not likely to embarrass Peel's trustees who in any case had been left £1,000 to cover the costs of administration. In the event, Susan Bonham lived only another six months after her brother's death. For the price of £20 (a half-year's remittance paid in advance in July 1863) the Peel trustees obtained what was probably the most important collection of confidential electoral correspondence between the first and second reform acts.[1] No sooner was it in the hands of the trustees than they destroyed the greater part of it: an act of historical vandalism all the more remarkable since Stanhope was an historian of repute, an examiner at Oxford University, founder of the historical essay-prize which bears his name, and the man largely responsible for the creation of the Historical Manuscripts Commission in 1869. What happened he may himself be left to explain.

> At the decease of my much valued friend Mr Bonham his very voluminous correspondence passed into mine and Mr Cardwell's hands. I went over it all, burning the greater portion as no longer of interest. But I reserved Sir Robert Peel's letters and some others for our joint preservation, and I also put apart and preserved my own. Stanhope July 1863.[2]

What survived from this literary holocaust was a scatter of letters from Stanhope, now in the Chevening archives, and two volumes of select correspondence, together with letters from Peel, presumably inserted in chronological order in the General Correspondence section of the Peel Papers, eventually deposited in the British Museum. The two bound volumes of Bonham correspondence comprise 373 letters of which more than half are from Sir James Graham. For the rest, one can only speculate from these remains and from other Bonham letters in separate collections, how large was the 'voluminous' mass of papers which Bonham left at his death.

Enough has been preserved fortunately to make clear the role which Bonham played in Peel's political career and in the organization of the Conservative party after the first Reform Act. What that role was appeared sometimes obscure to the general public of the day. Interestingly enough, he was on more than one occasion accused of being the secretary of the Carlton Club. His Whig opponent at Harwich made the charge on the hustings at the election of 1837 but Bonham immediately denied that he was the secretary or in any way the paid servant, of the club. This was true; Bonham, though one of the earliest members and on the committee in 1841, was not the club's secretary. Yet the legend persisted. In September a correspondent from Caernarvon wrote that 'it is reported in this country that I have offered my services to the secretary of the Carlton Club. I suppose I was seen calling on you there.' There was obviously something unusual

---

[1] 40,615 fos. 227–34.
[2] Chevening Papers. I owe this and other information about Bonham's correspondence with Lord Mahon to the kindness of Dr Aubrey Newman of Leicester University.

in his position for such rumours to circulate. His status was less official than the *Edinburgh Review* suggested and his influence on events more restricted than that spaciously indicated by Disraeli, who could not forget in writing *Lord George Bentinck* that he was also the author of *Coningsby*, the best piece of political fiction in the nineteenth century. Yet the ascertainable substance of Bonham's work entitled him to a place in the party's history which for over a century was ignored by historians. There was little doubt in the minds of his political contemporaries on this score even though a convention of silence shrouded his activities. In 1844, when launching a personal attack on Bonham in the Commons, Divett, the member for Exeter, endeavoured to bring his peculiar occupation before the public eye. An early insinuation of the difference between the 'official position' which Bonham held and 'the real functions which he discharged at the Carlton Club and in the Conservative Party' merely evoked the laughter of the House. A few days later the same Mr Divett made a more outspoken reference. 'It was well known', he said, 'that the hon. Gentleman was the confidential election agent of the Conservative party (laughter) . . . The fact was notorious in all political circles and . . . ought to be made notorious to the country.' The House was amused by this peevish reference to functions about which politicians usually displayed a decent reticence; but nobody denied the charge.

Francis Robert Bonham was MP for Rye 1830–1 and for Harwich 1835–7, Storekeeper to the Ordnance 1834–5 and 1841–5, and assistant Conservative Whip 1835–7. He was born 5 September 1785 in London and was baptized at St George's, Hanover Square, the son of Francis Warren Bonham by his second marriage with Dorothea Sophia Herbert. His father F. W. Bonham came of a Dublin family, was educated at Trinity College Dublin, and later called to the Irish bar. Some time before the end of the eighteenth century he settled in England, at first in London and later in Bath. He died on 8 September 1810 at Richmond Hill, London. By his first marriage, with Mary Ann Leslie, he had a son John who matriculated in 1785 at Merton College, Oxford, at the age of sixteen. It was this Bonham who was later suspected of complicity in seditious Irish nationalist activities against Pitt's government in 1798. A daughter Mary Ann (Joyce) died unmarried at Hammersmith in 1796. By his second marriage he had five children of whom only two survived infancy, Francis Robert and a daughter Susan born in 1780. Neither married and they lived together for at least the last thirty years of their lives. On his father's side, therefore, F. R. Bonham descended from a substantial though not outstanding Irish Protestant family, a branch of which (through his half-brother John) was until comparatively recently settled at the family seat of Ballintaggart, co. Kildare. On his mother's side he came of more distinguished stock. Dorothea Sophia, who died at Hertford St, Mayfair, on 23 June 1820, was a member of the famous Herbert family, being in the direct line of descent from Sir Richard Herbert of Coldbrook, brother of William Herbert of Raglan and ancestor of the earls of Pembroke and Montgomery. Her father, Edward Herbert, had sat in the latter years of the 1727–60 Irish parliament as a member for Innistioge, co. Kilkenny, and her grandfather, also Edward Herbert, had been member for Ludlow in the parliament of Great Britain from 1754 until his death in 1770. Her mother, the Hon. Mrs Herbert of Rutland Square, Dublin, was Nichola Sophia Cuffe, eldest daughter of Lord Desart of Kilkenny, who as a commoner sat for Thomastown, co. Kilkenny, in the Irish parliament of 1715–27; and her grandmother was a daughter of the second Viscount Kenmare. Bonham was thus a scion of the Anglo-Irish governing class of the eighteenth century with more than a tincture of aristocratic connection – he was kinsman to the Peelite Sidney Herbert, son of the eleventh earl of Pembroke – and some family tradition of parliamentary membership. Peel and Gladstone themselves were *novi homines* compared with the solid lineage of their political adviser. It is this background which explains the sturdy Tory Anglican views which he retained to the end of his life. He wrote once of himself as 'entertaining from infancy a strong (possibly) prejudice in favour of the Church' and a 'dread of any proposed reforms'. What is remarkable is not that he entered political life but that he reached the age of forty-five before he became an MP. About the early part of his life, however, information is very scanty and much remains to be discovered before a full biography can be written. In 1802 he was at Bath with a private tutor attending his father who was suffering from a severe attack of paralysis. Two years later he went to Oxford where he matriculated as a gentleman commoner at Corpus Christi College on 27 January 1804 at the age of eighteen. He took his BA degree in 1807 and his MA three years later. In 1808 he entered Lincoln's Inn and was called to the bar in 1814. Yet it does not appear that he ever practised as a barrister, if the absence of his name from the Law Lists during the next ten or fifteen years can be taken as evidence. That in itself, however, would not be ususual. 'Thirty or forty years ago,' wrote a barrister in 1851, 'gentlemen used to be called to the Bar without any view to practice or to any pecuniary advantage. It was simply the rank or honour of the degree of barrister which was sought.'[1] On the other hand there is no real indication of what Bonham was doing between 1814 and 1830 and how he lived. In a parliamentary guide for the latter year his occupation is given as that of landowner. But all ordinary MPs at this time were theoretically landowners and in view of the general evasion of the property qualification no particular importance can be attached to this description. In all probability he was living the life of an independent gentleman. His father had been a man of considerable means who, besides providing for his widow and elder son, left by his will in 1810 the sum of £5,000 each to Francis Robert and Susan. In addition F. R. Bonham received a further sum of £5,000 from the estate of his half-sister Mary Ann and was his father's residuary legatee. There is also a family record of certain property at Clongaffyn, co. Meath, which came to him on his father's death and which he sold. It is clear therefore that F. R. Bonham had from 1810 onwards a reasonable competence. In the earty 30s he was undoubtedly experiencing some financial difficulty but it is not clear how serious this was. In any case it was more likely to have been the result of living beyond his means than any absolute poverty.

His entry into politics in 1830 was the most important epoch of his life even though the motives for that step are unknown. By that time he was already moving in the political world and personally though not yet intimately acquainted with Peel. His first known communication with Peel, apparently in March 1829, conveyed a suggestion made to Bonham by an Irish Conservative relating to the changes in the Irish franchise then under consideration, 'to which you will give

[1] W. Johnston, *England as It Is* (1851), II, 149.

whatever consideration it may deserve'.[1] About eighteen months after that letter was written Bonham was in the House of Commons and the circumstances under which he was returned for Rye are not without their interest. Up to 1824 the borough had been a close constituency with influence shared between the Lamb family and the corporation. An unsuccessful attempt was made in 1825–6 to create an independent town interest but at the general election of 1826 the two corporation candidates were duly returned. One of them was a certain Henry Bonham, a member of the Essex family of that name, who had formerly been member for Leominster and Sandwich. He had not previously sat for Rye and the name does not appear in the list of members for the borough in the reigns of George III and IV. There was thus no apparent family connection with the borough; nor in any case was Henry Bonham even indirectly related to Francis Robert Bonham in the century or more over which their ancestries can be traced. Nevertheless when Henry died in 1830, having resigned from the House of Commons shortly beforehand, Francis Robert stood as corporation candidate at the following general election and was returned. It is by no means unlikely that the two Bonhams were acquainted. Francis Bonham was at that date resident at the Old Steyne, Brighton; Henry, though resident at Portland Place, London, with a family seat at Orsett, Essex, was a well-known figure in the Brighton district and actually died at another house he occupied near Hastings. Certainly in 1844 Francis Robert was on friendly enough terms with Henry's son Edward Walter, then British consul at Tabriz, Persia, for the latter to correspond with him.

Simultaneously, however, there is evidence of a marked intimacy between Francis Robert Bonham and the leaders of the government party. Henry Bonham died on Good Friday, 9 April 1830. On 20 April Peel, then on one of his frequent holiday visits to Brighton, gave a dinner at Orton House at which both Bonham and Planta, secretary to the Treasury and MP for the neighbouring borough of Hastings, were present. It was not perhaps a coincidence that up to the time of the Reform Act of 1832, Rye was regarded as one of the constituencies which invariably returned a nominee of the Treasury. In any event the following August saw Bonham's election for Rye. In September he was guest at a 'grand dinner party' given by Mr Lawrence and Lady Jane Peel (Robert Peel's brother and sister-in-law) and in November he was presented at a *levée* at St James's Palace by Sir Robert himself. By that time his friendship with Peel seems well established. 'But who,' wrote Greville acidly in his journal for 16 December 1830, 'are Peel's confidants, friends and parasites? Bonham, a stock-jobbing ex-merchant; Charles Ross, Chas. Grant, the refuse of society and of the H. of C.' This description of Bonham seems almost certainly based on a mistaken identification. Quite apart from Greville's frequent inaccuracies in putting down first impressions (often acknowledged and put right later), there is a strong presumption in this case that he was confusing F. R. Bonham with Henry Bonham, his predecessor at Rye, who in fact had been a considerable figure in the financial and commercial world. His remark, however, testifies to the degree of intimacy already existing between Peel and Bonham by this date.

From that point onward Bonham's career begins to take on the clear outline

[1] 40, 399 fo. 22.

that marked it for the next quarter of a century. His bent towards party management displayed itself immediately. In the spring of 1831 he was assisting Holmes and Planta, the two opposition whips, in the House of Commons. Not only was he a foundation member of the Carlton but his name was noted by Raikes as one of a select list of men who were present at a 'House dinner of Tories at the Carlton Club' in November 1832. That dinner was held on the eve of the general election, the first under the Reform Act, and by the time it took place Bonham was installed in the position he was to hold for the next fourteen years. Dawson, writing to his brother-in-law Peel in the previous month, referred to the election reports being sent in to Bonham from all quarters; and what survives of Bonham's own correspondence from this time shows him deeply involved in the general management of the election. The earliest letter in the Bonham MSS is dated October 1832 and it is probably not accidental that the series starts at this point. Absence of earlier correspondence does not of course prove that his activities as election manager began then; but other circumstances bear out the suggestion. In contrast to the assistance given by Bonham in Peel's unsuccessful candidacy for the Oxford Chancellorship in 1834, for example, there is no record of his having played any part in the much lengthier discussions that accompanied Peel's resignation, candidature and defeat at Oxford in 1829.

In 1834, when Peel formed his short-lived ministry, he appointed Bonham to the office of Storekeeper to the Ordnance, a post which carried with it a salary of £1,200 per annum. 'I never could have accepted office', added the prime minister in making the offer, 'without seeking your aid and offering you some appointment or other which might give me the frequent opportunity of communicating with you.' Bonham now for the second time secured election to parliament. With a Whig ministry in power he had been defeated at Rye in 1831 and appears to have made no effort to return to the Commons in 1832. But with Peel once more in office, he was selected to put up as the colleague of J. C. Herries at Harwich, a borough where government influence counted for much. He sat therefore in the 1835–7 parliament and throughout that time acted as assistant Conservative whip. At the next general election, though assisted by a grant from the party chest, he again lost his seat. Occupied as he was with the electioneering interests of the party, he had little time to devote to the position in his own constituency. Moreover, Bonham was temperamentally unsuited for the platform; he avoided publicity, was ill at ease on the hustings, and silent in the House of Commons. 'Bonham left yesterday for Harwich', wrote Granville Somerset to Peel on 18 July 1837, 'and Herries thinks they will carry both seats if B [MS torn] does not get into a Fright; which he has promised me not to do'. The veteran Herries, who had held his seat at Harwich since 1823, contrived to maintain himself but could not rescue his colleague. However, Hardinge reported that 'poor Bonham bears his defeat with great philosophy.'

How well Bonham acquitted himself as whip is not easy to determine. Perhaps none of the Conservative whips in the 1835–7 parliament covered themselves with glory. They were faced at the outset with the difficult and discouraging task of protecting a ministry which suffered a string of defeats at the hands of the majority opposition coalition; and Sir George Clerk, the chief whip, though a good man of business, lacked the cordiality of his successor Sir Thomas Fremantle. Greville, whose prejudice against Bonham only slowly subsided, remained an unsparing critic. At the time of the general election of 1835 he wrote that 'the Committee [sc. of the Conservative party] has been bad and negligent; then they did a very foolish thing in ousting Pattison from Harwich to make room for that offensive lump of uselessness Bonham'. At the next general election in 1837 he commented approvingly that 'the Tories have made one good exchange in the article of whippers-in for they have got Planta and Holmes instead of Bonham and Ross'. That there had been no question of 'ousting' Pattison from Harwich in 1835 and that Planta and Holmes did not succeed as whips in 1837 does not add to his credibility. There is other and possibly more trustworthy evidence of Bonham's standing in the House of Commons at this date. In the course of other matters of correspondence Gladstone moved to add a line of condolence on Bonham's defeat. 'I do not know how you personally are affected by your exclusion from Parliament, perhaps not much; but I for one deeply and sincerely regret no longer to have the chance of sitting in the House by one whose cordiality as well public and private was especially valuable where everything tends to coldness and heartlessness – and I am certain that this feeling is common to us all'. The compliment rings both youthful and sincere. Bonham perhaps was touched by it for he replied more openly on the subject of his defeat than he appears to have done to other political colleagues.

> I will not deny [he wrote back] that in spite of my dislike to late hours, and my inability to take that active part in public business to which my inclination would have urged me, I should have been very glad to have sat in the present Parl^t. But if my disappointment had been infinitely greater, the numberless expressions of kindness and goodwill I have received from much valued friends, and from none more than yourself, would go very far to reconcile me to it.[1]

As it was, it proved to be the end of his parliamentary life. Nevertheless it was not the end either of his party activities or of his official career. Indeed Bonham may well have discovered advantages in severing a connection with the Commons which scarcely assisted, and in some respects impeded, his primary political functions. In any case he did not try to return at the general election of 1841 when circumstances were more favourable to Conservative candidates than at any time since 1830. It was, therefore, an illuminating tribute to his position in the party that Peel again appointed him Storekeeper to the Ordnance when forming his second ministry in 1841. The post was not a sinecure and while it lasted the mention of flint-locks, mapping surveys, and hay lent an occasional exotic flavour to Bonham's correspondence with his chief. Indeed it is clear that Bonham took a pride in the efficiency of his department. In December 1841, not many months after he had been installed in office, he regretfully declined an invitation from Peel to spend Christmas at Drayton – 'yet some member of the Board ought always (it was *not* so in Whig times) to be on the spot to provide against Contingencies and I have undertaken this duty till the 3rd of Jany when I go to Stow for that week'. But his duties were not so onerous that he could not devote much of his time to party business.

He did not, however, keep his governmental post for the whole term of Peel's great ministry. In the course of 1844 and 1845 Bonham was three times subjected

---

[1] The correspondence between Gladstone and Bonham, extending from 1835 to 1860, is in 44, 110 fos. 146–323.

to personal attacks in parliament on his position. One of these concerned his party activities; another his private character; the third and fatal occasion his official conduct. The first attack, from Divett, has already been mentioned. It was provoked by an incident in the City of London bye-election in October 1843 when Bonham cancelled a 'pair', which had been arranged between Divett and a Conservative member, on being informed by the local Conservative committee that Divett was not qualified to vote in the election. The information proved to be wrong and in the event Divett duly recorded his vote at the cost of an unwelcome train journey up from Devonshire. Next session the indignant Whig moved for the dismissal of Bonham from his public employment. The motion was ludicrous and nobody would second it but the debate gave Peel the opportunity to pay a handsome tribute to his absent subordinate – 'a gentleman', he said, 'whom he was proud to call his personal friend. . . . He did not believe that a man of higher integrity or a purer sense of honour existed than Mr Bonham'. This incident was not forgotten. A year later, with a studied repetition of Peel's language, Disraeli taunted the prime minister with including in his ministry and publicly professing friendship with a man who had been implicated in a design against the state. 'Yes, one of the intimate friends of the right hon. Gentleman', continued the orator, 'was concerned in Despard's plot and now holds office in the right hon. Baronet's Administration.' Whatever the justice of the charge, it was a piece of ancient history. Despard was tried and executed for high treason in 1803. No person named Bonham was then implicated but Despard had previously been imprisoned without trial for several years on suspicion of treasonable activity and when he was originally arrested in 1798 an associate called Bonham was also detained. This however was not F. R. Bonham, who at that date was only twelve, but his half-brother John who was fifteen years his senior. Armed with these facts Peel was able the following night to refute with ease Disraeli's accusation and secure a complete retraction of the slander. Unlike Divett, of course, Disraeli was concerned with Bonham merely as a means of striking at Peel. But the personal imputation was there and could not be adequately answered by the ostensible victim of the charge since he was not in the House of Commons. Bonham's gratitude to Peel therefore was proportionately great. 'In plain fact,' he wrote to Peel the following day, 'my obligation to you last night was such that it cannot be overstated. I am sure you will have considered my silence this morning almost as expressive of my feelings as any letter could be.'

But a more explosive mine than the ingenious contrivances of Divett and Disraeli was about to be sprung. In June 1845 a petition from the South Eastern Railway was presented to the House of Commons complaining of corrupt partially shown by the Board of Ordnance to a rival company, the London, Chatham and North Kent Railway, in connection with a proposed new line across Woolwich Common. The evidence adduced to support the charge was a letter from a Mr Hignett, solicitor to the board, requesting the North Kent Railway to assign certain shares to Captain Boldero, Clerk of the Ordnance, and mentioning Bonham as another member of the board for whom shares might be sent. On the main charge both Bonham and Boldero were completely exonerated by the select committee of the House set up to examine the case. But in the course of the enquiry a more damaging story was brought forward. In 1836, when a bill for promoting the South-Eastern Railway was being considered by parliament, the company's legal agent, a solicitor named Wray who was also Receiver General of the Metropolitan Police, asked Bonham to use his influence on behalf of the bill. Bonham, at that time in the Commons and also a member of the committee examining the bill, had personal reasons for obliging Wray and did what he could in and out of the House to assist its progress. After it had become law the company, acting through Wray, gave Bonham an option on 100 reserved shares at par. These were shortly afterwards sold at a premium of 3 per cent by Wray and the profits (£300) put to Bonham's account. The truth of this was freely admitted by Bonham in his evidence and the day before the committee's report was made public, he unburdened himself to Peel in a letter which must have caused a degree of pain to both men.

9 July 1845

Pray forgive me if in this last and hurried letter I address you in terms not now becoming my position. The result of the pending investigations before the South-Eastern Committee will prove to demonstration my innocence as to the charge intended to be fixed on me. Of this I can most solemnly assure you, and that till Mr Hignett's letter of the 3rd of Feby. was sent to me last Thursday I had not the most remote suspicion of such a proposition and certainly none such was ever made by my authority, or with my knowledge. So far it may be satisfactory to you to know that my *official* career has been without blemish. But in the course of the investigations it transpired that Three Hundred Pounds was paid by the Directors of the S. Eastern Railway in 1836 for my benefit (tho' I did not actually receive the money which remained in the hands of the Receiver towards liquidating a debt due by me).

I cannot explain as I really do not now understand precisely the circumstances, as my friend who applied to me and to whom I was then under pecuniary obligations merely told me that he had made Three Hundred Pounds for me and probably my head is now too much confused to make me intelligible. However I consider the acts indefensible nor will I go down to the Committee with an useless (to myself) explanation, only tending to inculpate one who has served and assisted me during my severe pecuniary difficulties.

I do not intend to put myself in contact with any of my old friends, and have only to request that without waiting for the Report of the Committee, you will at once appoint my Successor as Storekeeper of the Ordnance. If the best wishes of the stricken and afflicted and he has nothing else left to offer be acceptable they will go to the grave with (I dare not add more)

Yours
F. Bonham

The one point in Bonham's favour was that there had been no previous promise or suggestion before the bill passed that he would be rewarded for his assistance. But the report of the committee published on 10 July reflected severely on his conduct and when some days later the Commons discussed the matter Peel announced that he had accepted Bonham's resignation. The House on the whole was sympathetic. Hume, whose principles scarcely erred on the side of laxity, said of the Wray–Bonham transaction that 'he did not believe that it showed any corruption'. Sir James Graham told the House that 'I have long been acquainted with Mr Bonham and I am proud to call that gentleman my friend. He has committed a very grave error and Mr Bonham never dissembled the extent of that error.' But the tribute that brought most consolation came from Peel. 'With respect to Mr

Bonham', said the prime minister, 'I have long been connected with him by ties of private friendship; and . . . impossible as it is to defend that act, my feelings towards him remain unaltered.' There were some at least in the party who privately thought that Bonham had been singled out for attack. Granville Somerset, who condemned the committee's report on 'my dear old friend Bonham' as 'harsh and unfair' told Peel that 'bitterness against him personally evidently influenced Roebuck and I doubt not others'.

So ended Bonham's official career under circumstances that seemed to disqualify him for ever after from public employment. At the time it seemed a personal disaster; for he could not foresee that the rainy summer when it happened was to wash his party out of power for a generation. Yet the event affected only his position in the government and there was no question of his abandoning his party activities. It was in these years, for example, that he was engaged in the long campaign to find a seat for Gladstone, who had to seek re-election on appointment as Colonial Secretary in December 1845 and was disinclined to seek renomination for Newark from his former patron the strongly protectionist duke of Newcastle. In the 1830s and early 1840s the relationship between the two men had been fairly conventional, Bonham made use of Gladstone's local knowledge to secure information, at first about the electoral state of Scotland (there is a characteristic query in 1839 about the progress of registration in the Orkneys) and later from Cheshire, Flint and Denbighshire. Gladstone, twenty-four years his junior, wrote at first in a polite, deferential style to the man whom he described as 'a centre both in respect of locality and information'. Not until the autumn of 1939 is the 'my dear sir' of the early years dropped in favour of 'my dear Bonham'. The hunt for a safe seat between 1845 and 1847, while it deepened their acquaintanceship, had a certain ironic twist when at the general election of 1847 Gladstone was eventually elected for Oxford University. Eight years earlier Bonham had feared that the publication of Gladstone's book *The State in its Relation with the Church* had damaged his chances of ever securing this blue riband of the electoral world. Though a High Churchman himself, he had been apprehensive of the tendency of the Oxford Tractarian movement to stray beyond the decent pastures of theological debate into the wilder ranges of religious politics. He dutifully obtained a copy of Gladstone's book as soon as it appeared but confessed to Mahon that he found it 'rather tougher reading than a fashionable novel'. What he mostly regretted was that one whom they loved and admired should have mixed himself in the quarrels of dons. Gladstone, on all other accounts marked out as a future university member, had by this 'ill-timed publication' shown a lack of the quality of discretion so highly prized by those who exercised authority in such matters.[1] Nevertheless, in 1847, the indiscretion of 1839 forgotten or forgiven, Bonham's intensive two-year search could at last be closed.

Throughout the year of the great party disruption of 1846 Bonham remained at his post, plying Peel with information on the strength of the protectionists and assuring people that the revolt of Bentinck and the 'Dizzyites' was only a temporary phenomenon. 'Before I left London,' Arbuthnot reported to his son in September 1846, 'I had a visit from Bonham. He takes rather a more sanguine view than I do. He says that everybody is leaving Lord G. Bentinck, and he

[1] Chevening Papers (Bonham to Mahon, 19 Dec. 1838, 10 Jan. 1839).

believes that the great mass of the Conservative Party will re-unite.' Even if this was an accurate account of the conversations, Bonham in private was holding very different language. Writing to Gladstone only a fortnight earlier he was talking of 'the possibility of things becoming worse and the extreme bitterness of a *select* but most active portion of the Protectionists *which extends to many Constituencies* and renders impossible any concert at the Elections between the different Sections of the Opposition.' A few weeks later he told Mahon that having been approached by Croker for material for his article in the *Quarterly*, he was astonished by the ferocity of the subsequent attack on his old friends and for the 'ultra-Bentinckite' spirit of the review. But he accepted the situation resignedly. The country, he opined, cared little for any party; it only wished to be well-governed. The probable explanation of these discrepancies in his utterances was that, quite rightly, he did not trust Arbuthnot's loyalty to Peel and was affecting more optimism than he felt in order not to give any comfort to the protectionists.[1]

It is unlikely that after 1846 he had many illusions about either his own future or that of the party he had served. Already he had a rival in his own familiar haunt. 'Major Beresford,' he reported to Peel in November of that year, 'who has been wonderfully "affable" to Cardwell and others, and perhaps still more to me, assures me that *their party* is in complete organization and certainly if I were to judge from the letters he writes all day at the Carlton his correspondence is most extensive.' A further blow came in December with the issue of the customary letters of attendance by both Stanley and Beresford to their respective Houses. He had not, he confessed to Mahon, expected that Stanley would commit himself so entirely to the protectionist alliance. Nevertheless, he busied himself with the promotion of Peelite candidates at the general election of 1847 and on 2 August refused Peel's invitation to go down to Drayton since 'I hold myself pledged to remain here the whole of this week with reference to the many elections still proceeding. And unfortunately there is not a soul here to answer questions or undertake various business contingent on the progress of the elections.' Only a month earlier he had performed a characteristic service for Gladstone in his Oxford University election. His aid had been invoked by Phillimore, one of Gladstone's London committee, to secure the vote of two wavering clerical brothers, the Rev. C. and the Rev. W. Palmer. The first of these had been presented to his living by the former Conservative Lord Chancellor, Lyndhurst. Bonham accordingly applied to that quarter and received a sprightly and satisfactory reply. 'My dear Bonham, I have, at the hazard of being prosecuted for a breach of the privileges of the Hon[l.] House, written to Mr C. Palmer. I return your letter and Phillimore's.' Cardwell was another Peelite (and future ornament of the Liberal party) whose electoral fortunes were receiving Bonham's attention at this time.

After the 1847 election his party and professional activities slowly withered away. For Peel, and such old friends as Graham, Ashley, Goulburn, Cardwell, Lincoln, and Gladstone, his unfailing store of political gossip and such electoral services as he could still render, were always at their disposal. But the mainspring of his existence had snapped and there was no indication from Peel that it would

---

[1] *Correspondence of Charles Arbuthnot* ed. A. Aspinall (Camden 3rd Series, LXV) p. 241; 44, 110 fo. 187; Chevening Papers (Bonham to Mahon, 8 Oct. 1846).

ever be mended again. In his election manifesto at Tamworth in 1847 the ex-prime minister had spoken of himself as 'without the intention or wish to resume either that authority which belongs, or ought to belong to the possession of office, or that influence which is conferred by the lead and guidance of a great political party aspiring to power'. Bonham, to whom a copy of this address was sent, replied with an unusual touch of irony that 'as the minor characters of the Play cannot make a House without a good Hamlet, and as I believe that Constituencies have at least as keen a relish for "favours expected" as their Representatives, I am not sure that they will be benefited by an intimation which tho' not new to them, will not be particularly agreeable to the Electors whose votes are sought for the Goulburns, Cardwells, etc.' Nevertheless, even without Hamlet, the play went on. Together with other second-line party men – Lincoln, Dalhousie, Cardwell and Young, he assisted in maintaining some kind of cohesion among the faithful hundred and twelve that had voted with Peel on the motion for the repeal of the Corn Laws and in keeping their unwilling leader primed with current political information.

The outcome of the general election brought some gratification in the number of Peelites who had maintained their ground and in the defeat of Protectionists in the boroughs and even some counties. Nevertheless, he viewed the future pessimistically and thought the prospects for a strong government slight. 'Numerically,' he wrote to Mahon in August, 'the government has of course gained a good deal, but the materials are such as I suspect Ld. John will find utterly unmanageable.' His own position in the political world was steadily shrinking. At the start of 1848 he was saying despondently that the only consolation he found, in the hostility he had encountered and the neglect to be expected by one no longer thought useful, was the steadfastness of his personal friends.[1] He was still a regular visitor to Drayton and in a lull between two inundations of fashionable guests there in the autumn of 1848 he wrote to Gladstone that 'I should compromise for a tenth part of our present *agrémens* with a Host who always shines most in his own little circle. He is in the highest health and spirits.'[2] That year Bonham was sounding the ground at Leicester, Liskeard and Leominster (a pleasantly alliterative list of boroughs) on behalf of Peel's second son Frederick, a hunt which ended with his election for the last of these constituencies in 1849. The irretrievable stroke was Peel's death in 1850. Thereafter most of the threads which still bound him to the active political world began to part. His fortunes fluctuated almost exactly with the 'great Conservative party that destroyed everything', its collapse put an end to the effective career of the man who more than any other had contributed to the 'unseen management' which had helped to create it.

That Peel ever really appointed him to anything so formal as a 'political secretaryship' is improbable. But the point is perhaps of no great importance. The functions of his position in the party seem to have developed with use and practice; perhaps they were largely what he made them. It is improbable, too, that he occupied a salaried post maintained out of party funds. His financial difficulties in the 1830s and again in the early 1850s suggest that his services had always

---

[1] Chevening Papers (to Mahon 17 Jan. 1848).
[2] 44, 110 fo. 221.

been unpaid except when the party was in power and could find him some minor government post. What is beyond doubt is his importance in the Conservative organization. His activities clearly had the approval of the party chiefs and from the start possessed something more than a temporary and limited character. In 1832, for example, Holmes was conducting some electoral correspondence of his own but it is perhaps significant that Peel evinced no interest in his doings. Certainly it was again Bonham who played a central part in the 1835 election, though as was usual at election time he was overshadowed by more aristocratic figures on the election committee such as the earl of Rosslyn and Lord Granville Somerset. But at that date there existed no permanent organization (other perhaps than Bonham himself) for the preparation of an election as distinct from the *ad hoc* committee set up to fight it. In May 1835, when advising the formation of a small standing election committee he clearly assumed that he would take a part, and in point of activity the leading part, in such preparations. The probability is therefore that Bonham was already in the position of a permanent electioneering expert within the party organization. To that extent the article in the *Edinburgh Review* which appeared the following autumn may have been substantially true. What Bonham obviously wanted was not any change in his own rôle but the reinforcement provided by a standing committee which should above all concern itself with the next registration of electors. 'One of the most important points for the attention of a committee', he wrote to Peel two days later, 'would be to ascertain precisely the comparative effect of the two registrations in each particular constituency.' Whether in this or in some other way the work was undoubtedly accomplished. In 1836 Bonham was writing optimistically of the state of Conservative preparations and told Peel that with a Conservative ministry in office the party would gain over fifty seats in England alone. At the end of the year, together with Granville Somerset, he made out a list of the places which the Conservatives were likely to win in the event of a dissolution. When the general election came the following year the strength which the party put into the field reflected the work carried out since 1835.

In the next few years the preparations of the party managers were even more intense and they were now powerfully aided by the organizing talents of Sir James Graham. In the autumn of 1840 Bonham was engaged in a 'rather extensive correspondence as to the Registrations, and the ensuing Municipal elections' which gave him grounds for confidence. Before the start of the new session he was able to give a comprehensive and definite answer to a request from Peel for a forecast of the result of a dissolution at the hands of a Whig, or alternatively a Conservative, ministry. The reply was clearly one which would have a direct bearing on Peel's parliamentary tactics, for the Melbourne ministry was now so weak that it rested virtually with Peel to decide the time and manner of its exit. Bonham's conclusion, reached after four pages of evidence, was that from the party viewpoint an early dissolution would be welcome and that it would make no difference what ministry actually dissolved. 'So entirely too are we prepared' he wrote, '(some elections will always regulate themselves at the last moment) that I should relatively to their preparation be glad Parl^{t.} was dissolved next week.' He added that though his calculations of actual numbers had been worked with every care, they were so favourable that he would like them checked by Granville Somerset and Graham, who were entirely *au fait* with the subject, with such aid as

Fremantle and Clerk might afford. Graham, who was kept informed by Bonham of this correspondence, warmly approved the suggestion and arranged to come down to London early in January 1841 to confer with the other party managers so that Peel could be put in possession of the most full and accurate information before parliament met. 'Thanks to you', he wrote to Bonham, 'and your indefatigable industry, no Party out of office ever before possessed such sources of intelligence and such means for active war.' When the general election came six months later the Conservative party machine functioned with the ease and effectiveness born of long preparation. Nearly 500 Conservative candidates took the field and Bonham was so deep in work that he even had to delegate some of his correspondence with Peel to other hands. 'Thirty-two letters this morning', he reported triumphantly on 23 June, 'and not one positively bad.' The result spoke for itself. Less than ten years after the Reform Act, that had seemed to put the Tories out for a generation, Peel led a party with a solid majority in the commons. Even Arbuthnot, who had no love for Bonham, was moved to write that 'you have laboured well and satisfactorily; & you ought to be proud'.

In the great triumph of '41, as at other general elections, Bonham's work did not merely consist in invigilating over registrations and preparing his annual 'book of knowledge' as Graham termed it, to guide the parliamentary tactics of his leader. A major part of his duties was to find seats for aspiring candidates and candidates for vacant seats and his correspondence amply demonstrates the cardinal position in the party organization which he had attained since 1832. Candidates in search of a safe seat; constituencies in search of an impressive candidate; provincial solicitors anxious to promote a lucrative contest; local Conservative associations with precise ideas on the kind of representative they wanted and no ideas on how to find him; able but indigent politicians looking for a cheap return; rich men prepared to spend freely in return for a seat in the House; these and more passed in a constant procession through the 'political secretary's' correspondence. Moreover Bonham's desk at the Carlton was not simply a clearing house for the better despatch of Conservative business; it was also the means for a measure of control. There was no lack of potential candidates, he told Peel in 1840, but 'out of possible changes might arise selfish discontents almost as dangerous as political crotchets and therefore with reference to both it requires some discrimination to select proper Candidates for rather permanent seats'. Hence Bonham's official recommendation of a candidate to a constituency became a badge of orthodoxy. In 1841, for example, when warning Bonham against putting up a certain Urquhart, 'a very ticklish and dangerous Personage', for an English constituency, Graham added that 'it would not do to have you his God-Father at any popular Election. If County or Leicester fancy him without any pledge from you, let them have him unbaptized; and he will be a degree better than a Whig-Radical; but I would say, avoid recommending him.' Considerations of prestige also entered into the question. Bonham was unwilling to start candidates in a hopeless contest because of the capital which the opposition might make of it. Thus in 1839 he told Peel that it would be 'utter insanity *on our part* to fight Birmingham'; if the local Conservatives wanted to put up a man, they could have all the consequent credit for victory or defeat.

There were of course borderline cases such as that of John Walter in the Nottingham bye-election of April 1841. Some Conservatives were disposed to look askance at the erratic figure of the proprietor of *The Times*; but Bonham, with whom Walter breakfasted and collected letters of recommendation before catching the train to the constituency, assured Peel that though 'abstractedly' the party might have a better MP, there could not be a better candidate for that place and the fact that he was fighting under the party banner might correct the deviousness of *The Times*. Earlier still an even more volatile figure had received Bonham's *imprimatur*. When Disraeli went down to Taunton in 1835 to contest (unsuccessfully) a bye-election against Labouchere, he was introduced to the Taunton Conservatives by Bonham in a letter in which he was referred to as 'a gentleman for whom all the Conservative Party were most anxious to obtain a seat in the House of Commons'.

This was a politic but scarcely truthful description; in fact Disraeli was not a candidate who had endeared himself to the party managers and he owed his official nomination to the influential backing of Lyndhurst. But the interest of the case is in the light it throws on the interlocking functions of the local party organization, which on the basis of the known registration figures could guarantee support in the constituency, and the party's London headquarters, a central office in all but name, which could produce on demand a candidate stamped with the hallmark of party approval.

Much of this electioneering activity was deliberately shrouded from general knowledge. Sometimes financial transactions were involved which it was particularly important to keep secret; partly because of the need to conceal any evidence that might lead to an appeal on grounds of bribery against an election return; and partly because party funds were limited and to draw attention to the few cases where money was provided by the party managers would be to invite a flow of applications for similar assistance which would necessarily be disappointed. In addition there were the tactical considerations which made much of the contemporary electioneering resemble an operation of war. So far from being an advantage it was frequently a handicap for a candidate to be first in the field. In some of the more corrupt constituencies a sudden attack at the eleventh hour with unexpected resources of money and influence could often carry the position by *coup de main* and even in less venal circumstances there seemed some advantage in concealing party intentions until the last minute. Knowledge of these more delicate election preparations was confined accordingly to Bonham himself and, apart from Peel, the three or four party officials with whom he acted in confidence such as Granville Somerset, Fremantle, and after 1837, Graham. Even therefore in relation to his own party, and in his own familiar haunt at the Carlton, Bonham was surrounded with something of the atmosphere of secrecy and mystery which Disraeli picturesquely described. How far this secrecy was maintained may be judged from an incident that occurred over the Newark bye-election of 1840 when a correspondent complained to Peel of the apparent indifference shown by the Carlton Club to the expressed desire of the local Conservatives to put up a candidate. Bonham, to whom the substance at any rate of this criticism was passed by Peel, good-humouredly defended himself. 'As I am somewhat in disgrace among some of our Carlton friends about an appearance of mystery', he wrote the following day,

let me observe in excuse that in a Club of 1100 persons, confidence if too widely diffused ceased to be confidence and one might as well send our intentions to the Treasury. I mention this with reference to Newark for which place Thesiger started last night and will be ushered into the Town with a procession this morning. I have no fear whatever of the result.

General elections, together with the crop of election petitions to which they gave rise, formed the recurrent crises of Bonham's work. But even in more peaceful times his interests were spread wide and his activities unending. To the primary task of watching over constituencies and candidates, anticipating and preparing for contests, was added a host of miscellaneous duties, sought and unsought. In November 1837 Ellenborough gave warning that a big Wiltshire estate had come on the market which might in whiggish and hostile hands turn the scale in that district, and suggested to Bonham that he should try to find a purchaser for it with the right political views.

Croker wrote to him in 1837 to say that if he had any interest with *The Times* or any other newspaper he should discuss with them the absurdity of the 4*d.* post scheme in areas round London and the other big towns which bore so hardly on districts outside the metropolitan area. When Peel appointed Lord Castlereagh as lord lieutenant of county Down, the son of the rival county magnate wrote indignantly to Bonham to ask for his opinion 'candidly, as a friend', whether it was not a deliberate slight on his father, the earl of Roden, since if so he should certainly resign from the government. It was Bonham from whom Graham enquired in 1840 whether he and Stanley should join the Carlton, and Lord Ashley in 1842 whether he should leave it.

Ashley indeed tried to use Bonham as a channel through which he could influence Peel on ecclesiastical matters, a rôle which Bonham wisely refused. He knew his leader better than his zealous correspondent and was not sympathetic to the latter's evangelical views. Ashley, a little piqued by his refusal, replied that he had considered Bonham 'a very fitting channel of communication' with Peel. 'As for myself I cannot undertake to ask any favour either with or without a hope of success; nor will I even state the case as one of ecclesiastical propriety, lest I should be misinterpreted, or by coming forward in the matter, injure the cause that I mean to serve.' Like most men of his generation Bonham did not wear his heart on his sleeve, especially in matters of religion; but he was not without strong sentiments. In the celebrated dispute over the chair of poetry at Oxford in 1841 he was an active supporter of the Puseyite candidate, Isaac Williams; and Ashley rallied him gently on this incursion into a species of election that did not normally come within his compass. Bonham seems to have reacted rather sharply to the insinuation and Ashley hastened to assure him that if his principles led him to support Mr Williams, he had as much right to support him as Ashley had to oppose him. 'I did not make the remark in any spirit of blaming you; tho' I deeply regret that a person whom I really respect so much as I do you, should differ from me on this most important point.' But whatever side Bonham favoured in the Tractarian controversy, he did not allow it to affect his political judgement. There is no trace of sectarian bias in the advice he gave to Peel a month later on the disposal of the vacant bishopric of Chichester and in his review of candidates Dr Gilbert, the anti-Puseyite Principal of Brasenose College, who was eventually appointed, was recommended as the leading personality within the university.

Nor, despite his Puseyite leanings, were his friendly relations with Ashley ever seriously affected and he continued from time to time to be the recipient of sorrowful complaints of the government's religious policy. Over the Dissenters Chapels bill in 1844 he was warned by Ashley that a disease had been introduced that would outlive Peel's administration and greatly embitter it. 'Say what they will, they have passed a law against the will of the Country to give to Socinians the funds assigned to the spiritual teaching of the Believers in the Holy Trinity – *they will pay the penalty of this Sin.*' The following year he received a pained and expostulating letter from the same source on Peel's appointment of the eminent geologist, Dr Buckland, to the Deanery of Westminster. 'Never have I heard, from all parties, such deep condemnation. Can he be called a clergyman except that he is in orders? is his life, his language, his learning, that of a Minister of the Church?' The letter ended, 'I never see you, so I write to you, tho' I hardly know why I bore you.'[1]

A contrast to the tortured conscience of Ashley was provided by Bonham's friendship with Viscount Mahon, later fifth Earl Stanhope and Peel's literary executor. Their intimacy seems to have started in the late 1830s when he was extracting from Mahon (as he used to do from many leading party members regardless of rank) a regular flow of electoral information on the part of England with which he was familiar: in this case Kent (where the family seat of the Stanhopes was located) and the Cinque Ports rather than the proprietary borough of Hertford which Mahon represented from 1835 to 1852 as the nominee of Lord Salisbury. But it was more than a political acquaintanceship. Mahon frequently invited Bonham to visit Chevening or dine with him in London, took him out driving, and sent him presents of game and fish. He sympathized with him over the Divett affair, even writing him a quick note from the House of Commons in February 1844 to tell him of Peel's warm defence. He asked Bonham's advice over a proposed mission to Madrid in 1843 and when in 1845, after mutterings of rebellion, Mahon eventually made his peace with Peel over the repeal of the Corn Laws, it was to Bonham he showed his letter before sending it to the prime minister. The fall of the ministry, in which Mahon served as secretary of the India Board, made no difference to their relationship, and they continued to exchange confidential gossip from time to time over events and personalities in the political world.

It was this ability to engage the confidence as well as the confidences of many different kinds of men that gave Bonham his success. Clearly he was in a central and ominscient position, deep in the inner Conservative counsels, and on an intimate footing with the grandees of the party. But he was also a frequent visitor at the great Tory country houses, one of the most familiar figures at the Carlton, and accessible to every member. His energy, enthusiasm and good humour, endeared him to a wide and varied range of acquaintances and he could always be called upon for such little services as getting an order to view Woolwich for Ashley's son and two nephews, or a seat in an upper window at the Carlton for Graham's two little girls to see the queen drive in state to the city. He had in fact the qualities of warmth, openness and easy friendliness that his leader signally lacked and even perhaps went some way towards supplying those deficiencies to

[1]   40,617 fos. 159, 206.

the party at large. Probably it was his sociability rather than his influence that gave him the *entrée* to circles such as that of the duke of Buckingham which were not conspicuous for loyalty to Peel. It was equally characteristic of the man that he was to be found at 'a large dinner-party of *quasi*-Protectionists' at the Kentish home of Lord Wynford in August 1846, and that he should duly report the tone of the conversation at table to his party leader. His annual cure at Brighton in September when he submitted to a regimen of sea-bathing and 'large potations of Marienbad water' was necessitated as much perhaps by the pleasures of the table as by close confinement to the clubrooms of the Carlton or his desk at the Ordnance Office. 'You must submit to discipline and avoid the temptations of Grant's Kitchen and Cellar,' wrote Graham on one occasion when under the plea of being unwell Bonham had declined an invitation to dine *en famille* and sample some of Graham's champagne. To the Wharncliffes, who gave nicknames to almost everybody within range of their family circle, he was 'mon ami' Bonham. 'Here we are dearest Missy & very *comfortable*,' wrote Lady Wharncliffe to her daughter from Strathfieldsaye in January 1839, 'I was in no small degree of anxiety before I arrived yesterday as to who I should meet . . . The only men are Lord Bathurst, 'mon ami' *Bonham*, & *Billy Holmes* – just such individuals as I should have *chosen*, since it produces quantities of political talk with the Duke and the Governor [Lord Wharncliffe].'[1] Not surprisingly therefore it was Bonahm again in more difficult days who at one time was urged by Graham to make Peel aware of the discontent prevalent in the party and at another to use his exceptional personal contacts whereby he was 'enabled to give the tone of feeling at the Carlton', to justify the conduct of the leaders and check insubordination.

In the matter of conveying information to Peel little urging was needed. One of the interesting aspects of his position was his intimate relation with his leader. By virtue of his duties Bonham was necessarily brought into constant communication with Peel; but beyond that there was a personal friendship which produced a marked confidence and frankness on both sides. Much of Bonham's work of course it was proper that Peel should not know; and in any case the 'management' that was the breath of life to Bonham was repugnant to his chief 'I am always unwilling to trouble you and the more so on Election matters to which I know you are not very much given', he wrote apologetically to Peel in 1839. And again in 1846, 'tho' I know your distaste to such matters', he sent Peel correspondence discussing the 'political state of Scotland.'

But though only major events and decisions in the field of electoral management were referred to Peel, in a more general way Bonham acted as his chief intelligence agent on all matters affecting the political scene. If Peel was guilty, as he has been accused, of being isolated from his followers, it was an isolation springing from personal habits and not from lack of knowledge. There was scarcely a ripple of opinion within the party which was not reported to him by his watchdog at the Carlton. The advantages of this constant flow of information were not lost on Peel. 'Your encouragement', wrote Bonham in 1841, 'entails the trouble to you of receiving my opinions *quantum valeant* without at all seeking to elicit yours.' In fact it is clear that Bonham was under express orders from Peel to keep him permanently informed of what was passing in the political world. 'Tho'

---

[1] *The First Lady Wharncliffe and Her Family* ed. C. Grosvenor & Lord Stuart (1927), II, 295.

there is absolutely no news which would justify my troubling you', he wrote to Peel in the summer recess of 1841, 'yet I think myself acting in the spirit of your instructions in doing so.' But his services to Peel were not confined to this 'chattering', as he himself once described it, on political topics. On a variety of subjects he was called in for active consultation especially where his wide know-ledge of local conditions and the subtle network of personal relationships within the party were directly relevant. This was particularly marked after the seals of office and power passed into Peel's hands in 1841. Bonham's counsel ranged over an extensive field, the selection of back-benchers for the reply to the royal speech at the beginning of session; the best way to deal with ambitious newspaper proprietors; the effect on university politics of the elevation to the bench of bishops of the head of an Oxford college; and the appointment of party whips. His peculiar position, in the party but outside the House of Commons, gave him a detached viewpoint which was not perhaps without its advantages. He once told Peel that he was in the position of the looker-on who sees and knows more of the game than the players. More than any other individual he acted as Peel's confiden-tial adviser in the delicate task of selecting a ministry when power was at last secured. At that crucial point in Peel's career, the summer of 1841, Bonham went down to Drayton to discuss at length with his leader the formation of the prospective Conservative government, and there is still preserved among the Peel papers a draft list in Bonham's writing, almost certainly dating from this time, of all the major and minor ministerial appointments together with the likely or possible candidates' names. 'I am very glad that you are going to Drayton', wrote Graham from his holiday retreat at Cowes on 2 August 1841, 'the more Peel is prepared with the whole detail of the scheme of his government, the better'. Inevitably, therefore, even Graham himself, not to speak of other knowledgeable but lesser politicians, made Bonham the recipient of their thoughts, self-inter-ested and otherwise, on the proper disposal of vacant offices.

A man in the position held by Bonham easily becomes a target for rancour and disappointment; yet he appears to have enjoyed an extraordinary degree of popularity. The exceptions are few and noteworthy. The case of Greville has already been recorded; though even his epithets grew milder after 1835. Disraeli perhaps was another enemy though possibly far less so than half-hinted by Monypenny. From 1841 onwards, of course, there was almost standing distrust and enmity between Disraeli and the party managers. Smythe is reputed in later years to have attributed Disraeli's exclusion from Peel's ministry to the interven-tion of 'the political parasites by whom it was the weakness of the great Minister to be surrounded' and in quoting this passage Monypenny suggests that the impli-cation is that Peel was dissuaded from giving office to Disraeli by 'the Crokers and Bonhams, and men of that type and standing'.

In fact there is no evidence at all that Peel ever contemplated taking Disraeli into the government; nor was there any valid reason why he should do so. The story deriving from Lord Houghton which Monypenny preferred, that it was Stanley who vetoed Disraeli's appointment, rests on an equally slender founda-tion. As between the two legends there is nothing to choose. Nevertheless there is clear evidence that Disraeli was distrusted by Bonham at the very time when Peel was forming his ministry in 1841. The immediate cause for this was the part played by Disraeli in the Speakership crisis of 1841. On the morrow of their victory in the general election the Conservatives were deeply divided on the question of challenging Shaw Lefevre's re-election as Speaker in the new parliament. Peel and the bulk of the party leaders and managers were against such a partisan demonstration; but a small though powerful 'country party' element including Sir John Tyrrell of Essex, Sir Richard Vyvyan of Cornwall, the two Neelds from Wiltshire, Blackstone of Wallingford, the Lowther set, and some Irish members, with the duke of Buckingham hovering uneasily on the outskirts of the movement, made a determined effort to whip up support for Lefevre's replacement. Party unity was eventually maintained after anxious consultations between the whips and their leader; but in summing up the affair in August Bonham warned Peel that though there were some credit items to be noted, '*per contra* you have to encounter a very *sly* but active hostility on the part of Sir R. Vyvyan and the most extraordinary and bitter abuse less at the Carlton than elsewhere (I hear) on the part of Disraeli who is the *Pittacus* of the *Times* and of whose lucubrations you will doubtless hear more.' Pittacus was the pseudonym adopted by the writer of a bitter anonymous letter to *The Times* arguing the case for opposing Lefevre. It created a considerable stir, and on Disraeli's own confession was universally ascribed to him – in the Conservative party at any rate. On returning to London from Buckinghamshire in the middle of August Disraeli met Bonham who informed him, as Disraeli described it to Peel, 'with that morose jocularity which he sometimes affects, that the party was flourishing notwithstanding my attempts to "stir up dissension on the Speakership" '. Disraeli immediately wrote to Peel to deny the authorship of 'a paper which I remember as one absolutely deficient in the commonest rules of composition'.[1]

On the *Pittacus* issue the verdict must be one of non-proven as between Disraeli and Bonham. The former's denial is of little value as evidence since Disraeli was on other occasions prepared to lie in defence of his own interests. If he had written the letter every prudential motive would have counselled secrecy at the time he was challenged by Bonham. For by the middle of August the Speakership issue was dead but the composition of the new Conservative ministry still remained to be settled. On the other hand Bonham had been recently in Buckinghamshire, Disraeli's own county, and had stayed with the duke of Buckingham who was Disraeli's friend. His categoric statement that Disraeli was *Pittacus* may have been wrong but it is difficult to accept that there was nothing in his report of Disraeli's 'extraordinary and bitter abuse'. The general ascription to Disraeli of the *Pittacus* letter is itself a measure of the views which the party in general attributed to him. Moreover Bonham's suspicions of Disraeli were almost certainly shared by all the other party officials. Granville Somerset had agreed with him about the authorship of the *Pittacus* letter. Fremantle, the chief whip, in discussing with Clerk the hostility to the government shown by *The Times* in the summer of 1843, added 'I suspect that yesterday's article against the *Quarterly Review* comes from the pen of Disraeli.'[2]

It was Fremantle again who suggested to Peel the omission of Disraeli and others of the malcontent Young England group from the list of those members of the House of Commons to whom the usual circular was sent at the opening of the

[1] 40, 486 fos. 7–8.
[2] Clerk Papers, 12 Sept. [1842].

1844 session. There is no need therefore to assume any special animosity on Disraeli's part against Bonham. His attack on the latter with the Despard allega- tion was entirely on the spur of the moment and handsomely apologized for the next evening. He told the House, probably with truth, that the reference had been perfectly unpremeditated but that 'a taunting cheer from the right hon. Baronet called my recollection to the circumstance, which I admit I thought might not be agreeable to him'. In the gallery of satiric political sketches drawn by Disraeli in *Coningsby* (1844), Bonham did not figure; or if he did he was not easily recog- nized. Moreover it should be remembered that Disraeli's tribute in *Lord George Bentinck*, while chiefly designed to detract from Peel's achievement, appeared during Bonham's lifetime.

Severe criticism of a rather different order once came from Arbuthnot in a letter to Peel dated 16 October 1839.

> What you say of Bonham I have long known to be perfectly true [he wrote]. He is so zealous & so good humoured that one listens to all he says with pleasure; but until confirmed by more cautious and better judging Persons, I aways keep my mind in suspence. He is what the French call a *Gobe Mouche*. He swallows readily whatever he wishes to be true. He wd. lead anyone into error who was not well aware of his Propensities. In this way he does a gt. deal of Mischief. He leads astray Men who ought to know better & to be on their guard against him. I saw a letter a little while ago from Ld Granville Somerset who had been stuffed by Bonham. Ld G. is a very right thinking Person; but he wrote that the Bank was to stop payment, to issue one Pound notes, & that Parlt. was to be called together forthwith. All this came from Bonham. I know also that he has been instilling his notions into Sir J. Graham. I know that Sir James pressed Ld. Burghersh (who is in the North) not to delay his visit to him as he was sure, by what he heard from London, that Parlt. wd. meet very soon. But habit is everything. Bonham's habit is to devour like a Ravenous Wolf all that everybody says to him. He then disgorges it – and don't take the trouble to judge whether what he has heard is true or false.[1]

What Peel said to provoke this tirade is not on record; but apart from the vagueness and inconsistency of the charges, there is a harsh note about them which may serve as a reminder that this was an old man speaking of a younger craftsman. Arbuthnot, who was now seventy-two, had served Lord Liverpool twenty years earlier in much the same capacity as Bonham was serving Peel. Some basis for the criticism no doubt did exist, for by nature Bonham was buoyant and optimistic. But at no time does his optimism seem to have led him seriously to misjudge the political situation. All the evidence is that he was well equipped by habits and temperament for the position he filled in the party. He could keep a secret; he was a good judge of men; and to take but one example of his professional work, his advice to Peel over his possible candidature for the Oxford chancell- orship in 1834 was a model of clearness and accuracy.

Moreover there can be no doubt that he was entirely trusted by the men for whom he worked. A small but illuminating instance of this occurred in 1837 over Peel's challenge to Captain Townshend in a quarrel arising from the election at Tamworth in that year. On the challenger's side the secret was confined to Hardinge (who conducted the negotiations which eventually produced an apology from the other party), the duke of Wellington and Bonham. The last-

[1] 40, 341 fos. 115–16.

named came into the affair by chance and his own native sagacity. 'Bonham,' explained Hardinge in a letter to Peel, 'by the accident of the servant giving me Capt. T's address in his presence immediately guessed the object of my Mission. He sees Members of yr. family in Town, & I found the safest course, knowing his honourable nature, was to bind him down to secrecy, rather than leave him at liberty to use his suspicions, which no contradiction which I in truth could make would have silenced.' But once in the secret Bonham played a part almost as important as that of Hardinge, verifying the reports of Townshend's speech which had given rise to the challenge, discovering his movements, and giving practical and moderating advice. For greater security Peel directed that the letters between himself and Hardinge should pass through Bonham; and at the height of the crisis it was Bonham who was entrusted with the delicate task of smuggling out of Peel's great library at Whitehall Gardens the case of duelling pistols that Peel had been afraid to take openly with him when he left London. It was typical too of his inexhaustible usefulness that Townshend's second, Alston, who told Hardinge that if their principals had gone out, he would not have allowed Townshend to fire, was another of Bonham's friends.[1]

Long after the events and personalities of the age of Peel had become a distant memory Lord John Manners wrote a description of Bonham which despite its brevity has the particular interest attaching to the impression of a contemporary who as a member of the Young England coterie had perhaps no special reason for thinking well of him. In response to a friend's enquiry in 1905, at a time when he must have been almost the last survivor of that political generation, the duke of Rutland as he than was set down in a few lines his sixty-year-old recollection of the forgotten Conservative party agent of the '40s.

> He was in 1841 an elderly man, dressed in a long brown coat and carrying a large strapped book, full of electioneering facts, figures, and calculations. He was not in Parliament but was Sir Robert Peel's trusted agent in matters relating to elections and party management; whether he held some subordinate post in one of the departments I forget. . . . For the rest my recollection of Mr Bonham is distinctly favourable – rough, faithful, honest, indefatigable, the depositary of a thousand secrets and the betrayer of none.[2]

But besides this, perhaps the only posthumous verdict on Bonham written from personal knowledge, there remains the general criterion. He was Peel's choice for a position of great trust; and Peel had little toleration for incompetent subordinates. The charge that this was an example of a great man's weakness for a mean creature, as Monypenny seems to imply, will not stand up to scrutiny. A man who could evoke tributes to his character from such different personalities as Graham the reformer and administrator, Leader the radical and art connoisseur, Granville Somerset the politician and sportsman, and Hardinge the soldier, to whom Ashley the evangelical applied for advice as 'a good hearted, honourable man', was not the Taper or Tadpole of contemporary political society. It is in any case inconceivable that a man of that stamp would have been admitted as an intimate friend of the Peel family. It was this relationship which made the unexpected death of Peel in 1850 so personal a blow. 'I can't forbear writing you', said Robert

[1] Cardwell Papers (PRO GD 48/53) Hardinge–Bonham letters fos. 103–10; 40, 314 fos. 189–92.
[2] See my *Politics in the Age of Peel*, p. 463.

Lamond, the leader of the Glasgow Conservatives, on receipt of the news, 'to you the loss will be dreadful'. Another friend, Lord Ashley, wrote in a similar strain – 'I know that you will be deeply afflicted'. Bonham was one of the small group of 'oldest and much attached friends' who were invited to the dead statesman's funeral. As late as 1855 the third Sir Robert Peel wrote personally to him 'as such an attached friend of my family for so many years' to tell of his engagement to Lady Emily Hay; and, not unfittingly, the last item in the collection of his correspondence is an invitation to attend the funeral of Lady Peel in 1859.

In the small circle of his intimate friends Peel was apt to show a warmth and affectionateness beyond the ordinary. Bonham was undoubtedly a member of that circle and it is equally certain that he felt for his leader a reciprocal devotion. Moreover beneath the outward joviality of his nature his feelings were simple, direct and partisan; he could not forget or forgive the disruptionists of 1846 and had no sympathy for those that did. In the autumn of 1848, three days after the sudden death of Lord George Bentinck, Gladstone wrote to Bonham to enquire into the chances of his brother John obtaining the seat at Lynn that had thus been made vacant. He thought fit to include in his letter a pious and almost gushing elegy on the dead protectionist leader which ended 'no thoughts, I trust, but those of peace and goodwill follow him to his melancholy grave'. The passage might have struck many people as sanctimonious. Written to Bonham, who had devoted his best years to building up the party destroyed by Bentinck and Disraeli in 1846, and who was a close personal friend of the man on whom they had poured unmeasured abuse, it was also lacking in tact. Replying fittingly enough from Drayton, where he was the guest of the late prime minister, Bonham made an honest and blunt retort.

> With reference [he wrote] to the late event I feel as in any other case of an individual suddenly cut off in the prime of life, with however the mitigating consideration that he has left neither wife or child to feel the privation. As I consider his public life to have been very mischievous it would be for *me* worse than affectation to allow any consideration of that sort to enhance his loss, and I regard myself as ministering more than enough to the spurious sensibility of the day in refraining from any comment on the idle and absurd praise that has been heaped on his memory.[1]

Nevertheless, he set to work to find out what the position was at Lynn and promised, if there was a chance, to do what he could for John Gladstone.

Peel's death was the second great epoch in Bonham's life. Yet even after that event he occasionally breathed the air of politics again. With Graham he maintained a desultory correspondence chiefly on parliamentary matters; and in 1852 his services were sought almost in the old style by Gladstone. The occasion was the general election of that year. On 21 July *The Times* published a list of the new House of Commons, as far as was then known, which divided MPs into liberals, ministerialists, and liberal-conservatives. To the last category the newspaper assigned sixty-three members; but in its leading article commented that 'Peelites can exist no more as a political party. In one sense we are all Peelites . . . but a political party cannot be held together upon sympathies and regrets.' On the same day that *The Time*'s analysis was published, Glastone wrote to Bonham asking for

---

[1] 44, 110 fos. 221–2.

his opinion. The simple tripartite formula of Printing House Square had not satisfied his subtle, disquisitive intellect. There ensued a long, detailed and meticulous discussion between the two (into which Sir John Young, Peel's former chief whip, was also brought), on the composition of the new House of Commons and its various shades of opinion. The hard core of loyal Peelites Bonham eventually put at twenty-three. Over the larger and more amorphous body of liberal-conservatives agreement was harder to come by. As Bonham sensibly observed at one point, 'the course of some at least of these must be regulated by the immediate questions submitted to them.' Where so few firm categories existed and so much depended on future developments, refined political arithmetic was of limited value. Gladstone concluded in the end that the only thing they could do was to keep together a party, however limited in numbers, for as long as possible in order to exercise some influence on events.

As the opening of the new session drew near there was a final discussion on the wisdom of calling a Peelite party meeting before parliament assembled. Bonham advised against such a step on the familiar grounds that a general invitation would meet with many refusals and a limited one with the grumbles of those omitted. It was known that Lord John Russell was going to summon a meeting of the official opposition and it seemed to Bonham in those circumstances that it would be imprudent to attempt a formal muster of Peelites – 'the more so as we have not an equally distinct and specified band of friends'.[1]

By the date of this correspondence Bonham had fallen on hard times. After 1850 the ill-health which had made an occasional appearance in earlier days was gaining on him and the decay of his political activities was accompanied by the sharper sting of poverty. At no time after 1830 were his affairs marked by affluence and it was now many years since he had drawn any official salary. On the formation of the Aberdeen coalition in 1852 the duke of Newcastle, who as Lord Lincoln had in the past been a frequent colleague of Bonham on party committees, approached him to enquire whether he could be of any service. But Bonham, too conscious of age and infirmity, felt unable to press any claims and nothing was done. In July 1853, however, he sent a pathetic letter to Sir James Graham asking for assistance.

> My dear Sir James, I will not waste your time with any apology for thus troubling you or indeed with any long story. I put myself into your hands and shall be guided by your advice and take the hint accordingly. My affairs are in a word such that without being at all in debt I am driven by duty to the one who has shared (not merely to myself for my wants are small) all my sorrows and sacrifices to the humiliation of stating them to you in confidence.
>
> My object is to solicit your influence with Ld. Aberdeen for any moderate permanent appointment to which he might feel himself disposed to appoint me. Broken in health, strength, and spirits, withdrawn altogether from general society as inclination and necessity have compelled, my aspirations are of a very limited kind. My suburban residence expires at Christmas next and it matters little to my sister or myself in what part of the Empire our destiny may be fixed hereafter, I fear not in London.
>
> If you think that you could serve me with Ld. Aberdeen, I feel that you will do so.

[1] Ibid. fos. 226–46. A detailed account of these discussions is given in J. B. Conacher, *The Peelites and the Party System 1846–52* (1972), pp. 119–21.

If not say so unreservedly and you will have no further trouble from me, but the worst certainly is better than my present state of which indeed this letter is no slight indication. I must add that I have never been in a position towards Ld. Aberdeen which would authorize my direct application to him with much hope of success. Very truly yours F. R. Bonham.

Graham answered immediately and encouragingly. He expressed his 'great pain' at hearing from Bonham in such circumstances and promised to call in the aid of Newcastle and Gladstone; 'no friend of Sir Robert Peel's can regard with indifference your difficulties and sorrows'. Graham was as good as his word. In the next few weeks he held consultations with the other Peelites in the government, Newcastle, Gladstone and Cardwell, which gave grounds for hope. 'You have a right', he wrote on 16 August, 'to expect the sympathy and kindness of all those who are really attached to the memory of our departed Chief.'

It fell to Gladstone to be the medium whereby the Peelites paid their debt to Peel's party manager. This in itself was neither unwelcome nor inappropriate. 'If I desired' Bonham had written to Graham in July 1852, 'to enlist a third person in my cause, Gladstone would be the man for I have the greatest esteem for him'. The post offered to Bonham was that of Commissioner of Income Tax and it was therefore Gladstone as chancellor of the exchequer who sent the official intimation to him together with a characteristically couched expression of 'the cordial pleasure with which I find myself the medium of this communication from Lord Aberdeen to so old & so highly valued a friend and of my readiness nay eagerness to bear any share of the responsibility of the appointment that may be thought to devolve upon me as the member of this Government peculiarly charged with the working of the Income Tax'. For a few days there was a slight but unexpected hitch in the negotiations, for Bonham despite his pressing needs at first obtained from one of the Treasury officials an unfavourable account of the duties of the office and the amount of help he was likely to receive from his other colleague in the department. 'I might,' he wrote cautiously to Gladstone, 'in my anxiety for many reasons to accept office have hoped to overcome the difficulty, for to me the employment would have been in itself a recommendation. But now I dread to bring discredit not only on myself but on the financial credit of the Gov^t.'

The fact was that Bonham, even more than he allowed Gladstone to realize, was reluctant to embark on an employment which he feared would be extremely arduous hampered by a septuagenarian colleague whose capabilities he had been given reason to distrust. However, further enquiries dispelled the first discouraging impression and on 22 August 1853 he wrote 'to accept (as far as in me lies) the office which Ld Aberdeen is likely to have very speedily at his disposal'. A month later he wrote cheerfully to Gladstone that he had secured enough experience in his new post to feel confident of his ability to perform its duties. 'In fact I feel perfectly happy in the conviction that there will be a fair proportion of business to occupy my time, and that of a nature not beyond the ordinary capacity of man'.[1] From Geneva the widowed Lady Peel wrote to congratulate him on his appointment. 'Amonst yr. many friends, no one more sincerely (and I really must be permitted to use the word) affectionately rejoices at any good that befalls so honourably minded, long tried and so true a friend as yourself.'

[1] 40, 616 fos. 350–61; 44, 110 fos. 253–71.

During the last ten years of Bonham's life he still maintained a political correspondence with Graham and Gladstone and since their duties kept them all in London, it is probable that there was more communication between them than the extant letters suggest. That Gladstone in particular continued to seek political advice from a man who had virtually retired from any kind of political life, may be taken as evidence of how lacking the Peelites were by that time in even the most rudimentary party organization. But there can be little doubt that Bonham's advice was genuinely sought; the more so perhaps since Gladstone's other parliamentary expert, Sir John Young, became chief secretary for Ireland under the Aberdeen government in December 1852 and in 1855 left parliament altogether to become chief commissioner of the Ionian Islands. On 30 January 1855, for example, the day after the defeat of the Aberdeen ministry, by 325 votes to 148, on the famous Roebuck motion, Gladstone asked Bonham for as close an analysis as possible of the fatal division, dividing the ministerialists into whigs, radicals and independent liberals, Peelites, and opposition; and the majority into opposition, whigs, and independent liberals and radicals. A request of this kind can scarcely be interpreted as a kindly but meaningless gesture to an obsolete political veteran. Or again, at the end of the year, Bonham was warning Gladstone against becoming involved with a certain Mr Snell, one of 'a parcel of Harpies calling themselves Election Agents with whom the Town abounds on the approach of an Election full of vague generalities meaning nothing but to catch the unwary, get their money by promises and I have known by a bold system of extortion.' Gladstone gratefully acknowledged the advice and submitted an answer for Bonham's approval before sending it on to Snell. And finally, as late as March 1857, after Palmerston's 'Chinese' general election, Gladstone was asking Bonham for anything he had in the way of a real analysis of the new House of Commons. The last recorded service of any note which Bonham performed for Gladstone came in January 1857 and by a fitting coincidence concerned his old enemy Disraeli, and a brother of his old leader the dead Sir Robert Peel. As is related by Morley, Disraeli made a characteristic move early in that year to split the Peelite strength by inviting General Peel to the official Conservative dinner on the eve of the parliamentary session. The general consulted Gladstone on the reply to this invitation and found him, as might have been expected, strongly averse to his acceptance. What Morley did not disclose, however, was in the first place that Disraeli in his letter to the general had scattered some groundbait in the shape of a remark that he would find many of his friends at the dinner. Perplexed by this ambiguous statement but by no means convinced that the Peelites as a body were being invited, General Peel thought it prudent to seek a second opinion. The second significant fact is that he did not apparently feel himself on such intimate terms with Gladstone as to justify a direct approach. It was Bonham who acted as the diplomatic intermediary between the two men, forwarding to Gladstone a note explaining the circumstances, together with Disraeli's guileless invitation and a copy of the draft reply to the queen's speech which was to be discussed at the dinner and which Disraeli had thoughtfully enclosed for General Peel's edification.[1]

After 1857 even this marginal political activity ceased. For this there were two

---

[1] 44, 110 fos. 274–314.

probable reasons. One is that the independent life of the Peelites had been virtually destroyed by the 1857 general election and formally ended with the junction of Gladstone and his followers with the Palmerston–Russell ministry in June 1859. Between 1846 and 1857 Bonham, despite the loss of his official position in the party in 1846 and the assumption of the commissionership of income-tax in 1853, had clearly continued to act as unofficial political adviser to the unofficial party of Peelites who still maintained a nebulous existence in the parliamentary world. But by 1859, if not earlier, even that slender basis for political activity had vanished. The other reason was purely personal. It is doubtful, even if there had been a real occasion for his services, whether his health would have permitted him to carry on an active interest in parliamentary and electoral affairs after 1857. Bonham seems never to have been a robust man nor did he come of robust stock. An accident that occurred to him at Liverpool in 1844 perhaps assisted the inevitable oncoming of old age. Certainly there was a noticeable decline in his health in the following decade. By 1850 his appearances at the Carlton were becoming rare. Two years later he confessed himself unequal to a journey to Hawarden suggested by Gladstone. 'Very many thanks,' he wrote on 24 July, 'for your kind invitation to Flintshire but these enjoyments are now beyond my reach and till I get rid of my suburban "Box" my aspirations dare not extend beyond the shady side of Kensington Gardens.'[1] His reluctance to take what at first sight appeared to be a laborious post as Income Tax Commissioner in 1853 was primarily due to the consciousness of his own failing energies; and in asking advice from an old friend on his suitability for the appointment he felt constrained to add the warning that 'in health strength and spirits I am a very different man from what you formerly knew me'. From 1855 onwards his sight was causing him trouble and he was frequently obliged to use his sister as an amanuensis. In the early spring of 1856 he had a bout of severe illness which made it difficult for him to write any but the most necessary papers; and at the end of the year he was again extremely ill and for some weeks could scarcely move except in a cab to his office. There were more complaints about his eyes in March 1857 and an apology in a letter to Gladstone for 'this miserably blind effort'. Some time before his death he retired from the civil service probably in accordance with the understanding on which he had entered his post in 1853 that he should only retain it as long as his health and strength enabled him to perform its functions to public satisfaction. He died in his seventy-eighth year on 26 April 1863 at his house in Knightsbridge from 'natural decay', according to the typically vague early-Victorian formula on his death certificate, after three days paralysis. His sister and for long his companion, Miss Susan Bonham, followed him only six months later and their common gravestone may still be seen in Brompton Cemetery.

In coming to Bonham's aid in 1853 the Peelites felt that he had deserved well of them. Certainly his position forms one of the most interesting aspects of the history of the Conservative party in the period 1832–47. Chronologically Bonham connects the political agents and managers of the eighteenth and early nineteenth centuries with the modern party central office founded by Disraeli after the Reform Act of 1867. In character, however, Bonham is nearer the latter for he lived in an age when the creation of local constituency associations and the

[1] Ibid. fo. 229. The suburban 'Box' was Bonham's house at 13 Albert Terrace, Knightsbridge.

obligatory registration of voters provided a new statistical basis for the work of the party managers and made possible for the first time the effective national organization of a party in opposition. Not the accidental defeat of the Wellington ministry in 1830 but the planned victory of 1841 is the first landmark in the process of subjecting government to the decision of the electorate, expressed and organized through party. Moreover, though the degree of specialization implicit in the establishment of a full-time salaried election manager had not yet been reached in this period, the differentiation clearly exhibited in Bonham's career between the work of the whips and patronage secretary inside, and the work of the election manager outside the House of Commons is a significant stage of development. Disraeli's tribute was not wholly unmerited; nor was the example perhaps wholly forgotten when in the course of time the author of *Lord George Bentinck* came himself to direct the organization of the Conservative party.

Part III

People and Society

11

A Glaswegian Criminologist: Patrick Colquhoun, 1745–1820[1]

Crime, like poverty, is always with us; perhaps more so. Affluent societies may have some success in eliminating poverty; there is little reason as yet to think that they are likely to eliminate crime. Yet the historical study of crime is not easy. Since it is by definition outside the law, the evidence for it is usually defective. Not until the state takes notice of the consequences of crime does our knowledge take a firm shape. In the eighteenth and early nineteenth centuries there are no statistics for crime in itself. What we have are statistics relating to the punishment of crime, which is a different matter. We can be morally certain that much crime went undetected, unreported or even unobserved; but how much is not even a matter of guesswork. It is completely unknowable. Even statistics for those crimes which resulted in the appearance of persons in court are fallacious. An apparent increase in crime may only be an increase in prosecutions; and that may be due to an increase in the zeal, skill and activity of law-enforcement agencies. Changes in the ratio of convictions and acquittals may only reflect changed attitudes among judges, juries and prosecutors. Statistics have to be interpreted; but it is often impossible to assess with accuracy the influences which decide that interpretation.

Yet crime and the treatment of crime is a significant aspect of the history of any society. The ramifications – social, economic, political, administrative, constitutional, religious, even philosophical – are endless. Crime is part of the problem of social discipline. The maintenance of an ordered framework of life is the prime internal task of government just as defence against attack is the prime external task. A society lulled by security and wealth may come to regard order as normal and natural; and crime as abnormal and curable. In rougher and more precarious ages crime is looked upon as a dangerous enemy against which the state has to mobilize all the forces it possesses. It was inevitable therefore that in the eighteenth century, when there was a general intellectual enquiry into the principles which ought to govern man in society, crime and punishment came under scrutiny. The Marquis de Beccaria, with his classic treatise on *Crime and Punishment*, may almost be said to have invented the science of penology. First published in 1764 it not only gained for its author a European reputation but became the canonical text beside which all other writings on the subject could be judged.

Among those in England influenced by his teaching, besides the well-known figures of Jeremy Bentham and Samuel Romilly, was Patrick Colquhoun. He was a Scot, born at Dumbarton in 1745, where his father was a magistrate and

[1] Not previously published.

registrar of county records. After an early spell in America he returned to
Scotland at the age of twenty-one and set up as a textile merchant. He became
Lord Provost of Glasgow (1782–4), was instrumental in establishing a Chamber of
Commerce, and became a justice of the peace. From the start his interests seem to
have been in a public rather than a commercial career; and about the year 1787 he
followed that road which (as Dr Johnson noted in memorably unkind words)
beckoned ambitious Scots to London. His intention – or hope – was probably to
secure a position under government where his knowledge of trade and America
might count as a qualification. Unsuccessful in this, he eventually obtained
appointment as a stipendiary magistrate, one of twenty-four distributed among
the eight metropolitan offices set by the Middlesex Justices Act of 1792. Attached
first to the office at Worship Street, Finsbury Square, he was transferred in 1797
to the Queen Square Office, Westminster, where he stayed until his retirement in
1818. He died two years later in April 1820.

A man with wide interests, strong views, and an enquiring mind, Colquhoun
was never content with the routine of a police-court even though he gained a name
as an active and assiduous magistrate. In the famine years of 1795–7 he helped to
establish soup-kitchens at Spitalfields (and characteristically wrote a pamphlet on
how to run them) and raised subscriptions for other distressed areas of London.
Loyal and patriotic, he busied himself with measures against radical societies and
in 1804 drew up plans for civil defence in the event of a French invasion. He
helped to found the Thames River Police and subsequently became their
Receiver-General. He started a police intelligence sheet, the *Hue and Cry*, the
forerunner of the *Police Gazette*; he sent legislative proposals to the prime
minister; and wrote books and pamphlets on subjects as diverse as the colonies,
indigence, ale-houses, model villages, education and economics. His last book, a
*Treatise on the Wealth, Power, and Resources of the British Empire in Every Quarter
of the World*, in which he made an attempt to measure national income, appeared
in 1814. It was, however, by his writings on police that he attracted most
attention: on *Commerce and Police of the Thames* in 1800, on the *Functions and
Duties of Constables* in 1803, and above all his *Treatise on the Police of the Metropolis*
which first appeared in 1796. Within twelve months it ran into four editions and
reached a seventh by 1806. It is a long, discursive book, furnished with tables of
criminal statistics, enlivened occasionally by anecdotal material, repetitious and
(though well-indexed) not always well-organized. His fundamental views and his
practical suggestions, however, are never in doubt.

A product of the same Scottish Enlightenment to which David Hume and
Adam Smith belonged, Colquhoun was in touch with the intellectual life of
Europe as well as Britain. He quotes from Montesquieu, prints an abstract of the
reformed criminal code of Emperor Joseph II promulgated in 1787, and was
deeply influenced by the Marquis de Beccaria – 'our favourite Beccaria', as he
describes him almost affectionately at one point. He was not himself a very
original thinker. Much of his theory of punishment was taken from Beccaria;
many of his practical suggestions from the reform proposals of the two Fielding
brothers, Henry and John, who between them virtually founded the system of
police offices in which Colquhoun found himself after 1792. His practical experience, energy and literary proclivities made him an outstanding popularizer,
however, of ideas which would otherwise have remained the province of a small

group of experts. In Britain his reputation brought him the acquaintanceship of such celebrities as Adam Smith, Burke, Gibbon, and the great Jeremy Bentham with whom he had strong intellectual affinities. Though the most productive period of his life was spent as an exiled Scot in London, his fame did not go unregarded by the city in which he first entered public life. In 1797 he was awarded an LLD by Glasgow University and in 1800 was given the freedom of the city. In 1818 he received the final accolade of a biography appearing in his own lifetime – G. D. Yeats's *A biographical sketch of the life and writings of P. Colquhoun, Esq.*[1]

Magistrate, moralist, economist, philanthropist, Benthamite utilitarian, and criminologist, Colquhoun is chiefly remembered for the idea of 'preventive police'. There is, however, a semantic trap here into which many have fallen. 'Police' did not mean to Colquhoun's generation what it means to us today. Failure to appreciate, or at any rate to explain, this vitiates a number of references to him which occur in modern histories of Scotland Yard and the metropolitan police. The word comes from the same root as policy, polity and politics; an association of ideas preserved in the former pronunciation of police (roughly the same as the Greek word *polis*) which has disappeared in England though still to be heard in its pristine purity in Scotland and Ireland. In Colquhoun's day and for some time after it meant the internal regulation of the manners, morals, and health of society. As late as 1849, twenty years after the foundation of Peel's metropolitan police, Craig's *Dictionary of the English Language* gave the primary definition of the word as 'the government of a city or town. It embraces the administration of the laws and regulations by which order, cleanliness, and health are preserved; the internal regulation of a kingdom or state.' Only after this come the secondary senses – 'the corporation or body of men governing a city; the municipal force under the control of the magistracy'. The early Police Boards set up by act of parliament at this time in various English towns, for example, had nothing to do with 'policing' in the modern sense. They were sanitary boards rather than constabulary boards.

When therefore Colquhoun writes[2] of the importance of a 'Legislative Authority, aided by a well-regulated and energetic Police' as 'a security against iniquity and depredation' he is thinking not of a body of men but of a body of regulations and regulatory agencies designed to safeguard the manners, morals, health and security of society. Chapter XIII of his famous *Treatise*, which is entitled 'The Police of the Metropolis considered and explained', deals with the magistracy in Middlesex and the City of London, suggestions for improvement, and comparisons with foreign systems. Chapter XIV, 'on municipal Police',

---

[1] G. D. Yeats, FRCP, FRS, was a graduate of Oxford who took a degree in medicine at Dublin and became private physician to the duke of Bedford when he was Lord Lieutenant of Ireland 1806–7. Yeats published books on medical and other topics.

[2] All the quotations which follow are taken from the 4th edition published by C. Dilly at the Poultry in 1797. The full title of the work is *A Treatise on the Police of the Metropolis, containing a detail of the Various Crimes and Misdemenours by which Public and Private Property and Security are, at present, injured and endangered: and Suggesting Remedies for their Prevention. The Fourth Edition, Revised and Englarged. By a Magistrate acting for the Counties of Middlesex, Surrey, Kent and Essex, for the City and Liberty of Westminster, and for the Liberty of the Tower of London.* Colquhoun's own name did not appear though it did in the 6th edition.

discusses the growth of London, the increase in the number of houses, the proportion of churches and chapels, schools, charitable institutions, law-courts, and prisons, with proposals for improving the judicial process for recovery of small debts, a discussion of the division of the metropolis into separate municipalities and the resulting high cost of upkeep for roads, pavements, watchmen, lighting and refuse-disposal. In effect, 'Police', for Colquhoun and his contemporaries, implied all the restraints and restraining agencies, private and voluntary as well as central and local government, which made up the totality of social disciplines. In that sense it will be used here.

That such restraints were necessary hardly anyone questioned. Though the eighteenth-century intellectuals were optimists, they were not for the most part sentimentalists, other than Rousseau and his followers. They took it for granted that human nature needed educative and coercive controls if a civilized social order was to be maintained. No false shame attached to a rational enquiry into the mechanics of such controls. In arguing for a preventive police Colquhoun was advocating a tighter and more permanent system of social constraints which would eliminate, or at least diminish, criminal and immoral tendencies in their early stages before actual or serious breaches of the law took place. In the context of what he was actually proposing, the contemporary debate, over whether 'preventive police' was reconcilable with the traditional freedom of the subject, constituted a genuine conflict of principle. The notion of the right of the individual to act as he thought fit, subject to his responsibilities to the law for the consequences of his actions, was deeply engrained in English society. The ability of the private citizen to go about his daily life free (in Paley's words), from 'inspection, scrutiny, and control', was at the heart of the much-vaunted British 'liberty'. Colquhoun's point was that this liberty could be purchased at too high a price and at the very least, had to be partially limited by other social considerations, if it was to remain a reality. Preventive action, even though it involved some degree of scrutiny and control, was not only more efficient but more humane.

All this had little to do with the modern concept of 'police' as a body of men, trained, organized and usually uniformed, operating as a kind of semi-independent law-enforcement agency separate from the courts and the magistrates. There is nothing to suggest in the *Treatise* that Colquhoun anticipated such a development. He devotes less than a couple of pages to 'Watchmen and Patroles', and the improvements he thought necessary in their organization and general efficiency. He provides statistics of the number of constables attached to the stipendiary magistrates' courts in London, of parochial constables and other parish officers, and of watchmen employed by private agencies. He suggests that there should be more *ad hoc* rewards and inducements for successful detection of crimes. But that is all. Even when dealing with the more technical aspects of crime, he is primarily interested in the magistracy, not in the men whom we would describe as constables but whom he designates as '*Officers of Justice* (parochial and stipendiary) who are appointed to watch over the Police of the Metropolis and its environs, in keeping the peace, and in detecting and apprehending offenders'. The stipendiary courts in Colquhoun's day had in fact only six constables each, other than the Bow Street office which had eight (the famous Bow Street runners). Together with the horse-patrol which guarded the main roads into London, the total force of full-time efficient officers for the whole of London amounted to only 117. Yet

Colquhoun makes no suggestion for an increase in their numbers, or even a consolidation of their organization. They are peripheral to the principal topic of the book. As one of the stipendiary magistrates himself, he was familiar with their work which was largely of a detective nature. They do not seem to have entered very much into his concept of preventive police, presumably because he thought of them primarily as thief-catchers. The links between Colquhoun and Peel's metropolitan police of 1829 is at best a tenuous one. Certainly Colquhoun did as much as anybody to popularize the theory of crime prevention and it was this which Peel and the first commissioners at Scotland Yard sought to instil into their new force. But 'preventive police' in this sense was a policy or an attitude. It is a misuse of the term to think of it as a designation for a body of men or of Colquhoun as a kind of proto-founder of the metropolitan police.[1]

II

Colquhoun's book appeared at a time when the war against revolutionary France was entering a new and dangerous stage. The first allied coalition had virtually collapsed; at home and in Ireland there was discontent, disaffection and sedition. The previous autumn the government had passed *Treasonable Practices* and *Seditious Meetings* acts; *Habeas Corpus* was already suspended. Colquhoun clearly shared the view of most educated people that there was a dangerous element of subversion in the advanced radical movements of the time. Yet he makes hardly any references to such matters and they do not seem to have coloured his general outlook on the specific problem of crime. When writing a new *Advertisement* for the fourth edition of his *Treatise* he suggested that the 'hordes of Emigrants' from France were partly responsible for the sudden increase in the number of gaming-houses in London and for the introduction of 'the foreign games of *Roulet* and *Rouge et Noir*'. In the body of the text he observes that the criminal classes in Paris, freed from the strict surveillance of royal officials, acted as confederates of the political factions in carrying out massacres and other atrocities of the Revolution and adds that as such men were much the same in all countries, similar scenes might be expected in London if government were overthrown. He prophesies also that the termination of the war would probably 'throw into this country a vast number of idle, profligate, and depraved characters, natives of this, as well as of other nations', presumably from the armed forces. But these incidental references apart, his outlook is conditioned by wider and more general eighteenth-century views on the nature of civil society. His book was not a *pièce d'occasion* but a considered practical and philosophical treatise.

He starts his classic book on the *Police of the Metropolis* with a criticism in general terms of the existing system. The first target is the mass of heterogeneous and ill-assorted criminal statutes. During the previous two centuries, he observes, the fault of the legislature had been in making too few laws to restrain acts of vice and crime and too many imposing severe penalties on those who committed them. This, he argued, was a false development in criminal jurisprudence and had caused an equally false reaction in the public. Private individ-

---

[1] As seems to be the argument in C. Reith, *A new Study of Police History* (Edinburgh, 1956) and G. Dilnot, *Scotland Yard 1829–1929* (1929). The section on Colquhoun in L. Radzinowicz, *History of English Criminal Law* vol. III (1956) pp. 211 seq., also seems to lean, albeit cautiously, in this direction.

uals would not prosecute, juries would not convict, judges would recommend to mercy, when the penalty prescribed by law seemed out of proportion to the offence committed. These two conflicting features, undue severity and undue lenity, simply fostered the growth of a large criminal population. The savage penal code (containing over 160 capital offences) not only defeated its own ends but failed to achieve what he thought should be the purpose of all law; namely, the prevention of crime.

Analysing the prevalence of crime and the lack of security for life and property, he suggests nine contributory causes: the faulty state of the criminal law; the lack of a single directing agency; the scarcity of paid magistrates in towns other than London; the absence of a public prosecutor; the lack of intelligence about known criminals, the retention of convicts in prison hulks; the defects in the system of transportation; the lack of institutions for the custody and rehabilitation of criminals; and the unseemliness of the existing mode of public executions. Of the judicial system itself it is not its harshness but its ineffectiveness of which he complains. Its single virtue was that, because of its antique procedures, 'it is scarcely possible that an honest or an innocent person can be convicted of a capital offence'. This remarkable expression of trust is, it is true, modified in a subsequent footnote admitting that there had been some instances of innocent men convicted; but he insists that these were rare and, when discovered, would always occasion a royal pardon. It is a limited consolation but he does not pursue the matter further.

The reason for Colquhoun's belief in the equity if not the efficiency of the courts was what he termed the great caution of the eighteenth-century criminal law – or what a less respectful critic might call its delays, confusions, complexities, and general procedural hazards which led Romilly to speak more tartly of a 'lottery of justice'. The duty imposed on the judges to scrutinize the proceedings in the prisoner's interests, the tiny details of indictment on which a prosecution might be overturned, and the sympathies of jurors, all reduced (in Colquhoun's opinion) almost to a minimum not only the chances of a wrongful verdict on the innocent but the prospects of a successful conviction of the guilty. For those brought to trial there was in fact statistically something like an even chance of acquittal. Colquhoun gives figures for Old Bailey trials, covering eight sessions, during the twelve months from April 1793 to March 1794. Of the 1,060 committed for trial, 567 were acquitted. Of the rest, 68 were condemned to death, 169 to transportation, 197 to minor punishments. In addition the sentences on 38 were suspended on condition of entering the armed forces and 21 others respited (probably on the same condition). Of the original 1,060, therefore, only 493 were punished and of these 197, after short periods of imprisonment, would be set at liberty again 'with little prospect of being better disposed to be useful to Society, than before'.

Even for those convicted on a capital charge there was a four to one chance of receiving a pardon, either on condition of entering the armed forces or being transported or – some cases – with no conditions at all. Indeed, almost as many people died in prison apparently as were actually hanged. Of the prisoners who came up for trial at the Old Bailey in 1790–91, 32 were executed, 25 died naturally. Of all the prisoners for the greater London area tried at various courts (the Old Bailey, the City, Southwark and Surrey) in 1794–5, 19 were executed and 22 died naturally. The haphazard system of granting pardons incurred Colquhoun's particular disapproval. 'No sooner does the punishment of the Law attach on a criminal,' he writes caustically, 'then false humanity becomes his friend.' Pardons were applied for, he continues; friends and relatives worked on the compassion (and ignorance) of the public. Often those who interested themselves on behalf of a condemned man had no knowledge of the facts of the case.

> If these humane individuals, who exert themselves in applications of this sort, were to be made acquainted with one half of the gross impositions practised upon the credulity, or of the extent of the evil consequences arising to Society from such pardons, they would shudder at the extent of the cruelty exercised towards the Public, and even, in many instances, to the Convicts themselves, by this false Humanity.

Though Colquhoun is careful not to attack the royal prerogative of mercy (and indeed, given the severity of the criminal law, thought it necessary to have it), the abuse of that power, as he saw it, constituted yet another count in his general criticism of the system. At the very least, he thought, pardons should not be granted unless the criminal made a full confession of his crimes and accomplices, and was either sent for transportation or made to pay proper compensation to the party injured by his action.

In general Colquhoun paints a melancholy picture, reflecting presumably his own experience, of the frustrations attending a zealous magistrate in his battle against crime. On average, he relates, the metropolitan magistrates annually committed between 2,500 and 3,000 persons of both sexes to the seven different courts of justice in or near the metropolis.

> But after fully convincing their own minds, from a careful, and in many instances, a most laborious investigation, that the parties are guilty, they are obliged, from experience, to prepare themselves for the mortification of seeing their labours and exertions in a great measure lost to the Community. The major part of these criminals being returned upon Society, without any effectual step adopted for their reformation, or any means used for the prevention of a repetition of their crimes.

Even if some of them suffered the inconvenience of temporary incarceration, this (he thought) would have no effect on them, other perhaps than teaching them new and better ways of committing crime. Despite the work of the professional magistrates (which as Colquhoun describes it resembled more the function of the continental examining magistrate than the rôle of judge), the system remained weighted in favour of the criminal. He knew even before he perpetrated his crime that he stood an excellent chance of escaping detection entirely. In Colquhoun's opinion less than a tenth of the offences committed within the jurisdiction of the Old Bailey court were followed by an arrest and commitment for trial. If, however, the criminal was unlucky enough to be detected, he would look to friends and accomplices to intimidate prosecutor and witnesses by threats of personal violence from pursuing the case. If he actually appeared in court, there was always the prospect that the indictment could be thrown out on a technicality. If the trial proceeded, perjured witnesses would come forward on his behalf. If, notwithstanding, he was convicted, he could still hope to cheat the gallows by playing on the humanitarian feelings of the public. If Colquhoun's assumptions and statistics were right, it followed that the odds of a capital offence being followed by the actual execution of the offender were in the region of 99 to 1 against.[1] It is not to be wondered at that capital punishment was not a deterrent.

III

If these were the faults of the system, what were Colquhoun's remedies? His response is to go back to first principles. 'Prevention of crimes and misdemeanours, it cannot be too often repeated, is the true essence of Police.' The only permanent cure for crime is better social discipline. He looked primarily to an improvement in the agencies, regulations and constraints operating within society rather than any charge in the existing machinery of criminal jurisprudence. It is characteristic that church and state are brought together in his observation that

> the foundation of all good Police throughout the nation rests upon those wise regulations which the Clergy and the Magistrate shall carry into execution for the preservation of morals, and the punishment of Crimes.

Reformation, that is to say, begins from below. He is at pains to stress that most crime is petty crime, committed by people who are not hardened offenders or professional criminals. The men whose activities loomed largest in the public's imagination – the highwayman, the footpad, the pickpocket – formed only a small proportion of the offenders who came before the courts. For Colquhoun the serious and significant fact was the existence of widespread, everyday dishonesty. This was the foundation on which the edifice of serious crime rested. The readiness of ordinary people, in homes, workplaces, shops, in town and country, in the ordinary course of business, to pilfer, take bribes, profit on the side from the criminality of others, turn a blind eye, ask no questions – this was the corrupting element in contemporary society which made crime in the more serious sense so difficult to prevent and so hard to detect. It is to reduce this nomansland of dishonesty rather than criminality that Colquhoun proposes, for example, to place under stricter supervision, preferably through some system of licensing and inspection, such trades as old-clothes dealers, scrap-metal merchants, night-coaches, cheap lodging-houses, and pawn-brokers.

He has other practical suggestions. The coinage should be made more equal in face value to its metallic value to reduce the profitableness of counterfeiting. The legal process for the recovery of small debts should be made simpler and cheaper – not only in the interests of the debtor but also of the honest and trusting creditor, who was often ruined by unscrupulous clients. Above all, he wanted to see the appointment of a Public Prosecutor, working under the supervision of the Attorney-General and aided by a staff of Deputy Prosecutors. This, he believed,

---

[1] Colquhoun does not make this statement himself but it is the logical conclusion from several scattered observations of his. At different points he suggests (a) that of every hundred crimes only ten result in a court appearance. (b) Of these, five on average end in an acquittal. (c) Of the five convicted, four on average are respited, leaving only one where the capital sentence is actually carried out. The calculation is so heavily dependent on the conjectural ratio of crimes committed to crimes prosecuted that it is of value only as the opinion of a professional magistrate and a contemporary. It is worth noting however that Colquhoun thought a large proportion of acquittals occurred in capital cases where the jury considered the legal penalty out of proportion to the offence charged.

would do much to remedy the deficiencies of a system which otherwise left too much to the initiative of the private individuals who had been victims of crime. In the absence of such an official, at least there should be provision for reimbursing the costs of private prosecutions and giving compensation for those who had suffered loss and damage as a result of criminal actions.

When he turns to a particular examination of the preventive agencies in the metropolitan area, his principal criticism is that the stipendiary magistrates had no power to prevent crime and no money to pay for the detection of the criminal when a crime had been committed. Their work was primarily judicial: the hearing and determining of a wide range of minor breaches of the law. They also had many miscellaneous and time-consuming administrative duties, including the licensing of public-houses, swearing-in and superintending parochial constables, making orders under the poor laws, arranging for the billetting of troops, attending general and quarter sessions, and inspecting prisons and workhouses. For crime-prevention they had neither the time nor the money. The annual grant of £2,000 for the upkeep of each office was spent on rents, rates, taxes, salaries and other administrative expenses leaving nothing over to meet the costs of pursuing criminals or rewarding informers. A tart and feeling comparison is drawn between the professional stipendiary magistrate and the amateur, part-time magistrates (the lord mayor and the alderman) in the City. The first had the experience and the knowledge but not the resources; the latter the resources but neither the time nor skill. Intelligent foreign visitors, according to Colquhoun, noted with surprise that the British capital possessed an organization for dealing with criminals after their crimes had been committed but did nothing to prevent those crimes from taking place.

What was needed, he thought, was greater centralization. The stipendiary magistrates themselves were indispensable but their work should be coordinated by a central board under the discretion of the Home Secretary. There would be no need for more than three officials – 'responsible Commissioners' or 'auxiliary Magistrates' as he variously calls them – provided they were men of businesslike habits, 'able, intelligent, prudent and indefatigable'. Their prime function would be to supply purpose and unity to the existing body of police magistrates. Colquhoun gives a list of suggested duties for them, arranged under twelve headings. He wants his Commissioners to make recommendations for any needed changes in the law; to devise more economical arrangements for prisons and transportations; to maintain a register of all known criminals; to collect intelligence on major criminal activities; to provide directives and information to the police-offices; to assist provincial magistrates in dealing with serious outbreaks of crime; to enforce better security in the port of London and the royal dockyards; to administer the parliamentary funds allotted for police offices, prisons, transportation, and rewards; to correspond with magistrates in every part of the United Kingdom; to make regulations for gaming-houses, brothels, public-houses, watchmen, night-coaches, receivers of stolen goods, and public weights and measures; to take over responsibility for convicts in hulks and awaiting transportation; and finally to make regular reports to the Home Secretary. In its centralized techniques of regulation, inspection and reporting, as well as in its comprehensiveness, it was a scheme that might have come from Jeremy Bentham himself. One can hardly quarrel with Colquhoun's final observation that if the plan were adopted, his Commissioners would 'have abundance of employment' with which to justify their existence.

IV

When all preventive measures failed, how was society to deal with the convicted offender? Three principles, according to Colquhoun, ought to govern the punishment of criminals: the reformation of the criminal, the deterring of others, and restitution or compensation for the wrong done. The first two are clearly preventive principles; the third one of natural justice. As a preliminary step he wanted greater discrimination in the scale of penalties laid down by law; or rather, since to talk of a 'scale' implied an order and symmetry in the criminal law which did not exist, he wanted a careful and rational scale of penalties drawn up. The central feature of his proposed reform of the law was what he called 'distributive justice', in other words, making the punishment fit the crime. The criminal law should be codified, partly to make it clearer, more importantly to allow a complete review of the punishments laid down by law. To execute criminals, he notes with what might be either Scots literalness or an unsuspected vein of irony, was useless as a method of reforming them. Even as a deterrent to others, execution had its limitations particularly in Britain. Colquhoun was not an abolitionist and seems to admit a fourth principle, that of retribution, as far as the supreme crime of murder is concerned. But for all other crimes, he insisted, the only justification for capital punishment lay in the deterrent effect. A multiplicity of capital offences and an inefficacious system of law-enforcement had little or no deterrent value, especially when executions, though carried out in public, were spectacles of public disorder and excess, a civil saturnalia rather than a vindication of public morality.

On the other hand, he did not think that the humanitarian criminal code of the Emperor Joseph II, which dispensed altogether with capital punishment, was applicable to Great Britain. Laws had to be adjusted to actual social conditions. His own preference was for the death penalty to be restricted to a small number of crimes where the public interest really required it.[1] Executions should be rare and, while remaining public, 'ought to be rendered as *terrific* and *solemn* in the eyes of the People as possible'. In general, however, his opinion seems to have been that public executions, however 'terrific', remained momentary events which were less of a deterrent than more permanent forms of punishment. He was an advocate therefore of the public exhibition of criminals. Convicts undergoing hard labour should, when feasible, be employed on public works where they could be constantly seen by the public. Life sentences would in those circumstances operate more as a deterrent than either executions or transportation. This, he thought, was a branch of penology which had been unduly neglected. Convicts labouring in full view of the public would furnish an excellent moral example. It could also, he said cannily, be used to make a profit, if not to the individual who had suffered from their actions then at least for society which had been put to

---

[1] It is not clear what Colquhoun thought this category of crime should include. In the *Introduction* (p. 7) he says that the 'highest crimes' are forgery, murder, arson and treason. In the text (p. 265) he suggests that it would be sufficient to retain the death penalty for treason, murder, mayhem (physical maiming of another person) and aggravated arson.

expense in bringing them to justice. Under proper management, the work of an individual convict would, he calculated, be worth £30 *per annum*, or more than the annual wage of a common labourer.

For those convicted of less serious offences and serving shorter terms of imprisonment (ten years or less), Colquhoun advocated confinement in a penitentiary or house of correction rather than transportation or the hulks. The idea of corrective punishment was, of course, not new. Indeed, it had been accepted by the legislature in a number of acts passed in the 1770s. But these had never been implemented in any effective manner and when between 1784 and 1790 the old system of transportation was revived in a slightly new form, the penitentiary system was largely abandoned. This in Colquhoun's view was a mistake; the system should be revived, extended, but at the same time applied more strictly to its original object of reformation. The inmates of these institutions should be set to useful and productive employment. To encourage effort, there should be a system of carrots and sticks – almost literally so, since he had no compunction in prescribing corporal punishment for those who would not work. For those who worked well, there was to be a small financial reward and the prospect of a remission of sentence. When discharged, moreover, the convict was to receive a suit of clothes and a sum of money to assist him in finding employment. In this way the lesser, and by implication, the more youthful offenders, not yet hardened to a life of crime, would

> be arrested in the career of villainy; and after a course of labour, sobriety, and religious and moral instruction, joined to good and judicious discipline, accurately carried into execution, they may be also restored to society, with minds freed from depravity, and with such habits of industry and such a disposition to lead a new life, as may enable them to hope for employment.

This is Colquhoun at his most hopeful. The object was humane, even if the conclusions were, on all subsequent experience, shown to be unduly optimistic.

IV

At heart Colquhoun was a moralist and a philanthropist. He exhibited the typical rational virtues of the eighteenth-century enlightenment. In common with more eminent figures such as Adam Smith and Jeremy Bentham, he approached his specialized topic from a broad ethical and philosophical standpoint. It was this which provided the framework of reference for all he wrote. Virtue and benevolence were the guiding principles to be followed. The amendment of society was to be pursued not romantically or sentimentally but calmly and rationally. Morality rather than compassion was the hallmark of his analysis of the problem of crime.

Like many other moralists he believed that civilization and opulence tended to corrupt human nature. 'Immorality, Licentiousness, and Crimes,' he says categorically, 'are known to advance in proportion to riches.' A great capital city like London was 'the centre of Fashion, Amusements, Dissipation, Extravagance, and Folly' and its great wealth was a lure for both the wicked and the weak. Innumerable temptations were present to excite and satisfy 'imaginary wants and improper gratifications'. A great deal of poverty was due simply to improvidence, profligacy, and wickedness. Hence, for example, a proper control of public-houses, 'those haunts of idleness and vice' was 'the groundwork of any rational plan of Reform'. Even the respectable middle classes, to which he himself belonged, did not escape censure.

> The idle vanity of being introduced into what is generally but erroneously termed genteel society . . . has been productive of more *domestic misery* and more *real distress, poverty*, and *wretchedness* to *families* in this great City (who but for their folly might have been easy and comfortable), than many volumes could detail.

Daniel Defoe at his most puritanical could not have been more scathing about middle-class pretentiousness.

Reform therefore was something which must begin with religion and morality. The real source of public crime was private wickedness; and the best way of preventing the first was to punish the second. This conviction led him on to express views more reminiscent of Calvin's Geneva than Hogarth's London.

> The only means, therefore, of securing the peace of Society, and of preventing more atrocious crimes, is, to enforce, by lesser punishments, the observance of religious and moral duties. Without this, Laws are but weak Guardians either of the State, or the persons or property of the Subject.

He even criticizes the law itself for attaching heavier penalties to 'what may be termed, *Political Crimes*, and crimes against property' than to those against 'religion and virtue'. In constructing his proposed scale of punishments, the legislature should have primary regard to '*the immorality of the action; and its evil tendency*', by the latter phrase presumably meaning its corrupting effect on others. In an appendix he explains in more detail how the corruption of morals could be better prevented. He is prepared to punish gamesters, control lotteries, impose legal sanctions on domestic servants for breaches of duty. In the sphere of sexual morality he proposes legal penalties for seduction, adultery, and cohabitation without marriage. For Colquhoun, at any rate, the contemporary decline in the disciplinary powers exercised by the clergy over the laity (evident even more in England than in Scotland), was clearly a cause for regret. He could hardly have expected, however, that a House of Commons stuffed with cheerful sinners would take his proposals seriously. In advocating these extreme forms of social control, he was asking the impossible. The Evangelical Revival was well under way in the 1790s but its emphasis was on persuasion rather than coercion as a means of moral regeneration. Yet, on the broader issue, his argument that there was a close link between ethical self-discipline and the public crime-rate must have won the approval of many people. Between 1790 and 1820 Hannah More, William Wilberforce and Jane Austen were better representatives of the educated classes than the Prince of Wales, Charles James Fox or Lady Holland.

Despite his strain of Calvinistic repressiveness, however, Colquhoun was fundamentally an humane and, beneath the dry manner, surprisingly sympathetic man. Much of English criminal law, he says flatly, was not in accord with either justice or morality.

> By punishing smaller offences with extraordinary severity, is there not a risque of inuring men to baseness; and of plunging them into the sink of infamy and despair, from whence they seldom fail to rise capital criminals; often to the destruction of their fellow creatures, and always to their own inevitable perdition?

He gives instances of the inequity of punishments laid down by law. An aggravated physical assault carried a smaller penalty than breaking down the side of a fishpond, cutting down an orchard tree, or stealing personal property to the value of one shilling – all of which were capital offences. He makes a plea to the wealthy and charitable to assist in setting up 'asylums' where discharged convicts and former prostitutes might be housed and furnished with honest employment. He has words of pity and indignation for the poor, the innocent, the industrious, who found themselves caught up in the toils of the law. Such unfortunates were far more likely to suffer in body and mind, he points out, than the 'worthless and profligate'. On imprisonment for debt, he writes with unusual emotion that 'Humanity, Justice, and Policy, plead for an improvement of the System'. And he concludes with a grim aphorism: 'Knaves are seldom victims to the Severity of the Law'. Even with the professional criminals – those who elsewhere he describes as 'in a state of depravity, arising from a long course of criminal turpitude' – he is able to display remarkable objectivity. He observes (and draws attention to the observation) that 'it rarely happens *that an atrocious offender, or a professed thief, is not an ingenious, clever man*'. Such professional wrong-doers were necessarily men of resource, courage and strength of mind: qualities which, if applied to honest pursuits, would raise them high in society.

Moreover, Colquhoun was not afraid to assign part of the blame for the existence of such men to society itself; and to do so in remarkably sharp language.

> To suffer the lower orders of the People to be ill educated – to be totally inattentive to those wise regulations of State Policy which might serve to guard and improve their morals; and then to punish them, with a severity unexampled in the history of the world, either ancient or modern, for crimes which have originated in bad habits, has too much the appearance of creating delinquents for the purpose of putting them to death.

It is obvious that in blaming society in these biting words, he was not looking for greater political equality, or a redistribution of wealth, as a cure for social evils. Such notions would have appeared to him at best chimerical, in practice socially destructive. Essentially he was a benevolent, paternalistic authoritarian who sought greater regulation and control because human nature in its fallen state made such restraints necessary in the interests of civilized order. He did not believe in the innate goodness of human nature or the perfectibility of man. He was not a Rousseauesque idealist but a practical utilitarian. The art of life, he says revealingly, is to conduct man to the maximum of happiness and the minimum of misery. It is the cardinal utilitarian maxim (though in this case, perhaps, taken from his favourite Beccaria rather than his English acquaintance Jeremy Bentham), applied to moral ends. In the hopeful spirit of the utilitarians he thought much could be achieved by good sense, sound philosophic principles, and enlightened legislation. But his hopefulness was tempered by realism.

> It will not be altogether possible, amid the various opposite attractions of pleasure and pain, to reduce the tumultuous activity of mankind to absolute regularity. We can only hope for a considerable reduction of the evils that exist.

Nevertheless, in the final paragraph of the book, clearly designed to leave his readers with a distillation of the essence of his teaching, he returns to the two issues which are never far away in the preceding pages: the moral responsibility of society for having allowed crime to reach its horrifying proportions, and the availability of practical remedies.

For those who may have been appalled by his long catalogue of the various aspects of contemporary criminality, he gives the reminder that the problem is the result not of an increased, or general, depravity of the human race but of the failure of the laws to keep pace with the growing luxury and wealth of society and the additional temptations they brought in their train. He bids them remember that despite all he has said about the criminal classes, 'the most deformed part of the human race', these people were once innocent and many of them had become what they were because of the defects of the social system into which they were born, particularly the defects in the social agencies designed to prevent crime. As a Scot, perhaps, Colquhoun was ready to think that, in human as in divine creation, a fall from grace should justly be followed by retribution and punishment. But as a Benthamite he could not accept either that guilt was predestined or that it should incur eternal damnation. The principle of Benevolence, he concludes, suggests that where remedies are possible and practicable, they should be put into effect. To subsequent generations the two deities of the eighteenth-century Enlightenment – Reason and Virtue – seemed increasingly arid and uninspiring concepts. Colquhoun's book shows that they could induce both humanity and efficient reform.[1]

[1] The only separate modern study of Colquhoun seems to be Dr Ralph Pieris's scholarly article 'The Contribution of Patrick Colquhoun to Social Theory and Social Philosophy' (*University of Ceylon Review*, XII, no. 3, 1954) which includes a sketch of his life, a list of Colquhoun's published works, and a general bibliography. About a third of its thirty pages is devoted to a discussion of Colquhoun's views on the criminal classes and social control under the general heading of 'Social Pathology and Social Control'. While I agree with most of what Dr Pieris has written in his useful paper, its comparative inaccessibility in this country, my own differing approach, and in some cases slightly varying conclusions, may justify (it is hoped) printing the present essay.

12

The Founder of Modern Conservatism[1]

A curious feature of the Conservative party is that though its practice has almost invariably been Peelite, its myth has been largely Disraelian. When Conservative speakers and writers wish to clothe their contemporary arguments with the mantle of historical authority, ten will bring in a reference to Disraeli for every one who mentions Peel or Salisbury. For historians this is a salutary reflection on the limitations of their subject. It is of little consequence now that Disraeli was the most cynical and unscrupulous of all the men who have held the leadership of the Conservative party; that his historical philosophy was fustian and his social philosophy artificial; or that he stood the party on its head over the second Reform Bill in 1867 for the sake not of any principle or considered political strategy but of opportunism and from motives of personal rivalry. It matters very little either that as a politician he was obsessed throughout his career with the pursuit of power but had very little notion of what to do when he had it. All this is unimportant compared with other things. In the first place he was ultimately successful. He led the party out of the wilderness. Only the elderly and unkind could occasionally reflect that he had originally led them into it. He died in an aura of respectability which soon became an odour of sanctity that would have astonished and amused the Victorian generations who had known him in his audacious prime. But this is not the whole explanation. Though success is the supreme contemporary virtue, something more is needed to create a legend. Something theatrical, romantic, and slightly larger than life, something that for good or bad oversteps the conventions of the age and in so doing makes those conventions seem narrow and humdrum. Disraeli had all this and more: wit, a flair for presentation, a gift for the unforgettable phrase, an eye for the weaknesses of mankind, and the authorship of some of the best political novels in the English language. It is a great thing, if one wishes to be remembered, to have delivered speeches which still sparkle in the faded print of *Hansard*, to have produced books which after a century can still entertain. One can almost write one's own history: in his *Life of Lord George Bentinck* he almost did. With posterity literature is more potent than history; and Disraeli, as more than one Victorian observer noted, was very much a literary figure. He was above all, as Lord Blake has percipiently remarked in his superb biography, a political impresario and actor-manager. It is not surprising that he can still hold the stage or that the paint and canvas in the background still deceive. As a Tory colleague of his said to the eighth duke of Argyll, "Disraeli is the greatest myth that I know".

It is easy on the other hand to understand why Peel never became a legend in

[1] Originally published in *Solon*, a short-lived magazine edited by Sir Anthony Meyer MP, in 1970.

the Conservative party. He was a man of his time. He came of a generation of politicians who were trained to regard the claims of party as less important than their duty to the crown and to the state. Party indeed was a noun he was apt to prefix with the adjective 'mere'. It was not an endearing trait and Peel was always less than grateful to the men who sustained him in power. Party he regarded as an adjunct to politics, not as an end in itself. He was interested not so much in the pursuit as in the use of power. His instincts therefore were administrative and his approach to political problems empirical. He was an intellectual with an occasional touch of intellectual contempt; a natural autocrat who had to school himself to patience and compromise; an idealist who in the last resort would not surrender or retreat. The follies and selfishness of human nature which amused Disraeli repelled rather than interested Peel. A proud, shy, self-conscious man, he kept the warmth, affection and loyalties of his nature for a small circle of friends and colleagues. With the larger mass of his party his relations were always difficult and sometimes brittle. Twice he made a sudden switch of policy which seemed to betray the deepest interests and convictions of his followers. His career as party leader ended with the disruption of 1846. He died four years later when the passions of that event were still running high; and he spent those last four years in propping up a Whig administration. Though, alone among the post-1815 party leaders, he left a school of younger politicians who acknowledged his example and took his name, it was a legacy which in due course was inherited not by the Conservative but by the Liberal party. Though he himself after 1846 became a political hero and after his death an object of popular sentiment, it was for the most part among the poor and unenfranchised. It is not, at first sight, an encouraging *curriculum vitae* to submit in support of entrance to a Tory pantheon.

Yet the fact remains that this stiff, controversial and unaccommodating figure was the real founder of the Conservative party. He first enunciated and then popularized the basic principles of modern political Conservatism. He rallied and united the scattered forces of the right after the confusion and demoralization of the defeat over the Reform Act of 1832. The Conservative victory in the general election of 1841 was the first time in British political history that an organized opposition party took over power from opponents previously in a majority in the House of Commons. When in the next generation Disraeli carried out his much advertised 're-education' of the party, it took the inevitable form of a return to Peelite principles. Inevitable because it was only on these terms that a Conservative party could obtain and keep power in the political conditions of Victorian Britain. For all his deficiencies in the management of men, Peel understood his own society, understood what most needed to be done and had the ability to do it. He was a political architect in a sense in which Disraeli never was or could have been. He had the advantage for an architect of living in an age of revolution and reconstruction; but the foundations he laid are still discernible.

The birthplace of modern Conservatism can easily be located. Its landmarks are Peel's first ministry and the publication of the *Tamworth Manifesto* in 1834. The name 'Conservative' of course was slightly older. It first came into use during the years 1828–32 when the old eighteenth-century constitution was reeling under the successive shocks of the repeal of the Test and Corporations Acts, Catholic Emancipation, and the Reform Act of 1832. But in the sense in which it was then used, often (as in the phrase '*parti conservateur*') unchanged from the French political vocabulary with which it originated, it was no more than a convenient description of those who opposed constitutional change. But a party which merely opposes change is left in a disadvantageous position when its opposition proves unsuccessful. Decimated, demoralized, divided and leaderless the Tory opposition was never so weak in the Commons during the whole of the nineteenth century as it was in the sessions of 1833 and 1834. With the passing of the Reform Act it was confidently predicted that the Tories were out for a generation. The political choice of the future seemed to lie between the moderate Whig-liberals and the Radicals of the extreme left, and the lot of the Tories to remain as helpless and angry spectators of events they could no longer influence. It was Peel's early and difficult task to drive home the elementary lesson that a party which will not accept change is opting out of politics. The Reform Bill was on the statute-book. To behave as though it was non-existent or reversible would merely ensure ridicule and impotence. Their duty, Peel told the thin and sullen ranks of the opposition, was to make the Reform Act work and save their Whig opponents from the consequences of their own folly. In the circumstances of the time it was an attitude of great courage and independence. It was also an act of great political sagacity. For the first time it stamped him in the public mind as a politician with reserves of statesmanlike resilience which had survived the reform crisis. But he was not yet party leader. Indeed there was no Conservative party and no acknowledged leader. In the dark days of 1833 and 1834, when the amorphous majority of reformers in the House of Commons and their vociferous radical supporters outside seemed bent on reforming and possibly disestablishing the Church of England, and reforming and possibly abolishing the House of Lords, Peel had to labour hard to instil into the restive Tory politicians the need for restraint. All he had to support him was the traditional Tory concern for law and order. If that was still their interest, he argued, they must support government, as the repository of those qualities, whenever it needed support. Their duty was to behave in opposition as though they themselves were the goverhment. They could not, if they were true to themselves, oppose simply for the sake of opposing. It was necessary even out of office to assist on occasions their political opponents, not for themselves but for the cause of government in general. It was a theme to which he continually recurred throughout the 1830s as the ability of the Conservative opposition to affect the actual course of legislation steadily increased. 'We adopt,' he told a great gathering of Conservative MPs at a Merchant Taylors Hall banquet in 1838, 'the principle used in the policy which ought to prevail in all administrations; for we not only follow out the principles on which government ought to act, we actually perform many of their functions.' In or out of office, therefore, ran his doctrine, the Conservative party ought to retain something of the character of a responsible national executive.

What Peel said in these early years he was saying as an individual politician. But he said it again, conclusively and authoritatively, in the *Tamworth Manifesto* of 1834 after William IV had summoned him home from Italy to be prime minister. That famous document was not a philosophic statement of the fundamentals of Conservatism. It was a practical production designed to assist his followers in the forthcoming general election. It was intended above all to efface the Wellingtonian image of blank reaction which still clung to the politicians of the right. It represented no sudden conversion on Peel's part. Everything in it he had said before. The difference was that he was saying it for the first time as prime minister, for the first time as the acknowledged leader of a political party, and in circumstances of nation-wide publicity.

It is difficult now to recapture the impact of the *Tamworth Manifesto* because we have forgotten the background and because its more permanent principles have long been absorbed into the general stock-in-trade of Conservative philosophy. To contemporaries however it had the shock and excitement of novelty. What it did in effect was to offer an alternative to the apparently irresistible course of the radical movement under their half-hearted and squeezable Whig allies. An alternative that would preserve the essential continuity of British life and institutions while bringing them more into harmony with the changing needs of a rapidly changing society. To the moderate members of the aristocracy who felt that the Whig ministers were being increasingly compromised by their Radical and Irish supporters, Peelite progressivism came as a safe and acceptable *via media*. To those who had supported the Reform Bill of 1831 but were growing uneasy at its consequences, the assurance was given that society could be reformed without being transformed. To the young and sympathetic minds of the rising generation of both Whig and Tory families the work of adapting old institutions to new conditions offered an idealistic challenge. What gave the Tamworth formula its special appeal were its dual ingredients. On the one side there was the emphasis on the need to eliminate defects, inefficiency and injustice in public life and the promise of a 'careful review of institutions civil and ecclesiastical', and the 'correction of proved abuses and the redress of real grievances'. On the other was the refusal to pander to every popular whim, to promise instant remedies for what anyone might allege to be an abuse, or to abandon 'that great aid of government, more powerful than either law or reason, the respect for ancient rights and the deference to prescriptive authority'. The second element was as significant as the first. Along with Peel's conviction that the rapid changes coming over British society called for strenuous, intelligent and discriminating government action, went his engrained respect for historic continuity and his sense of the organic unity of society. Not for nothing was Burke his most frequently quoted political author. It was this fundamental Tory side to his nature that enabled him to declare, as he did in his great Merchant Taylors Hall speech of 1838, that among the great Conservative principles was 'the preservation and defence of that combination of laws, of institutions, of usages, of habits and of manners which have contributed to mould and form the character of Englishmen.'

This then was the formula. How did Peel put it into practice? The first task was to create on that intellectual basis a great national party. Though the defence of Church and State was still the conventional rallying cry of the right, Peel realized that the day had passed when the traditional alliance of parson and squire was an adequate foundation for a political party aiming at power. In the expanding, semi-urbanized, semi-industrialized society of the young Queen Victoria the Tory party had either to widen its base or be content with permanent exclusion from office. In the 1830s Peel worked consistently to enlarge the party's area of support both by what he said and the kind of audience to whom he said it. In this he displayed a national leadership of a kind rare among politicians of his day or for many years to come. In an age when party programmes did not exist and it was unconventional if not actually unconstitutional for ministers to make speeches outside parliament or their constituencies, Peel showed notable initiative in seizing the few reputable opportunities that came his way to speak to the public at large. The *Tamworth Manifesto*, in form a letter to his constituents, in fact an appeal to the nation, was itself an unprecedented act by the head of a government. In it he frankly addressed himself to 'that class which is much less interested in the contentions of party than in the maintenance of order and the cause of good government'. Within a week of its publication he made a speech on the same theme to the merchants and bankers of the City at a Mansion House dinner. When he left office a few months later he delivered at another City dinner in May 1835 the most significant political speech he had ever made outside the walls of Westminster. When he was invited to stand as candidate for the Rectorship of Glasgow University in 1837 he accepted for the political advantages it offered; and he reserved his most important address not for the university students but for a great civic audience of over three thousand at a specially convened Glasgow banquet. To all these varied representatives of the professional, mercantile and industrial middle-classes he preached the same gospel. Those who had supported the Reform Act as a means to efficient government but had no wish to see it transformed into 'a platform from which a new battery is to be directed against the institutions of the country' were told that their natural political home was in the Conservative party. There was no real line of demarcation between them and the landed aristocracy; it was their interest also to maintain the fundamental institutions of society and the peaceful evolution of the mixed constitution under which this lived. He, just as much as they, wished to see the great machine of government functioning as it should: 'animating industry, encouraging production, rewarding toil, correcting what is irregular, purifying what is stagnant and corrupt'.

His efforts were not confined to speeches and manifestos. The same insistence on broadening the party's basis was evident both in his public patronage and in his private friendships. He deliberately set out to invade the liberal-radical monopoly of intellectuals and break the image of the 'stupid' Tory party. As prime minister in 1835, for example, he gave a baronetcy to John Barrow the geographer, and pensions to Mrs Somerville, the scientific blue-stocking whose book on *The Connection of the Physical Sciences* had appeared the previous year, to the wife of Professor Airy, the Cambridge astronomer, and to Sharon Turner, the aged and distinguished Anglo-Saxon historian. The list of guests at some of his house-parties at Drayton Manor read like a roll-call of the professional, scientific, literary and academic figures of the day: Playfair the chemist, Stephenson the rail-road engineer, Whewell the great Cambridge mathematician, Lyell the geologist, Fox Talbot the pioneer of Victorian photography. Wheatstone the physicist, Parkes the agricultural expert, Hallam the historian. It was a matter of importance, Peel told the king in 1835, that a Conservative government should encourage 'the application of great talents and great acquirements to the support of the ancient institutions of the country'. Even his own bourgeois family origins and industrial wealth he turned into electoral assets rather than aristocratic disadvantages. 'Ought it not to make you, gentlemen,' he asked his City audience in May 1835, 'do all you can to reserve to other sons of other cotton-spinners the same opportunities?' A hybrid himself, he tried to make the Conservative party a hybrid organization; and middle-class support was increasingly tapped to supply a wider membership and more liberalized tone to the parliamentary party. He had an undeniable partiality for the aristocracy, as his affectionate friendships with Lord Lincoln and Sidney Herbert demonstrated. But two of his most illustrious ministerial recruits were Gladstone and Cardwell, like himself Oxford double-firsts and sons of industrialists. Middle-class brains and middle-class votes were essential ingredients in the great Conservative victory of 1841.

When he secured political power, he translated his concepts into practical legislation. If Conservatism was to be a national party, it was not enough to enlarge the basis of electoral support. It was also necessary to have a policy which took all classes of society into account. He was not a democrat. He did not think that the poor and uneducated possessed peculiar qualifications for solving society's problems. Indeed he distrusted their ignorance and feared their proneness to violence and demagoguery. An extension of education took precedence in his mind over an extension of the franchise. It was to the aristocracy, the wealthy, and the educated that he looked to provide the governing classes of the country. But it was a cardinal axiom with him that those classes deserved their power only in proportion to their ability to rise above class and individual bias. For a ruling class to govern solely in its own interest was in his view the shortest road to unrestrained democracy. The landed aristocracy could only justify its practical and prescriptive authority by acting in the general interest. He did not trust the people; he wanted the people to trust the ruling classes and the ruling classes to deserve that trust. This in the age of Chartism and the Anti-Corn Law League was a difficult lesson to absorb. When the urban proletariat seemed arrayed against the manufacturers and the manufacturers against the landowners it was not easy for the Conservative party, as the great embodiment of the agricultural interest, to keep itself detached from the bitter class animosities of the period. Indeed the growth of the Agricultural Protection Societies which provided the basis of the revolt against Peel in 1846 was largely a reaction to the savage attacks of the League on the farmers and landed gentry. But the ingenuous formula of the Young England politicians – an alliance of the aristocracy and the working classes against the shopkeepers and the Manchester School – even if practical, which it was not, held no attractions for Peel. His constant theme was the interdependence of society. Ideally one might wish that Britain had remained an agricultural community with benevolent squires, stout yeomen and a smiling peasantry in a landscape unsullied by slag-heaps and factory chimneys. But the Industrial Revolution was a fact and no statesman could ignore it. Faced in 1841 and 1842 with a great industrial depression, widespread unemployment, endemic pauperism and social violence, he made his first task the restoration of national economic well-being. He resisted anything that threatened to constrict the recovery of British industry even when, as in the case of Ashley's campaign for shorter factory hours, his policy seemed to conflict with humanitarianism. On the other hand he rejected the dogmatic school of *laisser-faire* economists who regarded poverty as a product of surplus population and wholesale emigration as the only permanent solution. Peel would have none of this chill academicism. His was a more earthy solution. 'We must make this country,' he told Croker, the party's chief publicist, in 1842, 'a cheap country for living, and thus induce parties to remain and settle here, enable them to consume more, by having more to spend.' And again, 'the danger is not low prices from the tariff but low prices from inability to consume, from the poor man giving up his pint of beer and the man in the middling station giving up his joint of meat.' Peel's free-trade budgets, and the unprecedented imposition of an income-tax in time of peace, were all designed for one central purpose: to restore financial stability, to encourage commerce and manufacture, to provide employment, and to reduce the cost of living. When introducing his epoch-making budget of 1842 he warned the House of Commons that, 'whatever be your financial difficulties and necessities, you must so adapt and adjust your measures as not to bear on the comfort of the labouring classes of society'. The income-tax was a step towards government solvency. But it was more than that; it was a measure of social equity. 'It is for the interest of property,' ran Peel's dictum, 'that property should bear the burden'. It was significant that the income-tax, hysterically attacked by Cobden and the League, was welcomed by the working-class Chartists. Peel's apparent obsession with tariffs and finance had its profoundly human side. Indeed, among all the remedies for what Carlyle had christened the *Condition of England Question*, the road of economic recovery along which Peel led the country between 1842 and 1846 was perhaps the most immediate and comprehensive way out of the nation's miseries that any government in the Hungry Forties could have devised.

The repeal of the Corn Laws in 1846 was only a particular example of this general policy. By 1845 if not earlier Peel had come to believe that the policy of reducing tariffs in order to encourage consumption had been experimentally proved. He saw no reason why the success of the cheap food policy commenced with butter and meat should not be extended to corn; and he was convinced that the prosperity of British farming depended not on the artificial shelter of high tariffs but on the application of more scientific farming methods to meet the demands of a growing industrial market. The real issue of the Corn Laws in 1846 was not economic but political and psychological. The intensive propaganda of the Anti-Corn Law League had succeeded, as Lord Lincoln told Gladstone in 1845, in compromising the whole position of the aristocracy. Their title as governing class was impeached; their parliamentary party system jeopardized. The coming of the Irish Famine merely precipitated a crisis which had been growing in British society over many years. For the sake of the future of Conservatism as a political force and the Conservatives as a parliamentary party, it was necessary to remove the imputation of narrow class interest with which the League had clothed them. Peel claimed, with justice, that the repeal of the Corn Laws was one of the most conservative acts of his career. 'I have thought it,' he said at the start of the stormy session of 1846, 'consistent with true conservative policy, to promote so much of happiness and contentment among the people that the voice of disaffection should be no longer heard, and that thoughts of the dissolution of our institutions should be forgotten in the midst of physical enjoyment.' He had his way and proved his point. The pent-up social, class, and even religious passions of his generation were released in one dramatic climax. Those who feared that concessions to agitation would merely encourage fresh popular demands and those who thought that any split in the Conservative party would destroy the last barrier to democracy, found their answer in the years which followed. Chartism died down; the year 1848, which saw revolutions in every great state in Europe, produced only a pale and harmless gesture of imitation in Britain; the efforts of Cobden and Bright to carry the impetus of the League into a new radical party met with dispiriting failure. Peel died in 1850 and the Conservative party did not regain power until 1874. In political terms the man who inherited the fruits of Peel's work of conservation and conciliation was Palmerston, his former Tory and Canningite colleague. The protectionists who had rejected him were left in the backwater of political life. But it was the landed classes as a whole who were the true beneficiaries. British aristocratic parliamentary government, which it was Peel's object to preserve, enjoyed in the central decades of the century its last golden age.

To say that there was an element of concession and expediency in his public actions is true; but that it is only another way of saying that he was in the business of politics as a professional. The charge that his policy was no more than a series of periodic surrenders to successive waves of agitation is however one that does not survive serious examination. He fought the battle of the reform bill to the end. In the 1830s he yielded nothing to the radical attacks on the Church and House of Lords or to the radical demands for a further instalment of parliamentary reform. More than any one man he was responsible for rescuing the Church of England in the years of its greatest weakness and unpopularity between 1833 and 1837. The introduction of the income-tax in 1842 was an act of political courage which his political opponents never believed he would carry out. His conversion to the repeal of the Corn Laws was an intellectual process in which the decisive factors were not the propaganda arguments of the League but the success of his own free-trade budgets in the preceding years, the steady recovery of trade, industry and employment, and the growing conviction, which he shared with many other intelligent politicians, landowners and agricultural experts, that the Corn Laws had ceased to be of any practical economic value. His preoccupation with the *Condition of England Question* in the 1840s was prompted by more than a mere calculated policy of killing Chartism by prosperity. Underlying his concern for the poor was the same sense of social justice which he had shown in his Home Office administration in the 1820s. It was reinforced by his harrowing experience as prime minister in 1841–2, the most terrible year which British society endured between Waterloo and 1914.

For the rest of his career Peel made it his prime object to ensure that the violence, distress and starvation of 1841 and 1842 never returned. 'Are those winters effaced from your memory?' he asked the House of Commons when fighting with his back to the wall in 1846, 'From mine they never can be'. All his public and private utterances confirmed the sincerity of that statement.

It was this background which gave fire and content to Peel's Conservatism. The Tamworth formula of preservation and adaptation was only the beginning. The difficult question was what to preserve, how to adapt. The actual application of Conservative principles in that as in any other generation demanded hard thought, great political judgement, and constant effort. As he phrased it once in the House of Commons with reference to the repeal of the Corn Laws,

I trust that a territorial aristocracy, with all its just influence and authority will long be maintained. I believe such an aristocracy is essential to the purpose of good government. The question only is – what, in a certain state of public opinion, and in a certain position of society, is the most effectual way of maintaining the legitimate influence and authority of a territorial aristocracy?

It is the perennial question to which Conservatism must give a perennially changing reply: what 'in a certain state of public opinion and in a certain position of society' is the best thing to do in the light of its basic principles. In Peel's day those principles were the maintenance of the aristocratic ruling class, of the established Church, of the constitutional integrity of the Crown, House of Lords, and House of Commons, and the unity of the British Isles. But though the content of the formula changes, the equation remains the same; and in his own day Peel was its greatest exponent.

The battle between fixity of principles and flexibility of politics is the unending battle of Conservatism. It is also what keeps it alive as a political force. Peel drove his party in the 1840s too fast and too far. But bitter as it was, the disruption of the Conservative Party in 1846 was a profound process of political education. The moral was clear. Conservatism, if it was to survive, must offer an alternative government. To do that it must become a national and therefore a composite party and its policy must take the form of an intelligent and sophisticated approach to the problems of the day. It was the last and greatest lesson he had to teach his followers. A more skilful politician might have done it less brusquely and with less damage. But the peculiar circumstances of the fifteen years following the Reform Act of 1832 called for courage and leadership rather than flexibility and compromise. These in any case were the early difficult years of modern party development. If Peel had much to learn about the business of being a party leader, the Conservatives had something to learn about being a party. In the end, as he believed they would, they returned to the road along which he had guided them; but belatedly and without gratitude. Posterity may think another verdict possible. That Peel, if not a good, was paradoxically a great party leader; that he was not only an outstanding public servant, but the founder of modern Conservatism.

13

Lord George Bentinck and his Sporting World[1]

Lord George Bentinck died of a heart attack on the evening of 21 September 1848 while walking across meadows near Welbeck Abbey; he was only forty-six. The premature and dramatic death of one so prominent in the political world produced interest and sympathy. His critics stayed decently silent; his friends, and the press in general, vied in public tributes to the stern reformer of the Turf who in the Corn Law crisis of 1846 had sought to vindicate the principles of honour and integrity among statesmen. The duke of Newcastle wrote solemnly that his career had been 'like a meteor . . . purifying all it touched'. The duke of Newcastle did not race; the duke of Bedford, who did, had a different opinion. Writing to Greville, he commented that 'the *nauseum* that is written and spoken about George Bentinck surpasses anything I ever recollect'. Greville himself, who knew Bentinck as well as anyone, reflected that it was fortunate for his reputation that he died when he did. At the height of his fame, credited with more ability than he possessed, saddled with expectations he could never have fulfilled, the future would only have brought disappointment to him and disillusionment to the public. 'As it is, the world will never know anything of those serious blemishes which could not fail to dim the lustre of his character.'

The politically important part of Bentinck's career comprised in fact only two parliamentary sessions. His effective rôle in the Commons had already ended some nine months earlier when the Protectionist whips had virtually deposed him from the leadership. Even in 1846 his achievement was spectacular rather than real. It is difficult to believe that there would not have been large defections from Peel in the Conservative ranks over the repeal of the Corn Laws, whether Bentinck had put himself forward or not; and equally that the Liberal opposition would not have been able to exploit the breach between Conservatives to bring down the government even if Peel had survived the Irish crimes bill. Without Bentinck's intervention, however, the Corn Law crisis would have lost much of its theatrical quality. It turned a conflict of policy into something which in parliamentary life is far more exciting and memorable: a conflict of personalities. Yet, oddly enough, between Bentinck and the prime minister whom he attempted to frustrate, and succeeded in overthrowing, there were many resemblances, temperamental as well as physical. Both were big, impressive men, over six feet tall with auburn hair and long, resolute countenances. Both were stubborn, masterful men, with strong moral convictions, considerable willpower, enormous energy, and much native intelligence. Both had courage and self-reliance; neither was disposed to allow the opinions or interest of his followers

[1] Not previously published.

to override his own views; both lost their position in consequence. What Bentinck lacked in contrast to the prime minister were the qualities of self-discipline, objective judgement, a trained mind, and over thirty years political experience.

In several respects Bentinck, a descendant of the Dutchman who was William of Orange's close political adviser, was more of an oddity as Conservative leader than Peel himself. A moderate Whig when he first entered parliament in the 1820s, he warmly approved of Catholic Emancipation and was offered a post in Grey's reform ministry of 1830. Though he refused, he gave an independent support to the reform bill of 1831. When Stanley, a close friend, seceded from Grey's ministry in 1834, Bentinck followed him into the short-lived Fourth party and ultimately took his place among Peel's Conservatives. Protectionism apart, he had hardly any affinities with traditional 'Church and King' Toryism. He favoured state salaries for Irish Roman Catholic priests and it was his vote for the admission of Jews to parliament which finally brought to a head his quarrel with the whips and his own virtual cashiering from the leadership in the House of Commons. His original involvement in politics had been casual and half-hearted. As a platform speaker he was ill at ease, rambling and repetitive, with awkward gestures and a high-pitched voice. He was well aware of his own technical and temperamental disqualifications for a parliamentary career. He described himself in 1847 as 'virtually an uneducated man, never interested or attracted by taste for political life, in the House of Commons only by a pure accident, indeed by an inevitable and undesired chance'.[1]

The 'accident' had been the premature death of his elder brother in 1824. The second brother, a keen sportsman and traveller, but now heir to the dukedom of Portland, was reluctantly persuaded to take over the parliamentary seat at King's Lynn, a pocket borough, which his dead brother had held. Tiring of this, he resigned two years later and the third brother George took his place. He had reasons of his own at that time for wishing to please his family but it was not a position for which he felt any enthusiasm. Born to wealth and unquestioned social status, but without the prospect of title and family responsibilities, George Bentinck grew up in what was, even for a duke's son, a singularly undisciplined way. He spent his first seventeen years at Welbeck Abbey, the family seat in Nottinghamshire; he attended neither public school nor university. Since his father was one of the wealthiest men in the country, as the *Annual Register* delicately observed in 1848, 'it did not therefore become necessary for him to engage with much ardour in the pursuit of any laborious profession; still, it was thought desirable that he should have some avocation.' The army was the obvious answer and in due course he joined the 9th Dragoons as a cornet. There he showed himself arrogant, humourless, and conceited, careless of his regimental duties and intolerant of criticism. Receiving a private letter of remonstrance from his captain, he promptly demanded an official enquiry which acquitted him for lack of proof. His indignant superior followed him to Paris, where he had gone as private secretary to his uncle George Canning, in order to issue a challenge. A duel was only prevented by Canning who secured the intervention of the French police. Further prosecution of the quarrel in England was halted by another board of enquiry ordered by the commander-in-chief, the duke of York, who had

---

[1] *Croker Papers* ed. L. J. Jennings (1884) III, 144.

been approached by his racing manager Greville on behalf of the duke of Portland. The establishment, it must have appeared to Captain Ker, had ways of protecting the sons of dukes. That unfortunate but irascible officer was obliged to resign from the army. It was perhaps significant, however, that Bentinck himself subsequently transferred from the Dragoons to the 2nd Life Guards, from which he retired with the rank of major in 1827.

By that date he had already taken up the pursuit which was to make him famous in the sporting life of his time. It was in the world of leather and horseflesh, race-courses and training-stables, crooked jockeys, unscrupulous bookmakers and heavy gambling, that his character and temperament revealed themselves over the next twenty years. It is not difficult to see the attraction. Though the early nineteenth-century has been dubbed the Corinthian age of sport, it was governed by a different ethic than that which was the accepted ideal of later Victorian society. Many, perhaps most, regular sportsmen played, fought, shot and raced not merely to win, but to win money. Few sporting activities were carried on without money being staked on the outcome. Even the MCC rules of cricket at that time had a section on betting. The prospect of financial gain gave a sharp edge to competition; and in an age when rules of sport were loose, and even more loosely enforced, every variety of artful dodge or dishonest trick was brought into play to influence the result. Horse-racing in particular, where the fallible natures of horses, jockeys, trainers, owners, handicappers, starters and judges multiplied the opportunities for fraud, was no place for a greenhorn. The enormous sums won and lost in betting made the actual prize money almost insignificant. Often private matches were arranged between owners to decide wagers. It was the period of some of the highest gambling ever known in the history of the Turf. Admiral Rous, the dominant figure at the Jockey Club in the third quarter of the century, said once that betting had been at its peak between 1822 and 1845. These years almost exactly coincided with Bentinck's racing career and to their reputation he himself materially contributed.

He made his debut in 1824 when he rode a friend's horse to victory at Goodwood. He started to bet heavily and two years later he lost, it was rumoured, as much as £30,000 (five times a secretary of state's salary) on the beaten favourite in the St Leger. His family had to come to his financial rescue and the displeased duke of Portland tried to wean him from his regrettable proclivities by purchasing an estate for him in Ayrshire to divert his energies. Though a keen breeder and owner of a large part of Newmarket Heath, the duke did little racing himself (though he had won the Derby with Tiresias in 1819) and disapproved of gambling. Bentinck promised to abstain from amusements which carried any 'risk of fortune' but did nothing to keep his pledge. Indeed, the duke, by simultaneously making him a generous settlement, bringing him in an income of some £18,000 a year, provided him with the material basis for even larger involvement. He persuaded his brothers to guarantee his credit with his bankers, and to camouflage his activities began to race horses under the names of various friends, not always with their permission. His cousin, Charles Greville, joined forces with him after the death of the duke of York in 1827.

They had little to show for their combined efforts, however, until 1835 when their filly Preserve, running in Greville's name, won the 1,000 Guineas. Disagreements over the handling of the filly then brought the partnership to a close.

Left on his own Bentinck went from success to success. In 1836 he brought off his famous coup over the St Leger by taking his horse Elis in three days from Goodwood to Doncaster inside a van when all the pundits had concluded that the horse could not be walked up (as the custom then was) in time for the race. He considerably enlarged his racing establishment and from about 1838–9 began to run in his own name. Having quarrelled with John Day who had the stables at Danebury in Wiltshire where most of his horses trained, he transferred them to Goodwood, the seat of his friend and fellow-Stanleyite the duke of Richmond. Greville adds that Bentinck (who otherwise evinced few tender emotions) cherished a hopeless passion for the duchess of Richmond. His most recent biographer Seth Smith discounts this story for lack of corroboration; but Greville's circumstantial account, including a statement that the attachment was noticed by others and was even alluded to in the scandal-sheets of the day, has the ring of truth. Certainly it would help to explain the unusual position which Bentinck soon occupied at Goodwood where he was allowed to treat the house and estate as though they were his own. He never married and never had a home of his own, using his father's town house in Cavendish Square or Welbeck Abbey as occasion suited.

In the 1840s he became conspicuous as a Turf reformer. His success, particularly at Goodwood, Epsom and Newmarket, in expelling the more obnoxious characters who infested race-meetings, was inevitably somewhat transient. His more permanent reforms were those governing the start of races, the regulation of jockeys, the numbering of horses, and the creation of enclosures. His set of rules, brought out in 1844, was gradually adopted at courses all over England. Even so, once his presence was removed, there was a constant tendency for the old abuses to return. When Rous became official handicapper to the Jockey Club in 1855, he found that standards were falling again and that constant vigilance was needed to keep down fraud and corruption. The Jockey Club itself was in low esteem and nearly bankrupt, its authority minimal. Rous's new set of reforms, brought forward in 1850, took him nearly thirteen years to put into effect. Even Bentinck's system of starting races had broken down after his death, mainly because of the venality of course officials. Nevertheless, Bentinck had pointed the way, even if he did not live long enough to carry out all he would have liked to have done.

His prestige reached its zenith in 1844 with the part he played in exposing the Running Rein fraud. The Derby of that year was remarkable even in an age accustomed to a certain laxity on the Turf. Although it is a race for three-year-olds, the field on this occasion included a four-year-old Maccabeus (which had been substituted for the real Running Rein) and a five-year-old Leander. Ratan, one of the favourites (whom Bentinck had backed heavily) was held back by a dishonest jockey; Leander smashed his fetlock in a collision with Running Rein and had to be destroyed, his head being then cut off to conceal evidence of his age. Running Rein won the race with ease; a Jockey Club enquiry followed; and the result was overturned in favour of the second horse Orlando, owned by the prime minister's brother Colonel Jonathan Peel. Bentinck's unflagging efforts to expose the fraud earned him the formal thanks of the Jockey Club and election as Steward for the next three years. Then suddenly, at the Goodwood meeting of July 1846 following the great Corn Law repeal session, his racing career came to a halt. As indifferently and laconically as he would have placed a £100 bet, he offered his entire establishment, at the absurdly low price of £10,000, to a party of sportsmen gathered at the duke of Richmond's house. After some initial hesitation the offer was taken up by Lord Mostyn and the deal quickly concluded.

The one great prize which had eluded Bentinck was ironically achieved two years later by Surplice, one of the horses in the sale. Disraeli has described a scene in the House of Commons library between himself and Bentinck, the day after the 1848 Derby, in his best romantic vein. It was as well perhaps that it did not see print until 1851. One may doubt whether Bentinck would have relished a description of himself as giving 'a sort of superb groan' and 'moaning out' his regrets. Like most big gamblers he had schooled himself to meet victory and defeat without any outward show of emotion. More prosaically he went to Epsom to see Surplice run, though apparently he arrived a few minutes after the race had ended; but he had backed him as a yearling and made a handsome sum (one account mentions £11,000) on the result. Seth Smith suggests that he was less concerned at the outcome of the Derby in 1848 than he had been in 1843 when his fancied horse Gaper, whom he had backed heavily, faded in the final furlong and came in fourth. In any event, by the summer of 1848 he could afford to be in a sanguine mood since he was planning to take up racing again. It was only ownership he had given up; he had never stopped betting or attending meetings. A week before his death he had the satisfaction of watching Surplice win the St Leger and it was a characteristic touch that when they took his dead body back to Welbeck Abbey they found in his pockets along with a quantity of notes and coins his betting-book. Just previously he had been talking with his old trainer Kent and asked him to purchase eight or ten likely horses as the nucleus of a new establishment. At the age of forty-six he could reasonably look forward to another twenty years in which to enjoy his favourite occupation. The strain of the previous two parliamentary sessions had been as great for him as probably for Peel and he was glad to be out of national politics once more. He told one MP, after the abandonment of the Protectionist leadership in 1847 that 'far from feeling the least annoyed, I shall feel greatly relieved by a restoration to privacy and freedom', and referred with unusual seriousness to the effect on his health and nerves of his parliamentary efforts.[1]

At the height of his racing career in the early 1840s Bentinck was undoubtedly, in Greville's phrase, 'the leviathan of the Turf'. He had sixty to seventy horses in training (at a time when there were normally not more than about a thousand thorough-breds in training stables in the whole of England), an equal number of brood mares and almost as many foals and yearlings. For several years his establishment numbered over two hundred horses, distributed between Goodwood and other stables, including three stud farms. It is not surprising that in 1843, when he enlarged his string at Goodwood to seventy-three, the usually placid duke of Richmond was moved to protest at the strain on his stable accommodation; fifteen in consequence were sold. In 1845 his annual expenses, including training bills, stake money, forfeits, and jockey's fees, were reckoned by his trainer to be over £40,000. His extravagant style of racing had something to do with this as well as the actual size of his establishment. He habitually entered

[1] M. Seth Smith, *Lord Paramount of the Turf* (1972) p. 154.

horses almost indiscriminately for a large number of races even though most of them had subsequently to be withdrawn. In 1845 he entered as many as eighteen colts for the Derby and eight fillies for the Oaks. For the following year he had a nominal total of 479 engagements involving actual stakes of £35,000 and forfeits of £22,000. This was racing on a prodigal scale which, as his own trainer said, 'has, I believe, never been equalled in the history of the Turf by a single individual'.[1]

To have the reputation of being the 'Rothschild of Tattersalls' is a doubtful honour when unaccompanied by a Rothschild fortune. What Bentinck was spending on his racing in these years probably amounted to more than his private income and the prize money he won put together. In 1845, for example, he won fifty-eight races but the prize money totalled only £18,000. The gap between what he spent and what he got back from racing could only be bridged by heavy and successful betting. Systematic gambling, therefore, was a necessary part of his racing system. That year he was thought to have won nearly £100,000 in betting, much of it on horses other than his own. It was a phenomenally successful year for the Goodwood stables, however, and he could rarely have shown so profitable a season. On his beaten Derby horse Gaper in 1843 he stood to win about £135,000. Fortunately he had laid off some of this on the actual winner Cotherstone who retrieved for him a modest £8,000. Nevertheless, the accelerating expansion in the scale of his racing brought about a crisis in 1846 which was not unforeseen by his trainer. There were financial as well as political reasons behind Bentinck's decision to withdraw from ownership. To win enough by betting to finance his racing demanded the systematic gathering of racing intelligence, continual study of form, and careful calculation of odds. His new role in the House of Commons made it impossible for him to devote enough time and attention to this necessary work. It was not his inability to continue racing but his inability to go on winning enough money to finance his racing that made him give up in 1846. Though the action seemed impulsive, it was based on practical considerations. Writing to his brother William about the sale of his establishment, he admitted that

> I was dying to be out of it – they were costing me £40 a day and when I gave away the 200 Sovereign Stake to Gully and John Day through mismanagement in running Crozier instead of Planet for it, I was so disgusted and so satisfied I must be ruined if I went on with a racing establishment without having time to look after it and attend to it myself, that I felt quite a load off my mind as soon as they were sold.[2]

As it was, he had been running an overdraft of £17,000 at his bankers and though he had paid off £7,000, and hoped to pay off the remaining £10,000 with the money he received from Mostyn, (which accounts perhaps for setting that precise sum as the price), he still owed large amounts in fortunately less demanding quarters – £10,000 to the duke of Richmond and £7,000 to the brother to whom he was writing.

Bentinck did not race to win money; he had to have money in order to race. Yet it was part of his character to take a fierce pleasure in winning for its own sake. The money he won by his bets were the insignia of success. 'He counted the thousands he won after a great race,' observed Greville, 'as a general would count

---

[1] J. Kent, *Racing Life of Lord George Cavendish Bentinck* (1892), p. 238.
[2] Seth Smith, p. 146.

his prisoners and his cannon after a great victory.' Wealth in itself he treated with the carelessness of one accustomed to it all his life. When a testimonial fund was got up for him by the Jockey Club after the Running Rein case, he refused to accept any material gift and the money was used instead, with his approval, as a charitable fund for the dependents of deserving jockeys and trainers. Yet it was perhaps fortunate for him that his obsessive energies were diverted from racing to politics when they were. Had he continued to enlarge his already unprecedented racing empire, he might well have suffered a financial crash as many lesser men did, including his close friend William Gregory, grandson of Peel's old Irish under-secretary. His temperament always drove him to overdo things; it came out even in small and sometimes ludicrous incidents. Deciding that large sponges were needed on one occasion for treating some horses with inflamed legs, he sent his servant out to scour London for the largest and most expensive that could be found and sent half a dozen of them down to Goodwood. They proved too big for the stable-boys to handle and Kent preserved them in the stables as curiosities. A special training-diet he invented for his racers, of milk, flour and eggs, was prescribed so lavishly that the duke of Richmond observed dryly that he would soon be taking over the farm and dairy as well as the stables. He laid out so many new tracks at Goodwood that the jockeys became confused and many mistakes resulted.

For a man who disclaimed powers of oratory, moreover, Bentinck was notoriously long-winded, not to say tedious, both in speech and writing. On subjects where he regarded himself as expert he would deliver his opinions to all who he thought would benefit from them. He was known to harangue meetings of the Jockey Club for two hours at a stretch. After he had entrusted his horses to Kent at Goodwood, the unfortunate trainer was almost overwhelmed by the stream of letters descending on him, often running to seven or eight sheets and sometimes three in a day. To digest and reply to these was a severe tax on Kent's time and patience; the more so perhaps since his other employer, the duke of Richmond, was an uncommonly laconic correspondent who once sent his trainer a letter consisting of a single word. The younger Kent confessed afterwards that the strain of being Bentinck's trainer would have shortened his life had it gone on longer than the five years from 1841 to 1846.

Bentinck once said that 'I don't pretend to know much, but I do know men and horses.' Both claims perhaps need qualification. Even with horses Bentinck could make mistakes, though he was very loath to admit them and was apt to persist when wiser owners would have called a halt. His greatest miscalculation was over Bay Middleton, who won the Derby in 1836 for Lord Jersey. Bentinck paid what was then the record sum of 400 guineas for the colt, hoping to win the Gold Cup with him the following season, despite the fact that at the time of the sale the horse had a suspect foreleg. In the event Bay Middleton never raced again and proved a failure at stud. None of his progeny were worth anything up to the time Bentinck sold him in 1846 though the enormous sums spent on breeding them up and paying forfeits 'would have discouraged anyone else,' said his trainer feelingly, 'while to some it would have been absolutely fatal'. But judgement of blood-stock is littered with casualties. Against the failure of Bay Middleton can be set the purchase of Crucifix in 1838, purely on the strength of her pedigree, when she was, to quote his trainer again, 'one of the scraggiest and most unpromising foals ever seen'.[1] It was Bentinck's obstinate nature that made his errors of judgement worse than they need have been. He was so taken by the success of his 'vanning' ruse with Elis in 1836 that he afterwards used the device almost indiscriminately and would often 'van' mediocre racers who (in Kent's opinion) were inferior in value to the plebeian horses pulling the van. His proclivity for staging full-length trials just before an important race to guide his betting calculations frequently took the edge off some of his best runners. In general he habitually over-raced his horses; and the better they were, the more they were made to do. In 1845, for example, Miss Elis won first the Goodwood Stakes and then next day the Goodwood Cup. Both of these were long punishing races, the Stakes being 2 miles 2 furlongs and the Cup 2 miles 6 furlongs. Having won about £30,000 on Miss Elis in these two events Bentinck could not be restrained from entering her for the Chesterfield Cup on the last day. She finished almost last in a field of nineteen and was never the same horse again. Three weeks later she ran in the Great Yorkshire Stakes; Bentinck again backed her but she was beaten easily. He refused to listen to any excuses for Miss Elis and was therefore convinced that the filly which beat her, Miss Sarah, would win the St Leger. He placed £3,500 on her only to see her beaten by The Baron. Bentinck was even known to race a horse twice on the same day; to animals as to men he could be merciless.

There was another side to Bentinck's racing of which the public were unaware. For all his deserved reputation as a Turf reformer, in his own dealings he seems to have been guilty of practices which he would have been the first to condemn in others. What has to be remembered, of course, is that the Turf in his day was a rough and unscrupulous place. Bentinck's system of intensive racing and heavy betting would have made him prey to all the scoundrels and blacklegs who flourished on the sport had he not used his wits to protect himself against them. How far, in pursuit of his own ends, he overstepped the boundary between what was and was not generally acceptable by the standards of the time is another matter. There were some owners who would not have stooped to Bentinck's tactics – his own father, for example, the duke of Portland, his friend the duke of Richmond, Lord Spencer, Colonel Peel, Admiral Rous and others; many were less scrupulous. The line between deceit and deception is a fine one and much of what Bentinck did was merely self-defence. One of his reasons for entering his horses for so many races and paying out so much in forfeits was to conceal his real intentions. With the same object he would often run several horses in a race, leaving the betting public to guess which he thought would win. The same need for secrecy led him to spread his bets anonymously all round the country. His chief agent or 'commissioner' in this delicate task was a well-known bookmaker, Henry Hill, who was credited with unusual influence over a number of jockeys and trainers and the ability to influence the running of horses other than this own. Hill was one of the few visitors whom Bentinck would receive in his bedroom.

Bentinck took the view, and he was not alone in this among contemporary owners, that his horses existed to make money for the man who paid for their upkeep and training. He objected to others backing them heavily because it brought down the price for him in the betting-ring. He was sufficiently annoyed at times when this happened to seek some compensation. In 1836, for instance, he

---

[1] Kent, pp. 74, 130.

threatened to scratch Elis from the St Leger unless he was given odds of 12 to 1. In 1839 he was so incensed at the amount of money being placed on his promising filly Crucifix that he instructed his trainer (at that time Day) to tell other trainers that he was prepared to withdraw Crucifix if they would promise him half the stake money. He had other tricks up his sleeve. After his horse Gaper won the Criterion Stakes at Newmarket in 1842, it was clear that many fancied him to win the Derby the following year. To prevent the odds from shortening Bentinck announced that Gaper must be regarded as a doubtful starter for that race. He then began to back him heavily. Some devices were highly imaginative. Before the Oaks in 1835, for which Preserve was favourite, he tried to influence the market by letting it be known she had influenza. To impress the watching touts he instructed her trainer to send her out on training gallops with her nose plastered with a mixture of flour and water – a stratagem of which Greville, part-owner of the filly, did not altogether approve. Another less defensible trick he used to was to run bad or unprepared horses in the first race of an early-season meeting, at the same time expressing complete confidence in his ability to win. When their failure suggested to the racing public (including his own friends) that his horses were generally backward, he was able to get favourable odds on his better horses in subsequent races.

Tricking touts and bookmakers was one thing; deliberately deceiving friends and associates was another. Greville records his anger at a deception practised on him in 1840. The previous season Bentinck's filly Crucifix had damaged a leg in her box when away from her training stables. The local veterinary surgeon held out little prospect of her being able to race for some considerable time. When she was brought home, however, the damage seemed much slighter than at first feared. Bentinck, who meanwhile had hedged his bets on her for a considerable sum, naturally wanted to recover the money he had thrown away on the strength of a misleading report. He had the man put his pessimistic diagnosis down in writing and showed this round among his friends, including Greville. A copy was also sent down to his trainer with instructions to show it to any interested visitor. If Greville is to be believed, Bentinck's correspondence with his first trainer John Day was said to contain many instances of other questionable practices such as running horses with orders to lose (either to get a favourable handicap for later races or make money by betting against them); and making judicious presents of money to rival jockeys. Greville knew all this because some of the letters actually came into his possession in 1845. In that year a certain Mr Crommelin felt endangered by Bentinck's investigations into certain dubious happenings some four years earlier. Hearing of this the Days put their old correspondence with Bentinck at Crommelin's disposal so that he could threaten retaliation. Crommelin consulted Greville and lent him some of the letters. Greville advised against publication but a private hint was conveyed to Bentinck (presumably at Greville's suggestion) of the consequences to himself should he proceed. Bentinck and the Jockey Club then dropped the matter. Writing three years later Greville was emphatic that, while he could not remember all the details, the correspondence 'disclosed a systematic course of treachery, falsehood, and fraud which would have been far more than sufficient to destroy any reputation'.

How much of this is to be believed? The evidence for a shadier side to Bentinck's racing career comes from people, mainly Greville and the two Days, who had no love for Bentinck. This is not surprising. If he did commit such acts, they would have been known to only a few; and fewer still would have been prepared to speak about them. William Day's *Reminiscences of the Turf* was not published until the 1880s and Greville's more serious allegations were omitted from the Victorian editions of his *Journal*. As a diarist Greville made errors and sometimes delivered hasty judgements. In general, however, he was an accurate recorder of events and tried to give balanced assessments of men and motives. That he invented what he wrote about Bentinck is hardly credible. Over the Crommelin affair he admits that he took a personal pleasure in frustrating his old associate. This does not invalidate his story; if anything, the honesty of the admission strengthens it. The persons in the best position to know the truth were Bentinck's trainers and both have put their reminiscences into print. The Days support Greville's opinion and add details of their own; but they of course had their own grudge against Bentinck. Keen and sometimes bitter rivalry had existed between Danebury and Goodwood ever since Bentinck removed his string of horses from Wiltshire to Sussex in 1841; and over the Crommelin case Bentinck managed to have the younger Day warned off for a time by the Jockey Club. Kent, on the other hand, in his *Racing Life of Lord George Bentinck,* though discreetly critical of some of Bentinck's management of horses, provides no evidence of any real dishonesty. He had every reason, however, to avoid giving offence to either of the ducal households of Portland and Richmond when in old age he sat down to write his recollections. Bentinck's latest biographer, Seth Smith, accepts what one might call the Greville version. T. H. Bird, whose book on *Admiral Rous and the English Turf* came out in 1939, leaves his readers to judge for themselves, though by giving extensive quotations from Day and Greville and making no attempt to defend Bentinck's reputation, he seems to lean to their side. Greville conceded that Bentinck would not have consciously committed a dishonest act but 'he has made for himself a peculiar code of morality and honour, and what he has done, he thinks he has a right to do, that the game which he plays warrants deceit and falsehood to a certain extent and in a certain manner'. If so, he was probably not the only racing owner to think so. In Bentinck's case wilfulness and self-righteousness enabled him to regard his own behaviour in a different light to that of others.

What cannot seriously be doubted is the malevolent strain in Bentinck's nature. When he took up a quarrel he pursued it to the end; and he was not scrupulous in his methods. 'A lion of the Turf and a very dangerous customer' was one contemporary description. Seth Smith's summary of this side of his character is unequivocal; he was 'proud, arrogant, unrelenting, self-opinionated, and vindictive'. All these qualities are seen, for example, in his crusade against dishonest jockeys and bookmakers and in the various legal actions which arose out of that crusade. Take the celebrated *Qui Tam* case which was instigated in revenge for his expulsion of various undesirable characters from the Goodwood course. A group of these obtained writs against various owners, among them Bentinck, Anson, Colonel Peel, Gregory and Greville, under an obsolete statute of Queen Anne prohibiting betting. It is the manner of Bentinck's reaction which catches one's attention. 'I have registered a vow in heaven,' he writes passionately to a fellow-defendant in November 1843, 'to take signal vengeance upon these scoundrels and please God to favour my pursuits of these said devils, half of them shall be exterminated.'[1] In the Running Rein case he acted with single-minded tenacity and energy, travelling across to Ireland himself to gather evidence and altogether (as the defending counsel said in court) acting the multiple rôles of detective, attorney and procurer of witnesses. Though the suit was formally brought by Wood, the nominal owner of the colt, against Colonel Peel for the recovery of the stake-money, the moving spirit behind the Jockey Club's action and the subsequent legal defence of it in court was Bentinck. It was a contest in effect between him and the head of the syndicate which had engineered the fraud, a notorious character by the name of Abraham Levi Goodman who was the real owner of Running Rein.

Bentinck's wrath was directed with equal vehemence against his fellow-sportsmen when they acted in a manner of which he happened to disapprove. The Gurney affair of 1841–2 was a case in point. Gurney was a bookmaker who was unable to meet his creditors because he was unable to collect from his debtors. Under an arrangement sanctioned by the Jockey Club a committee of three was set up to put his affairs in order. A meeting of the Club, at which among others Rous, Colonel Peel, Anson and Greville were present, decided that all those who owed money to Gurney should hand it to the committee. Bentinck, who was one of them, at first refused to pay up and justified his refusal with a number of reasons reflecting on the good faith of the committee. Though in the end he settled his debt, at one stage he sent a letter to the *Morning Post* criticizing the Jockey Club's action. In private he complained angrily to Richmond of the 'blackguard conduct of Charles Greville and the unhandsome conduct of Rous and George Anson'. His language about the Jockey Club was equally intemperate. 'If it proceeds in the course in which it has of late been proceeding, the sooner for the sake of the Turf it is abolished, the better.' For his *Morning Post* letter Bentinck had in the end to offer a formal apology but he went on making difficulties on the Gurney matter until most of Club's members were exasperated at his obstinacy.[2]

It cannot be accident either that Bentinck's career was punctuated by quarrels involving old friends as indiscriminately as strangers. There was an early revelation of this vengeful side to his nature in 1828 after Canning's death and the failure of Goderich to hold the ministry together. George Villiers (the future earl of Clarendon) reported that both in private and in public Bentinck was behaving very violently against those of Canning's former followers (notably Huskisson) who had joined Wellington's new administration. Howard de Walden blamed some of this on Lady Canning who, he thought, had worked on her son-in-law Clanricarde and her nephew Bentinck to commit what he described as all sorts of follies and breaches of confidence and social decorum. He added that Bentinck's 'extreme excitability on all questions in which he takes an interest' made him an easy person to stir up in this way. These comments are all the more pertinent since they came from men who had no reason to favour either Wellington or Huskisson. Howard de Walden was a Canningite and Villiers a camouflaged Whig.[3]

It would be misleading to describe Bentinck as quarrelsome; he was not choleric by temperament. The root of the trouble was the rancour he displayed in

[1] Seth Smith, p. 73.
[2] *Ibid.* pp. 60–3.
[3] J. Bagot, *George Canning and His Friends* (1909) ii, 434–5.

any matter in which he conceived himself affronted. He never, for example, as far as we know, challenged anybody to a duel. But challenges are usually the recourse of the injured party. On different occasions his offensive behaviour provoked challenges from Ker and Osbaldeston, and might have brought about two more, from Greville and Sir Robert Peel. The case of Captain Ker has already been mentioned, that of Peel I have dealt with elsewhere.[1] The quarrel with George Osbaldeston originated with a race meeting at Heaton Park, Lord Wilton's seat near Manchester: Wilton gave large parties on these occasions and took care to include the official handicapper among his guests. It was generally thought that Wilton's horses, and those of the well-known northern trainer John Scott, enjoyed a certain advantage with judges and handicapper in the ensuing races. Osbaldeston, a hard-bitten little Yorkshireman and the most famous all-round sportsman of his day, determined to upset this comfortable arrangment. He took a good but unknown Irish horse Rush to Heaton, kept him back (or in plain English pulled him) in an early race, got good odds for him in the big race on the third day, and won in a canter. Bentinck, who had taken a side-bet of £200 to £100 with Osbaldeston on the result, chose not to settle the debt. When personally asked for the money at Newmarket the following spring, he handed it over with such insulting language that Osbaldeston promptly went off to find a second. The two men eventually met at Wormwood Scrubs. Accounts of what happened were written down long afterwards and differ substantially; the truth is now probably irrecoverable. It seems clear, however, that between them the seconds ensured that Osbaldeston (a crack pistol shot) did not inflict any damage on his opponent. Bentinck was left convinced that his own second, Anson, had saved his life.

There are three interesting features in the Osbaldeston affair. The first is that the Heaton Park trick was something Bentinck himself was accused of practising later on. The second is that many men thought the deception, though understandable, was not very defensible and that if Osbaldeston had killed Bentinck in a subsequent duel, his reputation would have been ruined. The third curiosity is the high moral tone which Bentinck adopted in the dispute. It was only with reluctance that he even consented to meet a man who, in his opinion, had forfeited the character of a gentleman. 'I trust,' he wrote to his father, 'you will . . . think I was at least right in morality as well as in honour when once I had uttered a charge, which in my conscience I believe to be just, to adhere to it and firmly refuse to retract or qualify it.' Not many aristocratic sportsmen of the time would have talked of morality as well as honour. But for Bentinck right was always on his side and his opponents invariably acted from the lowest motives. 'A strong difference from his views,' wrote his friend Gregory, 'was tantamount to a moral offence.' It was easier for him than for most to believe he was merely administering justice when others might have been forgiven for thinking that he was pursuing a private vendetta.[2]

The quarrel with Greville began in 1835 when Preserve lost the 2,000 Guinea for which she was favourite. Bentinck considered that his partner had interfered and given wrong instructions to her jockey. When the filly also lost the Goodwood Stakes later in the season he accused Greville of deliberately arranging for his own

---

[1] *Sir Robert Peel* (1972), pp. 595–8.

[2] *Squire Osbaldeston His Autobiography* ed. F. D. Cuming (1927 edn) pp. 187–91, 271–4; Kent, pp. 400–8; Seth Smith, pp. 32–7. *Sir William Gregory* ed. Lady Gregory (1894), p. 115.

horse Dacre to obstruct her. The elaborate letter in which he made this accusation was couched, recorded Greville many years later, 'in terms so savage and so virulently abusive' that with any other recipient there could only have been one response. Feeling, however, that he could not very well challenge his uncle's son, Greville brought in a third party and Bentinck was ultimately persuaded to withdraw the letter. The partnership came to an end but the outward appearances were maintained. Indeed, when in 1837 Bentinck assisted in trying out Greville's horse Mango for the St Leger (and subsequently netted £14,000 by backing him for that race) Greville thought there might be a reconciliation. The relationship broke down completely, however, in 1842 when (Greville relates) 'at a meeting of the Jockey Club I made a speech in opposition to him which he chose to construe into an intentional insult, and the next time we met he cut me dead.' Attempts by Greville and common friends to bring about a reconciliation failed and for the rest of his life Bentinck refused to have anything to do with him.[1]

We only have Greville's word for this affair but from a completely separate source there is an account of a small incident which fits exactly into the picture of Bentinck's temperament drawn by Greville and more briefly by Gregory. Assheton Smith, the celebrated fox-hunter, sometime Master of the Quorn, kept a pack of hounds at Tedworth in Wiltshire in his later life. Bentinck frequently hunted there during the parliamentary session and persuaded Assheton Smith to become a member of the Jockey Club. His membership did not last long since, according to his biographer, 'he loved the straightforward honesty of a fox-hunt but observed that the chicanery of racing was ungenial to him'. At one point, however, Bentinck pressed him to come up for a meeting to support him on some issue. Assheton Smith declined on the grounds both of his inexperience as a member and his ignorance of racing matters. Some time later he invited Bentinck to Tedworth and, knowing he had disposed of his hunters, offered to mount him on the best horse in his stables. This was Bentinck's reply.

> Dear Mr Smith. I have always been accustomed to drink out of a large cup, and cannot stoop to a little one. I decline hunting on another man's horse when I have no longer hunters of my own. Your letter reminds me that *you* are the *only* one of my father's old friends who, when solicited, would not support his son in his endeavour to reform the Augean stable.[2]

Even the easy-going William Gregory saw his friendship with Bentinck come to a sudden end in 1846 as a result of the latter's savage attack on the Peelites as janissaries and renegades. The breach lasted until just before Bentinck's death when a chance meeting at Doncaster seemed to restore them to their old footing.

When therefore Bentinck entered the parliamentary arena in the 1846 session, Peel found himself facing a remarkably dangerous man. The partnership between Bentinck and Disraeli is sometimes portrayed as though Disraeli were a kind of political mercenary hired by the aristocratic Bentinck on behalf of the landed gentry. This is an over-simplification. Disraeli was a professional politician coolly making the most of the finest opportunity which had so far come his way. He cared little for protectionism; the crisis for him was a stepping-stone in his career.

---

[1] Greville's main analysis of Bentinck will be found in his *Journal* under the date 28 Sept. 1848; but see also 6 June 1843 and 5 July 1844.
[2] Sir J. Eardley-Wilmot, *Reminiscences of T. Assheton Smith*, (1860) pp. 68–9.

It was Bentinck himself who acted more in the style of a political bravo, putting all his energy, ruthlessness and vindictiveness at the service of the Protectionists. The temper in which he undertook the task he revealed in his letter to Croker of October 1847.

> My sole ambition was to rally the broken and dispirited forces of a betrayed and insulted party, and to avenge the country gentlemen and landed aristocracy of England upon the Minister who, presuming upon their weakness, falsely flattered himself that they could be trampled upon with impunity.

Yet, however passionately he felt about what he regarded as a betrayal, the Corn Law battle could never have been more than a single and slightly unnatural episode in his life. He had few qualities necessary for a political leader and many which positively disqualified him for such a position. The gentry who followed him in 1846, though not always approving his language, were not sorry to see the back of him in 1848. Disraeli himself admitted to Greville that, much as Bentinck had failed as leader of the opposition, he would have failed as minister even more.

Bentinck was not able to prevent the repeal of the Corn Laws. What he did succeed in doing was to inject a peculiar venom into the crisis by the violence of his personal attacks on the prime minister.[1] The memory of them was still fresh in the mind of Sidney Herbert when six years later he delivered his brilliant and scornful speech on the Derby–Disraeli acceptance of free-trade in November 1852. Speaking of Peel he recalled how 'he was attacked by the foulest language, and accused of the meanest crimes'. It was this, far more than the studied sarcasms of Disraeli, that made it difficult for Peel's personal friends to return to the party which had condoned those attacks. That Bentinck had chosen to fight that battle in this way and by these methods, however, could have surprised nobody who had been acquainted with his character and temperament as revealed by his previous twenty years on the Turf. Nor was it only against Peel that he showed this violent and unscrupulous side to his nature. He made a charge against Lord Ripon in August 1846 (and subsequently had to withdraw it) of dishonest patronage bargains with Lyndhurst, the Lord Chancellor; and in June 1848 accused two Whig ministers, Grey and Hawes, of wilfully suppressing a colonial despatch and subsequently lying to conceal its existence. On the latter occasion Lord John Russell lost his temper and retorted that the mean frauds and tricks imputed to his colleagues were not the characteristics of men in high office. 'They are the characteristics of men who are engaged in pursuits which the noble Lord long followed.' It was an unfair and unwise generalization; but Russell was not the only one to feel that Bentinck had imported into the arts of parliamentary leadership a new and degrading element.

---

[1] Lord Mahon, who also commented on Bentinck's habit of treating political opponents as moral delinquents, gave as an example of his coarseness a comparison he made (in a speech at 'Mr Newdegate's festival') of Peel to a husband who procured his wife for immoral purposes and trafficked in her dishonour (Chevening Papers, Mahon to Bonham, 27 Aug., 12 Sept. 1846).

Epilogue

14

A Modest Defence of Historical Biography[1]

It is a paradox that while historical biography has never been more popular, reservations are still expressed about its legitimacy as a branch of history. Academic reviewers, especially younger ones, sometimes imply that for professional historians the attraction of biography is meretricious and its writing a soft option. This might be dismissed as intellectual snobbery were it not that more eminent historians have cast doubts on the value, or at any rate on the status, of biography as a professional study. The late Sir Lewis Namier once wrote that

> biographies have become the ritualist form of English historiography; they predominate as much as portraits do in English oil-painting; both answer a custom and a demand, and pay homage to the importance ascribed to individuals; but they may also be due to fear of unbounded fields or to a lack of creative imagination.[2]

A distinguished contemporary, Professor G. R. Elton, has argued that

> though biography is really a separate art, with rules and problems of its own, most people seem to think of it as simply a form of history . . . [But] even at its best biography is a poor way of writing history . . . The historian should know the histories and characters of many men, as he should know much else, but he should not write biography – or at least should not suppose that in writing biography he is writing history.[3]

Strictures from such sources demand attention.

Against them the classic nineteenth-century champions of biography, once influential, do not now enjoy much of a following. Carlyle's assertion in *Heroes and Hero Worship* that 'universal History, the history of what men have accomplished in this world, is at bottom the History of the Great Men who have worked here'; Disraeli's exhortation in *Contarini Fleming*, 'read no history, nothing but biography, for that is life without theory', nowadays seem decidedly fusty. Yet it would be perhaps unwise as well as a trifle conceited to hustle these Victorian sages ignominiously aside. Though neither was a professional historian (the term was scarcely known in their day) Disraeli wrote one and Carlyle no less than three biographies. Carlyle's further remark about the times calling out in vain for a great man is a reminder to our generation that the opportunity does not always create the man and that, conversely, when it does, the result is sometimes terrifying, as witness the career of Adolf Hitler. Disraeli's dictum is a succinct statement of one of the oldest justifications for the study of history: namely, that it

---

[1] Not previously published.
[2] In an essay on 'History' in *Avenues of History* (1952).
[3] In *The Practice of History* (1969 edn) p. 169.

is a case-book of examples from which we can all profit. If one of the attractions of history is that it is an extension of our more personal experience of life, we must at least admit that the study of other men's lives is of some relevance.

Nevertheless, these considerations are hardly enough to answer the criticisms levelled by Namier and Elton. Those criticisms must, however, be taken in their context. Namier was attacking not so much biography as such but bad biography. This is clear from his further accusation that 'the typical political biography mixes up three different functions, and in that mixture finds an excuse for doing each badly'. In Namier's view, such authors exploit the personal correspondence of their subject without giving it the critical treatment of a scholarly editor; they try to analyse a personality without any training, notably psychological training, in that difficult field; and they are content to fill in the historical background from the most superficial and elementary sources. These are magisterial rebukes and no doubt many biographies deserve them. Nor is it any defence to reply that there are many narrative or analytical histories against which equally severe criticisms could be brought. Namier, however, was less an opponent of biography than a perfectionist annoyed by the characteristic weaknesses of a certain type of popular biography. Yet he also wrote that 'true biography is a great and exacting art' and in the latter part of his life became the great exponent of collective biography as a 'new pattern of an aggregate character' to illuminate parliamentary history. Even more revealing is his definition that 'the subject matter of history is human affairs, men in action, things which have happened and how they have happened; concrete events fixed in time and space, and their grounding in the thoughts and feelings of men.' The emphasis here, one might think, places him, however incongruously, not far away from Disraeli and Carlyle.

Elton, in contrast, was constructing a definition which by its own terms excluded biography as a true branch of history. He freely admits that some biographies are good and all are historical; but, he argues, the biographer's province differs from that of an historian and 'in measure as he deserts his proper subject for what concerns the historian, that subject's age, he fails in his own task'. The question seems one of classification and the issue whether a definition of history which excludes biography is altogether satisfactory. If individuals do exercise significant influence over their age (as Elton accepts that they do), it seems artificial to regard their activities in certain circumstances as 'history' and other more private or less important activities as somehow 'not history'. To distinguish between the age and the individual is reasonable in theory; in practice it is one that is difficult to maintain. It is doubtful whether historians in the Eltonian sense and biographers would be happy with some sort of partition of human activities into a public domain and a private domain.

One may agree with Elton that there is an obvious difference between, say, a life of Gustavus Adolphus and a history of Sweden in the seventeenth century. The doubt is whether the immediate and palpable differences are sufficient to distinguish them as belonging to different fields or different techniques. Another well-known scholar, A. J. P. Taylor, once suggested that every historian should write at least one biography in order to learn the difference between the two. The experience no doubt would be educative but it would still not settle the real issue. Every botanist and zoologist knows that sometimes members of the same species have to all external appearance little in common. We may consent to class the story of an individual as biography and that a country as history; but what are we to do with all the other varieties of historical writing which fall between these two examples? Is the story of a family 'history' or merely a collection of biographies? In which category do we place the account of a parish, a business company, an infantry regiment? Does the *Victoria County History* deserve its title when its subject matter consists of separate descriptions of the territorial units into which England has historically been divided? Ascending the whole gamut of possible historical subjects from a single person to a whole civilization, at what point do we cross the line between what is, and what is not, 'history'? One only has to put the question to wonder whether it is worth putting. A search for definitions may simply end with inherently artificial and therefore inherently false categories. Even when we employ such useful terms as 'constitutional', or 'economic' or 'demographic' history, we are aware that to study those fields in isolation is unsatisfactory. All such concepts are merely guidelines which we have invented to steer our investigations in the confused, because undivided, world of reality.

Elton himself takes a wider and more humane view of his subject than a few isolated quotations abstracted from a particular line of argument might suggest. He has written approvingly of the frequent need to 'concentrate upon particular studies of restricted problems' and in another place has warned that 'a perfectly proper recognition that history is not simply the record of outstanding personalities – outstanding in position or in personal qualities – has in this century of the pretty common man been perverted into a notion that history knows no great men at all and that individuals do not affect the fortunes of mankind.'[1] The whole of this eloquent passage in fact seems to establish at least a *prima facie* case for historical biography. Though the historical importance of an individual may depend on a particular situation in which he found himself, the character and temperament which conditioned his behaviour at that juncture were not the products of that situation. To discover why a man acts in a particular way at a particular time it is usually necessary to go back many years, perhaps even to childhood or adolescence. The comprehensive study of such individuals must therefore be a proper function of the historian. Yet we can hardly create subdivisions in biography between the historically important, the less important, and the unimportant. Orthodox history itself conventionally covers a wide range of subjects from the sublime to the petty. To attempt to confine 'history' to what are deemed large and significant topics would be tedious for the reader, impractical for the historian, and dangerous for the subject.

What, one may suggest, lies behind much of the criticism of biography as a form of historical writing is that more than most it lends itself to popular and trivial treatment. A feature of our time has been the growth of what an American critic, L. P. Curtis then of Berkeley, christened *umclass* biography. He borrowed the expression from Mr B. Inglis who coined it to describe what he believed to be the dominant cultural class in modern Britain, characterized by its heterogeneous origins, upper-middle class status, intellectual pretentiousness, and social snobbery. Curtis views the *umclass* school of biographers as part of the London literary establishment, with a public school and Oxbridge background and close personal links with the parliamentary and publishing worlds. They are 'usually profes-

[1] *Political History* (1970) pp. 69–80.

sional writers with amateur standing who do not profess history for a living'. To be a woman in this field appears to be an advantage; to have a title is even better. Behind the satire one can recognize a certain element of truth. The production by non-historians of historical biographies has clearly become a major light industry. Equally clearly some of its practitioners are extremely good. To class them as 'not professional historians' is beside the point. History has always been the great amateur subject. Yet there are generic weaknesses in popular biography. Selection is all important; historical significance largely irrelevant; the prosaic and the commonplace something to be avoided. The many figures who have played a part in the world's affairs but who are in themselves not particularly exciting are rejected as unsuitable by this school of writers. What is needed to catch the public eye is the romantic and the dramatic; a whiff of crime and immorality does not come amiss, either. The *umclass* biographers, like butterflies flitting from flower to flower, move from century to century, country to country, in their endless quest for rewarding subjects.

At their worst these generic weaknesses result in serious defects from a professional historian's point of view. The authors, being non-specialists, usually lack adequate knowledge of the contemporary background and cannot therefore place their characters in a sensitive historical framework. If they have at their disposal a newly-discovered hoard of private letters (an event which frequently prompts a biography) they tend to make too much of that one source. They avoid comparison and analysis; they describe much and explain little. Their characters seem larger than life because they are shown on a strangely empty stage. They provide entertainment for the mind's eye but not for the mind's brain. Yet to be censorious, even when censure is deserved, is not enough. Alongside their typical defects, the *umclass* biographers should not be denied typical virtues. Though not professional historians, they are professional writers who are mindful of their public. They have to interest their readers and this means that they have to write reasonably well; style is important. If they do nothing else, they usually take pains with the character and psychology of their subject. They do not leave such important matters off-stage after the manner of the Victorian *Life and Letters* school of biographers. They make good, often skilful, use of narrative and description. Narrative, like biography, is regarded by some as an easy form of historical writing. At its best, however, it demands as much technique and even more imagination than analytical writing.

In all these respects professional historians can learn from popular biographers between whom and themselves there is in reality not a yawning gap but merely a variety of gradations. The professionals themselves, when they turn to biography, are not without certain occupational weaknesses against which they have to guard. The study of history accustoms one to dealing with situations, events, policies, organizations, administration, and legislation. The historian has less practice in analysing temperament and character and may for that reason be shy of making the attempt. Faced with the task of following a series of events which form the external life of an individual, the historian–biographer is apt to concentrate on the events (since he is accustomed to dealing with events) and neglect the personality of the man who forms their connecting link. Yet without that link the events themselves lack depth and cohesion.

The apparent linear simplicity of a biography is often delusory; it may more resemble a series of cross-sections as the subject moves from one field of action to another. The theory that serious biography is an easy form of writing will hardly survive the experience of attempting one. To know a man's society so that it becomes as familiar as one's own; to discover his true character and convey it convincingly to the reader, to describe the constant interplay of public issues and private motives; to explain with lucidity and authority the different spheres of activity and responsibility that a single career may traverse and yet maintain the constant presence of the man himself; to give the physical appearance, the voice, the gestures, the little human touches familiar to contemporaries; to bring to bear on dead evidence a disciplined imagination without which the biography itself remains dead; and to convey all this in readable prose without clogging the narrative, losing direction, or sacrificing depth – that is a task which requires all the skills of which an historian is master.

The defence of biography as a branch of history must rest, however, not on whether it is technically difficult but on other considerations. It may formally be justified on three separate grounds: as philosophically legitimate, as professionally valuable, and as humanly important. It is, in the first place, a demonstrably legitimate aspect of historiography. Unless we accept a deterministic view of history, we must be prepared to recognize the existence of chance and accident in human events. The actual question of determinism (in the sense that everything that happens is determined by an infinite and unbreakable chain of causation) is one for theologians, philosophers and physicists; but it is not clear to the layman that they are agreed on an answer. Meanwhile historians must work on the same assumptions that they make in everyday life; namely, that there are few things either certain or inevitable in human affairs. Unless an historian accepts that intellectual position and writes on that basis, his work has little meaning and not much justification; since all he can do in that case is to relate what was ordained from eternity and could not have been otherwise. This indeed may give food for moralizing about God's purpose in his Creation; but to do that is the province of theologians, not historians. On the other hand, to accept the role of accident is to argue not that all is chaos or blind chance, but merely that there is in man's activities an element of will and choice, the personal, the unpredictable and the fortuitous. If that is conceded, clearly the individual himself is one of those elements and therefore a proper subject for enquiry. In a field of knowledge so vast as that which we call 'history', there must be freedom to choose any topic from the fall of empires to the events of a single day. We may have our own private views on what is important in history and what is not; but it is all history and there can be no proscription of either subject or method. Biography is as allowable as any other form.

A case can also be made for biography as a scholarly discipline. It is perhaps the best corrective to the dangers of impersonal history – history, that is to say, which deals with large and general topics. To pursue broad topics, to deal with important aggregates, to survey long periods of time, to select what is typical and representative, to generalize from a mass of small detail – these are proper occupations for an historian. Yet there are dangers. Generalizations which ignore awkward exceptions soon begin to lose touch with reality. Abstractions such as 'movements', 'public opinion', 'class', 'party', 'nation', 'revolution', 'civilization', 'culture' may easily become substitutes for thought rather than what they are – useful but imprecise labels which in any given historical situation need to be analysed and refined. The examination of individuals, with all their oddities and perversities, helps to restore realism to the historical picture. To think in terms of people reminds us that events need not have happened as they did; it makes us reflect on the role of chance in human destiny. In the end all aggregates are composed of tiny particles; all historical events the result of human actions or reactions. The historian who neglects the small particulars of life hurts his own credibility.

For the professional historian the practice of biography offers a separate minor reward. The boundaries of such a subject are fixed not by the author but by the person whose life he sets out to describe. Where that goes he must follow. In the case of an important public figure this means that the biographer has often to make himself master of a number of different activities, in widely varying situations, which left to his own devices he might never have felt any inclination to explore. For the efficient performance of his task, however, he must address himself to these studies even if he lacks both personal interest and previous knowledge. It is usually a salutary experience. Given a human tendency, even among historians, to keep to familiar paths, anything that occasions a journey into unfamiliar territory has its value. The untidiness of life should be reflected in the heterogeneity of an historian's knowledge; he can hardly have too much miscellaneous information. In a paradoxical way, therefore, the uniqueness that is a quality of every biography is itself a mental stimulus.

The last, and perhaps the most persuasive, argument for biography is simply that it answers a profound human need. The historian Pieter Geyl wrote that what attracted him to the study of history was that it seemed 'a key to life . . . life in all its fullness, life in all its shadowing and aspects'. Biography by its own nature is the most valuable of these keys. It is not, of course, any more than history in the larger sense, the only key. Literature is as instructive, and for many a more entertaining, way of vicariously extending one's experience of human nature. Though historical characters once lived and literary characters are artefacts, the curious fact remains that the second are frequently more 'real' to us than the first. We feel we know, and in that sense we do know, Hamlet, Don Quixote, Anna Karenina with an emotional certainty and intimacy which is lacking in our apprehension of Francis Bacon, Philip II of Spain and Catherine the Great; and because we 'know' them in this vivid way, our perception of human nature is thereby enlarged. The explanation is of course simple. The conventions of creative literature allow, indeed almost demand, total vision. The author can show us his characters as they are seen by others, as they appear to themselves, and as they are known to their creator. For in fiction the writer is God, omnipotent and omniscient. He can present to us his creatures in the round; he supplies significant detail, brings in corroborative evidence, contrives the revealing episodes; he can even allow us to eavesdrop on their inner thoughts and emotions. All we need to know, he tells us; and what he tells us is absolute. We do not look beyond his words, for beyond there is nothing; his words are the only reality. We are consenting audiences to an illusion, the illusion which is art.

The historical biographer by contrast is clogged and limited. He is bound by a different set of rules. The discipline of the artist is in creating the appropriate material to produce the prescribed effect; of the historian in creating the appropriate effect from the prescribed material. He cannot invent what he needs; he must do what he can with what is given him. In practice his evidence, however voluminous, is always defective. He has to leave some things unexplored or unexplained. He looks at his subject from the outside, from a distance, and by a fitful light. Yet he has one consolation which may make up for these disadvantages. His subject is after all an historical figure, not a fictional character. He is dealing even at second-hand with reality, not the product of another man's imagination. The person he is writing about really did exist, said these things, had these experiences. Historical truth is sometimes stranger, though not necessarily more convincing, than literature; but even if it were not, it has a rough, homespun quality of its own which fiction with all its imagination and beauty cannot have. The novelist and the dramatist give us a distillation of their knowledge of human nature in the form of invented characters. The historical biographer, more crudely perhaps, gives us human nature in the raw. His account will be less polished, less penetrating, but it has a solidity and authenticity of its own. Biography, despite its unavoidable defects and limitations, gives therefore pleasure to those who are interested in the inexhaustible variety of human nature and human experience. Other forms of historical writing would not do this to the same degree. We have only to reflect on the state of history without biography to realize how much it would be impoverished.

15

Some Reflections on History[1]

History is a story. The difference in spelling is merely that between an etymologically more correct version and the shorter common form. This difference, however, has allowed a distinction to grow up between history as a relation of what purports to be true and story as any kind of narrative, even as a euphemism for what is an untruth. Yet that distinction in sense is a comparatively late development. There are many contexts in which the two spellings are interchangeable and other languages – French with *histoire*, for example, or German with *Geschichte* – find no difficulty in accommodating all these meanings in a single word.

To begin a discussion of history in this way is not mere pedantry. It is sensible, especially for the professional historians, to bear in mind that history is literature and its medium common prose. It has no special vocabulary of its own and has no need to invent a jargon to conceal poverty of thought. Its language, like its subject, is that of everyday life. The medium evolved by mankind to meet the uses and occasions of ordinary existence is the one best adapted to describe that existence. History needs the colour and flexibility of vernacular language; and also, one may add, its looseness and imprecision. By all means let what is quantifiable in history be quantified. For the most part the variety and mobility of human activity defy precise translation into any symbols known to man. We can depict and analyse but hardly ever define human behaviour. The plasticity of prose is wanted to convey the plasticity of events. Prose is therefore the natural medium of history and on the skill with which it is used depends much of its effect. The enduring histories – Thucydides, Tacitus, Gibbon – are the literary masterpieces.

Yet to regard history as simply a branch of literature is plainly unsatisfactory. Something is needed to identify the content of history as well as its form. If we look at what an historian does, we may for example conclude that it is the critical examination of the evidence for men's past activities. This austere formula is a useful one since it emphasizes the point that all history is 'contemporary' in the sense that when historians seek to find out what was once in the past, they can only look at what is still in the present. Their evidence, that is to say, can only consist of what is in existence now. The sources for history are things made by men: artefacts, we may say, using that term in the widest possible sense. Chief of those artefacts is writing. Though archaeology at one extreme and oral tradition at the other can supply some of the deficiences of written records, the absence of writing

[1] Unpublished essay which incorporates material from my inaugural lecture as Professor of History at St Andrews in 1956 on 'History and Credibility' and a subsequent paper on 'Use and Abuse of History'.

is the severest handicap under which an historian can labour. Historians look at these relics of the past and interpret them. The process is thus both personal and immediate. History depends not on whether human activities went on but on whether those activities have left any traces. Historians are looking not at events as they occurred but at the evidence for their occurrence. If no traces have survived, they are helpless; if some have, they can, so to speak, 'make' history. By interpreting the evidence, drawing reasonable inferences, and using their imagination, they can make statements about the past which they believe to be true. Logically therefore we can go one step further and define history as a relationship between an historian and his material. The nature of that relationship may be inferred from what he subsequently produces as 'history'.

It is here that doubts have arisen about the validity of the historical method. They come from men whose business it is (as it is not that of historians) to study the science of knowledge. Dilthey, Croce, Oakeshott and Collingwood have all in different ways suggested that history only teaches us something about historians. They have argued that the past is by definition unknowable; that 'history' is simply a relationship between the mind of the historian and the evidence he is scrutinizing; and that the product of that relationship is only a modification in that mind. When we read history we do not see the past but merely contemporary reflections in an historical mirror. Hence Oakeshott's contention that 'the past in history varies with the present' and Collingwood's view that each generation must rewrite its own history. These sceptical philosophers – though not all philosophers are sceptical on this issue – have by a different road reached the same position as that of the more intuitive French writer Paul Valéry when he spoke of 'the impossibility of separating the observer from the thing observed, and history from the historian'. In an attempt to secure a definition of history to which both sceptics and historians can subscribe, the formula has been suggested that history is society's view of its own past. This however is little more than the original criticism in a more collective form. In a simple sense, of course, the formula is true. But is history only that? If the implication is that there can be no objective truth in history, only a series of dissolving contemporary views, each to be replaced by the next, we are back in a state of philosophic scepticism again. It is not, of course, a question of the deliberate falsification of history. The elaborate rewriting of history by authoritarian states can be disregarded as patent and indefensible aberrations. The real issue is whether the relationship even between the most conscientious of historians and his evidence must by its nature remain essentially subjective.

The proposition that history is merely what historians write has an attractive simplicity. Like solipsism it is logically invulnerable. For practical purposes, however, it is incomplete as a definition and unsatisfactory as a concept. It is incomplete because it fails to meet the question of external evidence; unsatisfactory because we simply do not believe it. We use the word 'history' in several senses but perhaps the commonest is one which clearly implies the existence of an objective reality. When we talk of the history of Rome, the history of medicine, the history of the Peninsular War, we mean not so much what historians have written on those topics as a sequence of events about which they have written. It is even open for us to say, with no sense of absurdity, that for instance the history of Britain before the Bronze Age is largely unknown. In other words, we refer to things which we believe happened but which historians cannot write about because they lack the materials with which to do so. It is a sound instinct which leads us to use the word 'history' in this way. It represents the fundamental assumption on which all the activities of historians are based: the practical empirical view that history does not depend entirely on the historian; that actual events took place which it is his business to find out about if he can. That belief is based partly on inference, partly on actual evidence. What is postulated is that there is something to discover; the question is whether that task can be performed – or whether (to quote Paul Valéry again) – 'the whole of history is only composed of thoughts to which we affix the entirely mythical quality of representing something that once existed'.

Historians might think such a charge too exaggerated to be worth answering. Yet one ought not to be so conditioned by respect for academic history as to refuse to consider that there may be a point here which deserves discussion. There is after all, at first blush, a certain air of unreality about the whole business when dispassionately considered. Not only does the historian habitually talk of persons he has never met, and of events in which he did not take part, but these matters are commonly divided from him by a gulf of time and a world of difference. Philip Guedalla once amused himself by picturing 'strange encounters of historians with their history' and the embarrassment that might be caused by such unanticipated confrontations with the reality on which they are such authorities. 'It is delightful,' he wrote, 'to contemplate a medievalist projected into the Middle Ages or an amateur of revolutions adrift in a bread-riot', and – not to show partiality – 'a modern, just for once in waiting on his Queen, might droop along the tartan walls of Osborne and learn not to patronize his betters.' This is malicious but it also has a sting of truth.

Yet none of this seems an adequate justification for condemning history out of hand as defective in method or totally subjective in content. Historians cannot, of course, 'reconstruct the past'; the notion is absurd. It is impossible even to describe the sum of past human activities. The task would be physically out of the question even if the evidence were available; and for the most part the evidence is not available. The great mass of human actions falls into instant oblivion. At the most, all an historian can do is to look at the evidence which has survived, and from it select, combine, and recast to construct a verbal picture of certain events in the past. It is the only way in which history can be written. Yet this process is neither peculiar nor peculiarly faulty. The methods of the historian are not unique. Man is the measure, or at least the measurer, of all things. Knowledge in itself presupposes a relationship between man and the object of his enquiry. It is true that the historian works under special conditions. The irreversibility of time and the uniqueness of historical phenomena preclude either direct observation or experimental recapitulation. He has to deal with a past to which there is no access and from which there is no return. He can only be therefore an indirect observer. Like mythological justice, he limps along behind the press of events; he is a distant watcher not a participant. The experience of a spectator is very different from that of a player; yet it is proverbially the bystander who sees more of the game.

This characteristic of never being in direct contact with the object of his study is to the historian not a physical accident, a regrettable (or as Mr Guedalla suggested a fortunate) circumstance with which he must bear as best he can, but an undeclared advantage in his work. It is not an inherent defect but an inherent virtue. For indirect observation is the only kind of observation that suits the subject. The reason is simple enough. The historian has to deal with a mass of events scattered over a wide area of time and space. Even if he could be granted any direct contact, his immediate senses would be a frail and inadequate instrument for recording and judging them. If, as Professor Feiling said in his inaugural lecture at Oxford, C. H. Firth knew more about Cromwell's England than the Protector himself, it was because Firth was allowed an indirect observation to which Cromwell with all his authority could hardly have attained. Firth certainly lacked Cromwell's direct experience; but he understood the age as a contemporary could not; and he understood it because he was looking at it indirectly – that is to say looking at the events not directly but through the evidence for their occurrence. The flood of happenings cannot be caught by one man's eyes; it must be strained through the mesh of the historical method. The result, obviously, is not the same as the happenings themselves; it is an abstraction in a literal sense: a selection and assembling of ideas. Only in that way can history become intelligible. The great Leopold von Ranke has often and erroneously been criticized for his much-quoted remark that he wished to find out how things actually happened. In one sense, of course, it is an unrealizable task; but it is equally unrealizable for contemporaries and eye-witnesses. We never see anything as it 'actually is' or 'actually happened'; the phrases are meaningless. All we do is to record a mass of fragmentary data, whether scientific, sensory or historical. All that historians, including von Ranke, hope to do with their data is to elucidate the relevant facts and wrest from them an intelligible and defensible meaning. The abstractions of the historian, however, are more likely to catch the significant elements in a situation than the immediate impressions of a direct witness.

This is as true of contemporary as of past events. The business of a great department of state, for example, comes before the presiding minister in the shape of files of correspondence, digests of evidence, and summaries of opinions. Or take the conduct of war. Few modern generals see much of the battles they direct. A whole profession of staff officers, organized in successive echelons, exist to filter through to their commander the relevant evidence, in an assimilable form, on which he will have to make his decisions. Without that carefully processed information an historian, whether lying with front-line troops in a ditch or sitting in an operational HQ some miles back, would gain little through the medium of his direct senses. So little indeed that it is of no special consequence for an accurate analysis of the battle whether he was present or not. Few professional historians have had an experience comparable to that of S. E. Morison, professor of history at Harvard and historian of US Naval Operations in the last war. Appointed at the start of hostilities, to quote the sober language of his preface to that history, as part of his research he 'visited the various theaters of war on combat ships and has taken part in several amphibious operations and surface engagements with the enemy'. But Morison himself, though he thought that his operational experience was useful in teaching him the importance of chance in naval warfare, made no special claims for the validity of his history on the grounds of his participation in some of the actions he was commissioned to describe. 'If,' he wrote, 'I confined myself to personal impressions and oral testimony the work would not be history. As rigorous a study of the documents was made as if the war were a war of the last century. . . . A seaman's eye has been applied to the technique of a professional historian but the seaman has also learnt to discount the evidence of his eye.'

In all this there is nothing that should surprise us. The greater part of our working equipment of knowledge, and of the assumptions of which we order our daily life, is based on indirect evidence of a similar nature. We accept the existence of places and persons that we have never seen – and may never see – because of the abundance of indirect proof for their existence. When for the first time we book a passage to Australia or vote in an election for a candidate whose meetings we have never attended, it is with no sense of committing an act of faith. In our courts of law judges and juries examine past acts and pronounce on their nature and authorship in the light of historical evidence. The presence of the prisoner in the dock is only a material proof that there is someone to punish. The rôle of an historian is often compared to that of a court of law and the comparison is reasonable enough – except that the historian is prosecutor, counsel for the defence, jury, and judge in one; his verdict is reached at leisure; it entails no penalty; and is subject to indefinite argument and revision. To that extent we take greater risks in our law-courts than in our history-books. We have been accustomed in the past to hang a man on less evidence than would be required of a doctoral candidate in his research thesis.

No historian in fact would doubt the superiority of the indirect over the direct method. It is by examining evidence and not by personal observation that historical understanding is acquired. Understanding depends on accuracy, comprehensiveness and insight; and these are the results of enquiry and reflection, not of primary sensation or subsequent recollection. The fallibility of personal observation, even in honest, intelligent and disinterested witnesses, is a matter of common observation, as any policeman or psychologist knows. The evidence of participants in historical events, particularly when given after the events, is notoriously prone to bias and inaccuracy. To read the accounts by surviving German generals of the Battle of France, it might appear that it was a matter of common consent among them that Hitler was responsible for the famous 'halt of the armour' outside Dunkirk between 24 and 26 May 1940 and consequently for the failure to prevent the escape of the British Expeditionary Force and much of the 1st French Army; for missing, therefore, one of the great opportunities of winning the war in the west. Yet when British historians came to examine the captured German military records of the campaign, it became clear that the decision was taken by the commanders in the field; that Hitler merely assented to a decision already taken and put into effect by his subordinates; and that in any case the halt of the armoured divisions did not in itself explain the successful Allied evacuation. In more subtle instances than this it has been the indirect approach through the evidence that has made possible some of the most delicate and satisfying of historical achievements – the elucidation of matters that were unknown to contemporary society, or the refutation of evidence that deceived in its own time and was fabricated in order to deceive. To be able to demonstrate the fraudulent character of a Merovingian charter or to reconstruct the movement of prices in seventeenth-century Poland are examples of the historian's expertise which constitute their own reward.

That there is a subjective element in all historical writing is, of course, obvious. No two historians will describe a given set of events in exactly the same way; if they did we would suspect collusion or plagiarism. What troubles the historian when he contemplates a potential subject for research, however, is not that others will dispute his findings but that somebody may already be working on that subject and anticipate his findings. In the common experience of the profession two competent students researching on the same topic will tend to produce similar results. The preoccupation of historical debate with new material and new interpretations disguises the great mass of agreement on central issues. Were this not so, the teaching of history would become impossible. Historians are individuals but history as a subject has not yet disintegrated into a heap of personal interpretations. The greatest of historians only become influential if their conclusions are accepted by those of their colleagues in the best position to judge.

It is not true either that each generation has to reinterpret the past. Certainly there are continual changes and modifications in the teaching of history that result from the uncovery of fresh material, the re-examination of previously held views, shifts of intellectual interest, and the internal needs of the profession. But the process is irregular and unplanned, not to say haphazard and piecemeal. Historical writing at any one time is not monolithic; even the concept of a 'generation' in human society is artificial. Uniformity of outlook is only likely to happen where there is external political pressure. Clever and ambitious scholars do not naturally submit to a common discipline of either method or subject. They look for topics which have not already been explored, subjects on which new evidence has become available, debatable issues on which they can differ from previous authorities. All this keeps history as an academic subject intellectually alive. There is little excitement – or prospect of professional advancement – to be had by repeating the findings of others. That is why historians on the whole prefer to produce monographs rather than text-books. Yet, the fact that historical discussion among professionals inevitably revolves round what is new or controversial should not obscure the great body of established knowledge of which we are as sure as we can well be of anything. No reasonable person doubts that Hannibal crossed the Alps, that Harold was defeated at the battle of Hastings, or that Luther defied the Pope. The great bulk of our history books is composed of matters on which there is no dispute.

It can of course be argued that it is not as a rule the facts that are in doubt but their interpretation. To dismiss 'mere facts' and imply that history is concerned with something else may be a way of suggesting that history is not a valid system of knowledge but it is also a way of begging the question. In practice the distinction between fact and truth, or between events and interpretation, is extremely difficult to draw. Though historians are not content to supply summaries of dates and events, those dates and events are essential to their work. One common method of interpretation is to present facts in a certain grouping; another is by the discovery of hitherto unknown facts, or the demonstration by inference of facts which cannot be directly proved. An historian is not a passive recipient but an active questioner. Yet the evidence he is questioning has an authority of its own. It is true that when he interprets and generalizes, his judgement may be faulty or his evidence incomplete. In any case human activity is not so simple that it can be exhausted of meaning by the activity of one group of scholars. History is a branch of knowledge in which certainty, probability, and speculation all have their part. What may properly be required of an historian is that he distinguishes between certainties and uncertainties. If it is one of his functions to dispel doubt, another is to indicate where doubt must persist.

Historical doubt does not arise merely from deficiency of evidence or partiality of judgement. It also comes from the nature of the subject. The historian is presented with facts which need explanation and may to that extent be regarded as results. He does not necessarily know, however, what produced those results. He is continually working backwards from effect to cause, from the known to the unknown. He is a man reconstructing a calculation of which the object is never stated and the method of computation only imperfectly preserved. Of the answer to his sum there is no doubt, since that is his starting-point. But he cannot test the validity of his calculation since there is no way of repeating it to discover whether it always produces the same result. If he examines the fall of the Roman Empire, the fall is the fixed mark from which he sets out in search of the explanation for the fall. But though he can define the first, he cannot so easily prove the second. Indeed he is not even certain that he will recognize the causes when he comes across them. He can describe antecedent events which may have been causes; but to demonstrate the causal connection is another matter. In fact it is impossible to distinguish the causes in any scientific way because they are embedded in a mass of other circumstances from which they cannot be isolated. At most he can invite reasonable belief that what he describes had more to do with the fall of the Roman Empire than any other factors. An historian must look for causes because that is an essential part of the business of explaining and understanding. Yet he must recognize that in so doing his technique faces one of its most difficult tasks. The pattern of historical events is often so intricate as to defy analysis. The causes of the First World War are still a matter for debate; and though we may with some trouble agree on what we mean by 'The Renaissance', we can only tentatively suggest why it occurred when it did. In such matters historians are reaching the limits of their craft.

II

From the validity of the historical method one can turn to another question. What is the value of history? A few centuries ago people were in little doubt. History was for instruction and edification; its purpose was moral and didactic. From the storehouse of the past could be extracted examples of piety and nobility, sin and retribution. Not only was history in Gibbon's famous words 'the register of the crimes, follies and misfortunes of mankind' but that record could be used to point a moral for succeeding generations. Such considerations could hardly survive the rise of the professional historian. Yet it would suggest a certain academic insularity not to recognize that for the ordinary public the interest of history is precisely in this quality of being a case-book of examples, a gallery of portraits, a collection of stories. The exploitation of history takes various forms from frivolous entertainment to inspiring tales (whether *Lives of the Saints* or *Deeds that Won the Empire*), and even deliberate manipulation for political purposes. What societies think about their own past is always important and because it is of contemporary importance, it is a political matter.

This, however, is not so much a question of the value of history as of the use to which it can be put. If history is not to be a mere repository of facts and fables from which those with special interests to serve can take what suits them, what more reputable purpose can it be made to serve? Truth for truth's sake perhaps? An answer which may satisfy the professionals but is hardly sufficient for the society which provides them with their livelihood and accords them a certain prestige. To train the mind, develop analytical skill and power of literary expression in the young? No doubt it does all these things; but the same could be said of most other arts subjects. If we look for qualities peculiar to history a better justification is that it is an extension of our experience of humanity. It enlarges our knowledge and deepens our appreciation of the nature of man and his activities. History does this well for collective activities; it is perhaps less illuminating on individual psychology. This comes from the nature of the evidence. We can describe character and temperament but to be convincing such descriptions require a knowledge of motive. Yet motive is a difficult problem for the historian. It does not help him very much that historical figures are often at pains to explain their motives, either at the time or in subsequent writings for posterity, since he does not know whether they are telling the truth or even whether they are sufficiently aware of the truth to be able to tell it. This is not to say that autobiographies, for example, are useless; on the contrary. But the most important things they tell us are not what the writers set out to relate but what they unconsciously reveal. Even so, compared with fictional literature, history is a less satisfying guide to human nature. The novelist or dramatist, if he is skilled in his art, can not only inform our minds but leave us with a greater sense of revelation than an historian can hope to do.

The strength of history is in dealing with people in the mass, with the behaviour of societies and the actions of governments. It has therefore been deemed to be a particularly appropriate education for those who wish to enter almost any branch of public service. There is nothing demeaning in this. The concept of preparation for some future occupation, which was the original concept behind all arts subjects, cannot be excluded from any sensible assessment of the rôle of history in society. Its claims, however, should not be exaggerated. Politics, administration, diplomacy (the professions for which history was once – and perhaps still is – thought useful) deal with the present and future; history with the past. It offers no clear guide to what lies ahead and to look back for guidance is usually a prescription for disaster. The tendency of the military mind to fight the last war has become proverbial, however undeservedly. Historical situations are unique; even if we understood them in their entirety, such knowledge would have no practical application. Yet there is a justification for history as a training for certain professions. It toughens the mind to meet future situations by familiarizing it with a knowledge of what has happened similarly in the past. Generals are none the worse for being acquainted with military history, or politicians with past political events, or diplomats with the vicissitudes of international relations. History, as an extension of experience rather than as a specific guide, may be, and probably is, a good preparation for public life.

One must, however, distinguish between the study of history and professional historical research. It would be difficult otherwise to explain why such good political historians as Clarendon in the seventeenth century, Macaulay in the nineteenth, and Sir Lewis Namier in our own time, should have been such failures as practical politicians. The explanation is not that history is a poor preparation for politics but that there is an essential difference between the reading and writing of history. The qualities necessary for success as a professional historian are not only not the same as but in many respects the exact opposite of those required by the politician. The historian works in isolation, at leisure, with inert material. He is looking back, not forward. He can postpone his judgements; his mistakes affect only himself. The statesman or diplomat works in a living world of interests and passions, of difficulties at home and accidents abroad; he is only partially informed about the present and can only guess about the future. Yet he must make his decisions now, knowing that his actions may, and often will, have effects other than those he intended. In such a world temperament, character, even instinct, may serve him better than an academic education.

While therefore it is proper to commend an historical training, it does not follow that a multiplication of professional scholars or research students has in itself any particular social value. It is not necessary to know everything that is knowable, either in history or in any other branch of learning. A great deal of historical writing today is done by professionals for professionals and apart from that has very little importance. There is a tendency in most professions to become ends in themselves and unconsciously assume a social utility which it would not be easy to demonstrate. To ask why we should study history is a perfectly legitimate question. Some historians may simply answer that we do it because we want to. This modest reply has the advantage of stopping further argument but it tells us nothing about history itself. The same could be said about any human activity, intellectual or not. It is a valid reply but unsatisfactory because uninformative. In the case of history we can readily accept that mankind has a natural curiosity about its past and that society without history is like a man without his memory. Yet even that well-known comparison is not absolute. A man who has lost his memory is at a peculiar disadvantage in society; but communities with no more knowledge of the past than what their grandparents told them are not so disadvantaged. Historically, societies have been able to exist tolerably well without the help of an organized body of knowledge about the past. History as a study in its own right and the emergence of a profession of historians are the marks of a developed civilization; they are not antecedent to it.

There is, nevertheless, a case for arguing that history is not only a valuable study but one which occupies a unique place in the field of human knowledge. It is a case based not so much on utility as on the actual nature of the subject. As a branch of learning it falls somewhere between the natural sciences and the pure humanities. Natural sciences – a study of plants, for example, or of animals – have more stable and uniform material to examine, more open to systematic observation and classification and to the formulation of general rules. The traditional arts subjects, on the other hand, are concerned with systems of knowledge, theories of behaviour, and certain cultural manifestations: language, literature, painting, music and the rest. The historian does not set out to construct logical theories. Those who do, like Marx, are only pseudo-historians. Nor does he allow the study of any special cultural activity, whether numismatics or poetry, to become an end in itself though he is happy to make use of the scholarship of those who do. He is a generalist in that he takes any evidence which helps him to understand what he is studying; but his object of study is individual and unique. The rigours of source interpretation at one pole, the anarchy of human action at the other, constitute the tension of his work. He provides explanations and without them a mere recital of events would lose both interest and depth; but historical explanations are rooted in the evidence for a given time and place; they have a specific, not a common, application.

It is, however, exactly this specific character of history which gives it its general value. History is the basic humane subject since everything relating to man in society falls within its province. It occupies, in relation to other arts subjects, something of the same position as mathematics to the other sciences. It is the common language, the essential framework. To some degree or other it enters into the treatment of all studies relating to mankind, whether language, philosophy, economics, or the fine arts. All such studies, if they are to be complete, must provide some perspective for their subject; and that means giving an historical background. History is the common element, inseparable from the condition of man himself, and inseparable therefore from any study of mankind.

For this central position of history in the humanities there is a price to be paid. The historian proper (that is to say, without any further qualification) finds today that large parts of his intellectual territory are being invaded by others. There are two reasons for these incursions. In the first place certain aspects of history cannot be properly explored without bringing in experts with particular qualifications such as doctors, artists and archaeologists. The universal nature of history soon exposes the limitations of any individual historian. It is not possible for him to write with authority on, for example, epidemics or inflation without the guidance of physicians and economists. It is not possible either, one may add, for doctors and economists to write medical or economic history in any comprehensive way without more historical knowledge than their own particular expertise affords. But at least history is everyman's subject and the field is open to all. Its technical tools are few and can quickly be mastered. This leads to the second reason. Because experts in other subjects do not face any formidable difficulties in becoming historians on their own account, it is tempting for them to turn to history to provide depth and insight to their own formal studies. A natural desire for intellectual autonomy tends to lead to a policy of academic annexation. Indeed the expansion of sociology, politics and anthropology (to name only a few) has at times raised the question whether 'history' in its traditional form can long survive. The danger – in this country at least – has perhaps been exaggerated and the question may only be rhetorical. But if it is asked seriously, the answer is that history can only survive as a discipline in its traditional autonomous form. Anything less would impoverish its standards and lessen its importance. History is an elemental but not an elementary subject. All students of the traditional arts subjects are to some extent students of history. Historians should not object to this since it is a recognition of the fundamental nature of their own craft. Their duty is to maintain the autonomy of the subject as a branch of learning. Failure to do so would profit nobody; and that autonomy can only be maintained if history is taught by historians. If the subject is to be of value to others, it must be studied for its own sake by those who have no other motive.

Index

Principal abbreviations

Bn – Baron
Bp – Bishop
Bt – Baronet
CJ – Chief Justice

D – Duke
E – Earl
Ld – Lord
Vt – Viscount